A Sport for Every Kid

Also by Nicole Sperekas

But He Says He Loves Me
Girls Speak Out on Dating Abuse

SuicideWise
Taking Steps Against Teen Suicide

A Sport for Every Kid

Finding the Right Sport, Team, and Coach
for Children of All Abilities

Nicole Sperekas, PhD

The Lyons Press
Guilford, Connecticut
An imprint of The Globe Pequot Press

The Lyons Press is an imprint of The Globe Pequot Press.

10 9 8 7 6 5 4 3 2 1

Printed in the United States of America

Designed by Mimi LaPoint

Quotes on pages 33, 37, 41, 43, 45, 48, 49, 54, 60, 61, 92, 96, 233, 236, and 288 are from Doren, Kim, and Charlie Jones. *If Winning Were Easy, Everyone Would Do It: Motivational Quotes for Athletes.* Kansas City, MO: Andrews McMeel Publishing, 2002. Used by permission.

Quotes on pages 6, 35, 36, 48, 60, and 274 are from Doren, Kim, and Charlie Jones. *You Go Girl! The Winning Way.* Santa Anna, CA: Seven Locks Press, 2003. Used by permission.

Library of Congress Cataloging-in-Publication Data

Sperekas, Nicole B.
  A sport for every kid : finding the right sport, team, and coach for children of all abilities / Nicole Sperekas.
     p. cm.
  Includes bibliographical references and index.
  ISBN 1-59228-759-X (trade paper)
  1. Sports for children. I. Title.
GV709.2.S62 2005
796'.083--dc22

2005010686

To all the parents and youth sports coaches
who strive to make youth sports
a fun and positive experience for children
of all athletic abilities—
from the klutzes to the natural athletes.
When they help children do their best
and have fun at the same time,
everyone wins!

You will never know what you are capable of doing—or being—until you start.

If you try hard and you have fun and you're a good sport, you're a success no matter what the score or where you finish.

Contents

Acknowledgments

MANY PEOPLE HELPED me with this book. I am grateful to Drs. Suzanne Kincaid and Hannah Evans who read my first draft. Both are enthusiastic fans and good athletes themselves. Flor Estela Farwell, Mary Williams, and Kate Duarte kindly looked over a near-final draft. When a child, Flor assumed her gym teacher didn't think much of her athleticism when he assigned her to shortstop. Only years later did she learn that the shortstop is considered one of the better athletes in baseball. Pat Gartland plays lacrosse and helps coach a high school lacrosse team. Because of his knowledge of team sports, he was able to provide important insights that helped with the writing of this book. Over the years, I've learned a lot about many sports from Bob Moroney and Marc Burke. Both played basketball seriously in their younger days and can expound on the sport and its players nonstop, for hours on end. Lois Barnes is always a good listening post.

My family continues to give me steady support and encouragement. They are enthusiastic and knowledgeable sports fans. We often spend hours together watching games, often rooting for the underdogs.

The librarians at the Virginia Village Library—my local branch of the Denver Public Library—were very helpful. Their ability to track down references and other materials was impressive, and they always managed to do their work with a smile.

My literary agent, Stephany Evans, saw promise in my early manuscript. Working with her was a pleasure, and she always gave good advice and answered my questions promptly. I couldn't have asked for a more caring and thoughtful agent.

I was lucky to draw a seasoned editor, Rob Kirkpatrick. His background as a fan and a player helped him point out more than just the occasional dangling participle. This is a better book because of him.

A Sport for Every Kid

*I believe that most children, no matter their athletic abilities,
have the potential to enjoy modest success in sports.*

WE KNEW MY COUSIN was nonathletic when he was eight years old. He teetered, tripped, bumped, stumbled, crashed, and fell—frequently, and with apparent ease. Some family members said that David could trip on air. His mother became quite good at administering first aid while soothing her whimpering son. We hoped that perhaps by adolescence he would grow out of his clumsiness. He didn't.

By the time he was thirteen, his awkwardness had become worse. We wondered if he would reach adulthood without some life-limiting injury. He never showed an interest in sports, and we were all very relieved about that.

Imagine our shock when he came home from his youth group one day and announced that he wanted to go skiing with the group. The program provided lessons in the mornings and on-your-own skiing in the afternoons. We thought he had lost his mind.

With a heavy heart and great trepidation, his mother signed the permission slip and paid for ten Sundays of skiing. She checked out the instructors and was assured that they were the best and would proceed slowly and cautiously with the beginning skiers.

Three weeks later, David's mother drove him to the parking lot where the driver of the chartered bus was ready to take the kids up to the mountains. After tense and worried good-byes, the bus took off. It was 6:00 a.m.

At 5:30 p.m., David's mother headed to the community center's parking lot and waited for the bus to return from the mountains. She had spent a long day by the phone, sure that someone would call her and tell her that David had broken his leg. The bus turned in to the parking lot, and the children began to leave it. No sign of David. After a thousand teenagers had left the bus (or so it seemed), David emerged. He was smiling, laughing, and chatting with several other kids. He didn't look as if he were hurt—no crutches or bandages. He wasn't even limping as he walked. "How did it go?" asked his mother. "It was a blast," David replied.

For the first time in his life, David felt included. He went on to become a very good skier, and he even made Ski Patrol when he was eighteen. Now in his forties, he still skis and enjoys taking his children skiing.

It's difficult to explain how a nonathletic child mastered a very difficult sport without killing himself. In fact, David has never suffered a ski injury. I know that many parents have a child like David. He may be clumsy and not very interested in sports. He may be too embarrassed to play in front of his peers. He may sit on the sidelines, always watching his more athletic friends compete on the field. Because he doesn't have natural athletic ability, he may resign himself to always feeling excluded when his friends play sports. He may even put on a good front and pretend that he doesn't mind being left out even though he secretly harbors the desire to play.

It seems logical that parents would not encourage such a child to sign up for soccer or baseball or tennis. However, since great athletic ability is a rare occurrence, most parents have children who either have good athletic skills or who are quite limited athletically and afraid to pursue a sport. While minimally athletic, with motivation and good instructors, David was able to become a good skier. What I learned from David's experience is that there is a sport for every child—even one who is not very athletic. It's just a matter of finding the right sport for him.

Of course, there are children who are naturally athletic or those who have above-average athletic skills. They may want to participate in many different sports, and this is good as most sports experts prefer that young athletes engage in several sports and not specialize in only one. Furthermore, because they are athletically talented, they probably can experience success in most sports. However, even these athletes might pause before signing up for multiple sports. There may be situations when a child must pare down his choices. For example, your son may only have time to play one sport a season. However, he may be interested in playing football and soccer in the fall. Which one is he going to play? By evaluating his athletic strengths and weaknesses, his temperament, and emotional makeup, your son and you may be able to identify the best choice—the sport in the fall that best fits his athletic skills and emotional makeup. This is only one of many scenarios whereby a child may have to narrow his choices.

This book is for parents who have children of various athletic abilities who are interested in playing a sport. It is also for parents who may have a "nonathletic" child who may seldom express an interest in sports but who can be encouraged to try to play one. I put "nonathletic" in quotation marks because I believe that there are truly no nonathletic children. Most children, no matter their athletic abilities, have the potential to enjoy modest success in certain sports. With encouragement, patience, and some trial and error, there's a sport for every kid.

I will suggest thoughtful, gentle, nonpressuring ways to find the right sport or sports for your children. She may decide to never compete and only pursue a sport recreationally. Or she may want to compete. She may participate in it only through grade school or middle school. Some children may play through high school or college. Few will become Olympians or professional athletes. Nevertheless, I strongly believe that all children should have the opportunity to participate in sports and to experience the excitement and joy that comes with learning and playing a sport.

Part 1 contains a general introduction to the task at hand—finding the right sport for your child. I will cover a number of preliminary issues and questions that should be considered before actually learning about the different sports.

Part 2 is devoted to fact sheets on fifty-one sports. You can leaf through this section with your child to begin to familiarize yourselves with various sports. By researching sports and understanding the different physical and mental elements that are required for each sport, you may be able to find the best sport or sports for your son or daughter.

Once a sport has been chosen, it's important for the child to have a positive experience playing it. To bring this about, just choosing the right sport or two is not enough. You have to find the right level of play, the right coach or instructor, the right team, league, or club. In addition, there are a number of issues and situations that will arise from playing sports. A few of these are the overweight child, the depressed athlete, the foul-tempered athlete, conflict with the coach, burnout, noncompetitiveness, raising a champion, and cutthroat soccer. I will address these concerns and many others in Part 3. Whether your child opts to just learn a sport and play it recreationally or whether he goes the organized sports route leading to more and more competition, many situations will require knowledge, sensitivity, and thoughtfulness on the part of the parent. I hope that parents will find this a useful guide to help them navigate their children through the world of youth sports.

I write with insights gleaned from over thirty years as a child psychologist and as a former competitive swimmer and coach. I believe that my experiences in these areas give me an invaluable perspective that will be helpful to parents.

First, let's look at the various reasons for and benefits of learning and playing sports. That sports are played all over the world is a testimony to the universality of the values inherent in athletic pursuits.

PART 1

Getting Started

1   The Importance of Sports

Imagine the sense of wonder when a child goes from missing the ball all the time to actually hitting it occasionally.

MANY SPORTS BEGAN as games invented and played by children. A child began to hop. At some point the game of hopscotch developed. Then a child thought of jumping. Soon he experimented with seeing how far he could jump. This skill or ability eventually became known as the long jump. It is in the Olympics—one of many track and field events. The many sports I write about in this book all involve physical activity, usually have various levels of skill or performance, and can be learned, at least on a beginner level, by most children.

Sports Involve Abilities or Games That Are Played for Fun

One of the first reasons for sports is that they involve abilities or games that are played for fun. Children find skipping, jumping, throwing a ball, and swimming enjoyable and fun. Watch some young children engaging in these activities—they are usually laughing and smiling. Their exuberance is contagious and brings a smile to your face. They are having fun.

Games Present Challenges

After a child first skips or jumps or throws a ball, she will begin to experiment. She tries to vary the skips, the jumps, or the throws. If she didn't do this, these motions would become boring. Soon she tries to see if she can skip differently, jump longer, and throw the ball farther. Developing these abilities becomes a challenge. This is the second reason for sports. They present challenges and children enjoy challenges. Most kids will see some improvement in their athletic abilities over time. Almost all children are able to learn to skip, run, throw a ball, swim, and ride a bike.

Children Develop Confidence in Their Ability to Master a Skill

Eventually, some children will go from challenge to mastery. They notice that the more they try to do something, the better they get. They begin to develop confidence in their ability to master the skill. Have you ever watched small children learn to play tennis? Most of the time they miss hitting the ball altogether. After a while, some begin returning the ball. Of course, most of these returns go into the net or land outside the court. But imagine the sense of wonder when a child goes from missing the ball all the time to actually hitting it occasionally. After much practice, he begins to hit the ball over the net and it actually lands inside the court! Maybe that doesn't happen very often, but there's a noticeable improvement. Soon, he hits the ball most of the time, and he can return the ball accurately 10 percent of the time. A sense of mastery begins to develop. Even small amounts of mastery are thrilling for children. "Last week I could never hit the ball over the net. This week some of them go over. Wow!" (Some kids expect to "get it" right away and give up if they don't. They require lots of encouragement when they show small gains in their skills.)

Sports Are Natural Avenues to Learning Social Skills

Among the most important skills in life are social skills: the ability to get along with others. Many studies suggest that good social skills are essential for success and happiness in life. When children don't fit in or are left out for whatever reason, they lose opportunities to develop their social skills. Most sports are natural avenues to learning social skills, and team sports present many opportunities for developing them. But even individual sports involve interacting with others: an instructor or coach, other children in the class or on the team, opponents, scorekeepers, referees, and judges. I have seen some children with Asperger's Disorder, a type of autistic disorder resulting in the inability to read social cues, slowly show improvement in their social skills through playing sports. Some progress to the point where their social skills are passable, if not great. Sports usually involve interacting in various ways with others:

> **Give-and-take**—"You can use my bat after I'm through; then can I use your glove?"
>
> **Patience**—"I'll help you with your serve in a minute."
>
> **Accepting help**—"Maybe if you hold your racquet like this, you'll have better control."
>
> **Giving help**—"Mark, will you help Joey with his free throws?"
>
> **Teamwork**—"If you see her open, pass the puck to her."

Sports can help teach countless social skills, preparing children for success in life.

Children Experience Competition—Winning and Losing—by Playing Sports

American society involves a certain amount of competition, but most of us are disturbed when competition and winning become too important. The corporate scandals of the past several years provided us with examples in the business world of competition gone wrong. The use of performance-enhancing drugs is an example in the sports world. When the edge in competition is gained through unethical behavior rather than through merit, we all suffer. In recent years, the concern with winning has resulted in parents venting their anger at officials, coaches, other children and their parents, and even at their own children. Parents must teach their children that while winning is more fun than losing, the benefits of playing sports or engaging in some athletic activity go far beyond the won-lost column. To do this, parents must learn to be better role models when it comes to sportsmanship and being good fans.

Having said that, there is nothing wrong with competition. Learning to win and learning to lose are natural and important life experiences. It's a rare person who wins—or loses—all of life's "events."

- The baseball team that wins the World Series on the average loses over one-third of its regular season's games. The Florida Marlins, winners of the 2003 World Series, for example, lost over 40 percent of their games.

- Even the best hitters in professional baseball fail to get a hit more than 60 percent of the time. And the best hitters can strike out many times. Babe Ruth hit 714 home runs, but he struck out 1,330 times.

- World record holders can fail to win in the Olympics or even fail to qualify for the Olympics altogether. Marion Jones won two individual gold medals for the 100-meter and the 200-meter races in the 2000 Sidney Olympics, but she failed to qualify in those events for the 2004 Olympics in Athens.

But losing can still be a positive experience. A child who swims competitively can lose a race and yet improve his best time by two seconds. Competition does not always mean competition against others; competition also refers to self-competition—working hard to improve one's best time, or distance, weight, or performance. So, another value of sports is to experience competition and to experience winning and losing.

> *"On any given day you'll get beat, because that's just sports."*
>
> —Nancy Lieberman-Cline,
> member of the Basketball Hall of Fame

Sports Help Children Obtain Adequate Exercise and Conditioning

Participation in sports is a good way for children to obtain adequate exercise and conditioning. Physical fitness and regular exercise are necessary for good health for all age groups. Studies show that many children are too sedentary, resulting in poor physical condition and, in many cases, obesity. By age seventeen, the average child has spent

38 percent more time in front of the TV than in school. The Centers for Disease Control indicates that the rates for overweight children have tripled since 1980. Only 5 percent of kids were overweight twenty years ago. Now, about 15 percent of all U.S. children aged six to nineteen are overweight and another 15 percent are headed that way.[1] This is a serious problem since obesity increases the risk for diabetes, heart disease, high blood pressure, osteoporosis, and joint problems. In the past, most of these conditions were associated with aging. Sadly, they are now increasingly seen in children as young as elementary school age. For many children, their only exercise is limited to their physical education classes. Though some PE classes meet three or four times a week, many do not provide enough exercise for even minimal fitness. Even if children do take PE classes, many of them never exercise outside of school. Making matters even worse, many school districts have had to eliminate or reduce the number of PE classes because of budget cuts. For example, a recent Commission on School Nutrition and Physical Activity in Denver, Colorado, was told that students at one school participated in gym classes only 30 days out of a 184-day school calendar.[2] That's an average of about once a week.

In an article on children, their lack of exercise, and their resulting obesity, well-known sports columnist for *Sports Illustrated*, Rick Reilly, wrote, "We've got kids who not only can spell myocardial infarction but also will have one by their 30th birthday." To parents, "Stop jumping up and driving the kids three blocks to their friend's house. Let them take that cobweb-covered contraption in the garage. It's called a bike."[3] Parents should not let Reilly's wit obscure the seriousness of his concerns.

Unfortunately, sedentary tendencies in childhood become ingrained habits by adulthood. Along with their unhealthy eating styles, it's no wonder that our children are becoming fat and at risk for a number of health problems. Rallie McAllister, a physician, has recently predicted that for the first time in a century, "children in this generation will have a lower life expectancy than their parents."[4] Fitness should be a lifelong goal, and participation in sports can help children develop active lifestyles that will help them be fit all their lives.

Sports Provide Emotional Benefits

Besides physical benefits, there are also emotional benefits of exercise and fitness. We know that regular exercise can help reduce depression and stress. With some exceptions, many athletic activities can be played or engaged in for pleasure long into a person's eighties or nineties. Swimming and golf are good examples.

Participation in Sports Can Have a Therapeutic Value

Sometimes there may be very child-specific reasons to encourage your child to play sports. For example, I have recommended that parents of a child with attention deficit and hyperactivity find an individual sport or physical activity for the child. The one-on-one attention or lesson, the reduced stimuli, the small wait times, the required attention in short periods of time, all seem to help these children. Some aggressive children appear to benefit from playing sports that are competitive and very physical. Their aggression is channeled in acceptable ways, and inappropriate, aggressive, or hostile behaviors are reduced. I have found that some oppositional children can accept the guidance of a strict but caring coach or instructor. Some of these children, bent on acting out and opposing everything their parents say, seem to thrive in these situations. The coaches sometimes are amazed when the parents tell them of their frustrations in dealing with their kids. Such children are often described as "street angels, home devils." Thus, for many of these children, participation in sports can have a therapeutic value.

The Whole Family Can Benefit When Children Participate in Sports

Even though your child is the one participating in a sport, you will find that the whole family can benefit in subtle and not-so-subtle ways. Driving a child to soccer practice gives you some alone time to talk. Watching a practice session or game allows you the chance to see her learn and try hard. Sitting with other parents can become a social occasion— a time to visit with other parents, compare notes, and root for the team, your child, or other children. Occasionally the whole team and the parents have ice cream or go out for pizza after a game. These are usually enjoyable times for the whole family, whether the team wins and whether your child does well. You can model good sportsmanship after your child's team loses or when your child loses an individual event. You can link a loss to times in your life when things didn't go right, you didn't receive a coveted promotion or lost a race. Then you can share with your child how you handled it. These times together can be meaningful occasions for conversation, commiseration, and encouragement. They are opportunities to show your child that you respect her efforts and you respect her separately from how well or not well she performs in sports.

Sports Can Help Increase a Child's Self-Esteem and Self-Confidence

Perhaps the most important reason to encourage a child to learn and play some sport is that even small amounts of achievement or mastery in sports can result in enhanced self-esteem and self-confidence. Learning something, practicing, and becoming more skilled are bits and pieces of many tasks in life. The self-confidence that comes from learning a sport, practicing it, and getting better at it can spill over into other life activities. Self-confidence helps when we face new challenges. It is not much of a stretch for a child to say to himself, "I was terrible in tennis at first, but by really working at it, I got pretty good. This physics class is really difficult, but if I just work at it, like I did tennis, maybe it'll get easier."

Sometimes kids who are failing in school or in other areas of their lives have little confidence in themselves. After they take up a sport, they develop or regain their belief in themselves, apply the discipline of their sport to the rest of their lives, and begin to turn their lives around.

Sports Build Character

It is often said that sports build character. Some of the character traits they can help develop include self-discipline, personal responsibility, loyalty, hard work, integrity, dedication, and never giving up. Some people believe that sports don't build character as much as they reveal character. Sports can do both. With good coaches or instructors who lead in healthy ways and who demand that players always do their best, most children will develop and learn important lessons—lessons that can build character. There are also situations that come up in sports that will reveal character—a strength or determination that was not previously evident in the athlete.

Playing Sports Can Lead to a Lifelong Interest in Sports

Finally, participation in sports, if only on a beginner level or if only for a couple of years, may be enough to develop a lifelong interest in sports—an interest that can be expressed in ways other than playing a sport. For example, various occupations involve sports and the knowledge of sports. Some of these careers include sportscaster, sports writer, sports photographer, sports lawyer, coach/instructor, official/referee, sports psychologist, statistician, sports agent, sports medicine physician, athletic director, and personal trainer. Of course, becoming a lifelong and enthusiastic fan is a worthy outcome of playing sports as a child.

For all these reasons, involvement in sports is an excellent investment of time, effort, and in some cases, money. Your child, and you, can reap many benefits. You don't have to sacrifice other values to have a child involved in sports. For example, if you value education, you can make it clear that keeping up good grades is a requisite for continued participation in sports. Many schools have a sports eligibility requirement based upon grades so you don't always have to do the enforcing. Playing sports may require some prioritizing on the part of both you and your child. This is good. If you keep a healthy perspective and encourage a proper balance of activities, there are few downsides to sports at this level.

Can sports help build self-esteem? Can losing, which is inevitable in athletic competition, damage self-esteem? Self-esteem is a complex but important subject for parents to understand. I discuss this topic in the next chapter.

2   Sports and Self-Esteem

Winning and losing are a part of life, and
realizing that some people are better than
you in some areas is also a part of life.

SELF-ESTEEM is a controversial and hot topic in both psychology and
education. There are several differing positions.

- Some believe that a child cannot achieve without self-esteem.
  "How can my child possibly succeed at anything unless he feels
  good about himself first?"
- Others believe that a child cannot develop self-esteem without
  achievement. "How can my child possibly feel good about himself
  unless he can do or learn something first?"
- Still others believe that any negative experience can lower a child's
  self-esteem. "Any negative experience or failure will harm my
  child's self-esteem."

Self-esteem has to do with how a person feels about himself. Of
course, we want our children to feel good about themselves. We want
them to grow up to be individuals who are competent, happy, and who
have developed good self-esteem. How is self-esteem achieved? Is a
person born with it? Is it taught? Is it caught?

Children are more likely to develop healthy self-esteem if they
have the following:

1. Loving, nurturing, supportive parents

2. Positive experiences in life, especially in childhood

3. Opportunities to be successful in some areas, such as school and sports

4. Friendships and learning that successes don't necessarily come automatically without hard work

Competition and Self-Esteem

That seems straightforward enough, but the devil is in the details and the details are where the differing views come in.

There is some controversy regarding the need for children to have only positive experiences and success. Some people fear that any negative experience or failure in life may harm children and prevent them from developing positive self-esteem. Those who hold this view seek to cushion their children from any setbacks in life. They try to do this in a number of ways: they discourage letter or number report cards, as well as failing grades, and they support only competition that awards every participant equally. A good example of this occurred when an educator in California worried that if schoolchildren played the game of tag it could cause them emotional damage, especially the loss of self-esteem. The educator contended that this would happen since not all children can win when playing tag.

Ironically, many young children have the need to know who won and who lost. Five-year-old Matt entered his pumpkin in a pumpkin-decorating contest for Halloween at school. All the pumpkins received the same black-and-gold ribbon. He asked his mother, "Which pumpkin won? Where's the winner?" She told him that it looked like everyone won. "Yeah, but who won?" he asked again. Even this five-year-old wondered what the point was if everybody won.[5]

If parents believe that any competition or failure or comparison among children is bad for their child, then they will be unlikely to encourage, much less allow, the child to learn or play a sport. This point of view may be even stronger when it comes to team sports.

However, the development of self-esteem is more complex than parents may realize. For example, we know that Japanese children score better on standardized tests than American children do; yet

Japanese children score low on self-esteem measures while American children score high. Most people think that criminals commit crimes because of low self-esteem, yet a surprising number of criminals have high self-esteem scores.

Can a child's self-esteem be crushed by receiving an F in math? Can a child's self-esteem be ruined by losing a race? There is little evidence for this. In fact, the reverse may be true. For example, a child can be an excellent student or an outstanding athlete yet still have low self-esteem. How a parent or coach reacts to and handles a child when he loses a race may be more important in determining the impact of the loss on him than the loss itself. Self-esteem can also be influenced by how a parent or coach responds to a win.

Your child doesn't raise her self-esteem by lowballing life's tasks or by saying "I can't." She doesn't need to win in order to build her self-esteem. She does have to learn to say "I can" or "I can try." She can be taught to set small goals that are likely to be met if she tries. She should learn that she can feel good about herself through her efforts, taking note of any improvement.

A child's self-esteem isn't helped if he is constantly told how well he does certain things, even when he knows he is having difficulty doing them or does them poorly. Constant praise when not backed up by some achievement, however small, contributes little to a child's self-esteem. When this happens, children "feel good about themselves for no reason. We've given them this cotton candy sense of self with no basis in reality."[6] I worked with a young child whose learning disability affected his ability to read. We played a game where I printed some simple words. He read "hit" correctly but had trouble reading "head," pronouncing it with a long *e*, as in *leader*. He was beginning to be down on himself. I asked him if when he was born did he know how to read "hit"? He laughed, and said no. I pointed out that he has learned how to read "hit" and that it was only a matter of time before he would be able to read harder words. This encouraged him and raised his spirits. Rather than allowing him to focus on what he thought was a failure, I had him focus on the fact that he has been able to learn; he's gone from zero ability to read to being able to read "hit." (Note that I did not tell him he's a poor reader—he knows this already. Nor did I tell him that he's a great reader—he knows he's not and would eventually not trust me if I said things that were not true.) Feeling good when showing slow progress or small gains in some ability or skill is the same for sports. Even the most uncoordinated child can learn how to catch a ball. It may take him longer than other children, but step by step, he can do something that he had at one time thought he couldn't. A child doesn't have to win or be totally adept at something to build his self-esteem. Rather, even small improvements in a skill or ability can begin to build self-esteem and self-confidence.

Sports and Self-Esteem

Some parents are reluctant to allow their children to play sports because they fear that losing a race or being compared unfavorably to other players will hurt their child's self-esteem.

Winning and losing are a part of life. Realizing that some people are better than you in some areas is also a part of life. If your child joins a soccer team, unless he is a natural athlete, he will quickly notice that some of the kids seem to catch on more quickly and perform better than he. But with good coaching and determined effort on the child's part, he will soon see that he's getting better. Occasionally, he will do something during a game that helps his team win. Or he may do something that contributes to a loss. In both instances, he won't be the only player helping to win or contributing to a loss. He sees that playing soccer is a team effort and that he can have a positive contribution. There's little in this scenario that makes for lowered self-esteem. He can feel good about himself by being a good team member. He can feel good about himself by seeing his improved performance. Yes, he may look around and compare himself to the other team members. He may even rate himself as one of the poorer players on the team. But if the parent and coach handle the situation correctly, he will not automatically feel bad about himself.

It's a rare child who is crushed at the realization that some kids are better at sports than he is. Ten-year-old Andrew Somerville acknowledges this fact almost philosophically, "I play a lot of sports but I don't excel. I can admit that I stink because I'm good at other things, and that's just me."[7] Indeed, parents may be surprised to learn that there is considerable research that shows that participation in sports can increase the self-esteem and motivation of young players. This increase in self-esteem and motivation often translates into academic achievement, lower school dropout rates, and reduced incidence of high-risk behaviors such as drug and alcohol abuse and smoking.

Natalie was a freshman in high school with all Fs and was in danger of flunking out. She took up boxing and it turned her life around. She is now seventeen, receiving all As, and plans to go to college and become an attorney. The discipline of boxing taught her lessons that she applied to school and life.[8]

Protecting your child from competition does not guarantee high self-esteem. Encouraging her to learn a sport or athletic skill, within a healthy, supportive context, with the right coach or instructor and the right team or league, can help build her self-esteem. Accomplishments, however small, can help improve her self-esteem and self-confidence. Participation in sports can also help prepare her for life. It is said that sports are a metaphor for life—a life that includes successes along with failures.

3 Conversations about Sports

*Unbeknownst to his parent, Brian had thought
about playing baseball before but rejected
it because he thought he was too klutzy.*

CHILDREN WHO ARE ATHLETIC will often show an interest in sports and tell you that they want to play or join a team. However, the child who is uncoordinated may not express the desire to try a sport. It is helpful for his parents to realize that there may be a number of reasons for this. If they have a conversation with him to explore the possibility of playing, they may be surprised to find out that he has been thinking about playing a sport—the idea has been percolating— for a while. Obviously, such a conversation needs to be conducted in an inquiring and gentle manner. Parents don't want to come across as though they are pressuring or forcing a child to participate in sports.

There are several possible scenarios for such conversations. The following are reconstructions of conversations that four parents had with their children—children who could have been described as "clumsy," and whom I had been seeing in therapy. Since I felt that playing sports would be therapeutic for these children, I had recommended to their parents that they introduce the idea of playing sports to their children. Then, I advised the parents how to bring this up with their kids. After the parents had spoken with their children, they reported back to me how it went. (The names of the children have been changed.)

Here's the conversation Brian's father had with his son.

PARENT: I wonder, Brian, if you have ever thought about playing some sport?

CHILD: Well, yes, but I'm awfully clumsy. I could never be as good as Mike.

PARENT: What do you think about the other kids on the team? Are they all as good as Mike?

CHILD: No way! Phil can hardly catch the ball.

PARENT: Sounds like there are some really good players, like Mike, and then there are some players who aren't as good.

CHILD: Yeah. Most are not as good as Mike.

PARENT: Not all team members can be stars. A team has all kinds of players or else . . .

CHILD: There wouldn't be a team.

PARENT: That's right. So, do you think you'd like to try basketball?

CHILD: No. But maybe I could try baseball.

Unbeknownst to his dad, Brian had thought about playing baseball before but rejected it because he thought he wasn't good enough. By exploring the idea of playing a sport, Brian's father was able to support his son's interest.

This was an easy conversation because Brian already had thought about playing a sport and he even had the sport picked out.

Here is a similar conversation, but with a child who has not thought seriously about playing any sport or game, partly because she was minimally athletic but also because she had thought only in terms of team sports.

PARENT: Susan, have you ever considered playing a sport?

CHILD: Oh, Dad, you know I can barely ride my bike!

PARENT: I know it's taken you a while to get the hang of it, but you've gotten much better lately.

CHILD: That's true. But I think I'm a hopeless case when it comes to sports.

PARENT: I know that you think you're pretty awkward.

CHILD: I don't think I'm awkward. I know I am. Look at Paula. She can do just about anything.

PARENT: Paula and some of your other friends seem to be more athletic than you, but that doesn't mean that there isn't some sport you could play that you might enjoy and over time even get better at—like with biking.

CHILD: I don't know. I think I'd be embarrassed being on the soccer team.

PARENT: Maybe you'd be more comfortable if you thought about participating in an individual sport or game.

CHILD: Umm. Toby's learning tae kwon do. She's a blue belt. She loves it.

PARENT: Is that something you think you'd like to try—maybe eight to ten sessions? Just to try it, see if you like it?

CHILD: Yeah. I'd like that.

Because Susan was awkward, she had automatically ruled out playing any sport. By pointing out to Susan that she had been getting better riding her bike and by redirecting her thinking toward individual sports, Susan's father was able to tease out an interest that Susan had in tae kwon do.

The next child seems to draw a blank during this conversation with his mother.

PARENT: Joe, do you ever think about joining one of the teams at school?

CHILD: I'd rather read. Besides, you know I'm not good at sports.

PARENT: Well, I don't know that for sure since you've never played any sports.

CHILD: I just don't think I'm very athletic.

PARENT: You know, most kids aren't great athletes, but they play some sport anyway. They get better at it and they seem to be having fun.

CHILD: What do you think I'd be good at?

PARENT: Does that mean you'd like to try some sport?

CHILD: Well, maybe, if I could think of something I'd be interested in. Right now I'm clueless.

PARENT: Perhaps we can put our heads together and study various sports. Maybe we can find a sport or game that interests you or fits in with some of your strengths. Are there some sports you like to watch on TV? You might have to try several different sports before you find one that seems right for you.

CHILD: Maybe something nobody else does.

Like Susan, Joe ruled out sports because he wasn't very athletic. Unlike Susan, he never thought beyond that. He had never considered a sport he might like to play. Following this conversation with his mother, Joe doesn't appear to be very excited, but he seems open. His mother did not pressure him; rather, she opened the door just by having this conversation with him. And, she didn't start to narrow his choices by suggesting any specific sports. Now, the hard part—researching various sports with Joe to find a sport or game that interests him and fits in with the strengths he may have.

Brian and Susan had never openly expressed their interest in playing a sport. Both apparently had shut the door on this possibility because they assumed that if they were awkward they couldn't play a sport. Interestingly, each one even had a sport picked out. The third child, Joe, had shut the door so hard that he never went any further and never thought about a specific sport that he might want to play. By having these conversations with their children, the three parents found out something about their children that they didn't know before, and they were able to open doors for them without pressuring them.

Let's look at a conversation with a fourth child.

PARENT: Sheila, have you ever wanted to learn or play a sport?

CHILD: No.

PARENT: I wonder if you're not interested because you're not very athletic.

CHILD: You can say it, Dad, I'm the biggest klutz on the block! But that's not the reason I don't want to play sports—look at my friend Jill—she's *really* a klutz, but she's gotten pretty good at soccer. No, I'm having too much fun with my art and flute lessons. Besides, I just don't have the time.

PARENT: That's fine. I just wanted to make sure that you didn't rule out sports because you weren't very athletic. I'm glad you're enjoying your art and flute lessons. That song you played on the flute a while ago was really pretty. You really play the flute well.

Sheila knows she's a klutz, and she has no interest in sports. Her disinterest is not related to her being awkward. She knows that even clumsy children can play sports. Just as some athletic children do not play sports, some children have no interest in playing sports, klutz or not. Sheila's father opens the door by exploring the possibility of participating in sports. He finds out that she has not ruled it out because she is a klutz or has assumed that a klutz can't play. Rather, she has other interests that she finds enjoyable. His agenda was not to get her to be active in sports. He just wanted to make sure that she didn't have a hidden, unexpressed interest in sports—an interest that had been shelved by her because of her awkwardness.

When is the best time to pursue youth sports? While no one answer fits all sizes or ages, in the next chapter I offer some guidelines that can help parents with this question.

4	# When to Start?

> You may have a child who is ten who is not
> ready to play any sport; but you may have
> a younger child who is seven who is ready.

AT WHAT AGE should a child begin to play a sport or learn some athletic skill? While a good question, it is a difficult one to answer. By the end of this chapter, you will see that the answer to this question depends upon a number of factors.

Children begin developing their physical abilities—abilities that are necessary for sports—almost at birth. They crawl, stand, totter, walk, then they run, then they see who can run the farthest or the fastest. All this is through trial and error and without formal instruction.

The question "When to Start?" needs to be broken down in two: When can my child begin to learn the basics or fundamentals of a sport? and When can my child play in some organized sport involving teams or leagues and some low-level competition?

Playing Continuum
It is useful to think of learning or participating in sports at different levels.

Readiness:
Learning sports readiness usually applies to children four and under. At this level, they are not necessarily learning the basic moves or skills of the sport. Being comfortable in the water, not minding getting water

in their eyes, blowing bubbles in the water, are all examples of swimming readiness skills. Doing somersaults, tumbling, and bouncing on the trampoline are some of the readiness moves that introduce children to gymnastics. Learning to catch balloons and throw Nerf balls are a couple of the readiness abilities that lead to some of the basic skills for baseball. Often parents can work with their children at the readiness level.

Basic moves of a sport:
Children are taught the basic movements, skills, and rules of a sport. Often they are not taught all the components of the game. They may just learn how to do a forehand, a backhand, a rudimentary serve, and how to run to the ball and get their feet placed correctly.

Basic moves of a sport, learning to play a game or perform an event, but with no scoring or competition:
Here children learn all the basic movements of a sport and the rules, they play or perform on a real court or field, play a game, and learn about scoring, but no scores are kept, and no one wins or loses. Depending upon the sport, some simple scrimmaging plays may be conducted.

Basic moves of a sport, learning to play a game or perform an event, but with actual scoring or competition:
At this point, children are able to engage in competition and know all the basic moves and rules of the sport or game.

The level of a sport a child may begin with may depend on the child's age, readiness level, basic athletic skills, personality, and the teams, instructors, and coaches available in your locale. For example, many children are able to skip the readiness instruction because they already have the readiness skills and/or have natural athletic ability. Or, you might have a child who has learned the basic moves of a sport, but you prefer that he play on a team that doesn't compete. However, there may be no teams around that don't compete.

Readiness and Beginning Lessons

We know that when his son was only two years old, Tiger Woods's father was showing him the basics of playing golf. At that age, Tiger once putted with Bob Hope. Chris Evert began playing tennis at five. Scott Hamilton got his start a little later. He began skating when he was nine, and though not thought to be very athletic at the time (he was a sickly child), he seemed to take to it and his parents arranged for lessons shortly thereafter. There are many other examples of star athletes beginning to learn a sport or athletic skill at an early age.

If your child is four and shows an interest in playing, and you've identified a sport she'd like to learn, then just learning the basic movements at this age may be OK. Keep in mind that there may not be any team or instructor in your area who will take on children this young, so you might have to wait until she is older.

As mentioned, some children can be exposed to a physical activity/ sport *without* learning the basics of the sport. The American Academy of Pediatrics says that children under four are not developmentally ready to have formal swim lessons. That said, it is perfectly OK to teach swimming readiness at an early age. For example, many programs instill readiness with children as young as six months. The main idea of these programs is to increase the child's comfort in the water. (The Red Cross and the YMCA and YWCA are the leaders in providing such classes.) Then, when the child is a little older, swim instructors can build on this confidence to teach the child how to swim. Children as young as two or three can get ready to learn gymnastics by first being in a class that shows them how to tumble, balance, and jump. This same concept—teaching sport readiness—applies to many other sports.

There *are* some coaches or teachers who do have programs for very young children, programs that focus on teaching some of the basic skills of the sport.

One program in Denver teaches girls from kindergarten to fourth grade the basics of playing basketball. Sponsored by the University of Denver, it is a summer camp for the girls and their parents and the DU women's basketball coach is in charge of it. Women on DU's basketball team are the coach's assistants. They emphasize movement drills, listening skills, and the basic skills of the sport. The instructors turn the skill drills into games, like Simon Says. The girls are taught a few of the moves and mechanics of the game. For example, only three defensive plays are taught: guarding the player who has the ball, preventing a pass, and blocking a player who has managed to elude a teammate. The teachers don't just show how to make certain moves. They also explain the why of certain skills and moves. Having fun is emphasized.

A graduate of this program does not, by any means, learn all the plays and moves of the game. She is certainly not a complete player. But she has received excellent instruction, with lots of opportunities to practice skills and moves in an entertaining way.[9] Many cities have similar programs for very young children.

When children six and under play on a team, be prepared to see the kids look like little atoms moving about at random. It seems as if each child is playing an individual sport. They are a team in name only. For example, in basketball, it's difficult for kids this young to make the basic movements *and* include their team members by passing to them, blocking or screening their opponents, or always noting where their teammates are on the court. The child who half runs, half dribbles from one end of the court to the other and then shoots at the basket may look like he's selfishly hogging the ball. In actuality, he is so focused on making his basic moves that he forgets he has team members. Most children his age seldom understand the concept of cooperative play or teamwork. Nor can they understand concepts such as strategizing or positioning. This is OK and should be expected at this age.

Not all children are developmentally or emotionally ready to learn a sport when they are four or five. Parents must be sensitive to individual differences. If your daughter has developed slowly or is less mature than other kids her age, you may want to wait until she is older before placing her in a sport. With young children, taking up a sport or athletic skill is usually exploratory, so there is absolutely no need to rush to begin.

Playing in Organized Sports

Once a child has learned the fundamentals of a sport, when can he join a team or play at a competitive level? Generally, it is not recommended that a very young child participate in organized sports or competitive teams, even low-competition teams. The experts vary on when it is appropriate for a child to start playing organized sports; generally, the earliest ages recommended are six to eight. But some experts warn that kids should begin when they are older, especially if there is significant exposure to competition. Parents need to resist placing their children on competitive teams or leagues before they are ready. This may be difficult for many parents since competition is often what's fun for them. Check to see if your child thinks competition would be fun. If he is not ready for competition, try to locate a team or place where the game is played but with no competition.

If it seems to you that your child may be ready to play competitively, talk with him first about what it means to go from learning the basics to actually competing. Does it sound like fun? If after this discussion you are satisfied that he is physically and emotionally ready for competition, you can begin looking for a competitive league or team.

Again, a great deal depends upon the individual child, the nature of the sport, the coach, and the team. Parents need to understand which level of organized sports as well as competition their child is ready for. A parent might have a ten-year-old child who is not ready to play organized sports or to compete. Another parent might have a seven-year-old child who *is* ready. All that experts can offer are some rules of thumb. You should take their advice seriously, but you also need to be able to evaluate your child and make your own judgments.

The Older Child

What if your teenager has just now expressed an interest in learning to play a sport and play it competitively? There may be many reasons it's taken him so long to show an interest in athletics. Maybe he's now more coordinated than he was as a child. Perhaps he's gained some confidence in some other, nonathletic endeavors, and now is emotionally ready to face learning something that he's not a natural in. He may have just heard of an uncommon sport that he's interested in. It may be that when younger, he was involved in some nonsport activity but has lost interest and now wants to play a sport.

You may be able to locate programs that offer lessons or instruction for teenage novices. However, finding a high school team or comparable youth league team with teenage players that take on kids who are new to the game may be a challenge. By this time, most players on these teams have been playing for a number of years and are no longer beginners. There may be no teams or leagues available for the teenager who has never played the sport before, especially if it is a team sport.

Certain sports—individual and team—are often only offered in middle school or high school athletic programs. This way, even though your child has just now indicated an interest in sports, she may be able to get in on the ground floor if she is interested in one of the sports that tend to be taught in the later school years. Depending upon where you live, some of these sports are wrestling, field hockey, lacrosse, golf, swimming, tennis, and track and field. Additionally, some high schools offer PE classes in which certain team and individual sports are taught. For some kids, this may be their first real exposure to a sport, and it's conceivable that a few of them may become quite good over time. I know several adults who first played a team sport when they were taught lacrosse in high school PE classes. They went on to play on their college teams.

If your child is interested in a team sport but you cannot find any that are available to him at his age and beginner level, he may have to consider learning an individual sport instead. There are more opportunities for the older child who is a beginner to play and/or compete in individual sports than in team sports. For example, many opportunities exist for a teenager to learn golf, tennis, or one of the martial arts. Thus, if your child had his heart set on playing a team sport and you can't find an appropriate team for him to play on, you may have to help him compromise and encourage him to look into individual sports.

What are the ingredients necessary for playing sports? The next chapter delves into this topic.

5

Physical Ability and Then Some

Playing sports and games involves
more than sheer athletic ability.

WHAT FACTORS ARE INVOLVED when playing sports or participating in some athletic endeavor? The main ingredients are:

- Athletic ability
- Instruction/practice
- Motivation/effort/attitude
- Tactical and/or strategic abilities

Let's look at each of these in more depth.

Athletic Ability

For many sports, some of the basic physical abilities and physical attributes or capacities (for example, body type, size, and aerobic capacity) are partially determined by genetics. Michael Jordan did not become the basketball player he was without tremendous athletic ability as well as certain physical attributes or qualities. We often call this natural ability. By this we mean that he had much of the natural ability and physical features to play basketball before he ever picked up a ball. These features included quickness, speed, good eye-hand coordination, and height. Genetics determined these. Obviously, enhancing these natural abilities and turning them into skills required hours of instruction in the game's basics as well as the finer points, and considerable practice over the years. However, if he hadn't started out with that natural talent, physical ability, and physical build, all the instruction and all the hours of practice would not have been enough to make him the star he was.

Let's take a look at the genetic contributions for another super athlete. Lance Armstrong is the first and only seven-time winner of cycling's Tour de France—a feat no other cyclist has accomplished. When he was sixteen, his aerobic power was tested at the Cooper Institute in Dallas, an athletic fitness and conditioning center. This test, called the VO_2 Max, measures the maximum amount of oxygen the lungs can consume during exercise. The more oxygen a person is able to use, the more energy he produces and the faster he can run, swim, or ride. Armstrong's VO_2 Max levels were the highest ever recorded at the clinic.[10] Training and conditioning have, no doubt, improved his VO_2 Max levels even further, but clearly, the fact that his lungs can consume huge amounts of oxygen during races is a genetic gift. Another genetic gift—long thighbones—enables him to apply ideal amounts of torque to his pedals when racing. No amount of practice would lengthen his thighbones. These physical attributes are obviously quite helpful for optimal cycling performance.

Olympic gold medalist Amanda Beard was a natural athlete and a fish in water early on. When she was five years old she told her parents that she was going to swim in the Olympics. By the time she was thirteen it was apparent she was a natural, and her coach encouraged her to train full-time. She won her first Olympic gold medal in 1996 when she was fifteen.

John McEnroe preferred team sports when he was younger; he liked the camaraderie they provided. However, his natural abilities and physical gifts—quick feet, superb hand-eye coordination—gave him an advantage in tennis. He found the right sport for himself and went on to become one of the great tennis stars of his day.

Ice skater Tara Lipinski began roller skating when she was three and took up ice skating when she was six. While she also enjoyed horseback riding and baton twirling, skating was her first love. Lipinski began winning important competitions at twelve. She won the gold medal at the 1998 Olympics when she was only fifteen. At that time, she was the youngest gold medalist in figure skating history.

Most professional athletes and Olympians exhibited natural athletic abilities at an early age. While they were good at several sports when younger, they eventually focused on one sport—the one of several they were best in.

If your child is a natural or above-average athlete, she can probably do well in a number of sports as she already has many of the physical abilities needed for success. At this point, you and your child may want to narrow down the choices since it may not be realistic for her to play more than one or two sports a season. (The fact sheets in Part 2 will help with this process.) Many young children with average to above-average athletic ability *will* want to play several sports, and this should be encouraged since sport specialization at an early age is not advised.

However, not all natural athletes are good in more than one sport. Counterintuitive? Yes, but true. I've seen a number of children who appear to be naturally athletic. They pick up and master one sport quickly, but they never seem to do very well in other sports.

What are the implications for the minimally athletic child? Clearly, this child does not start out with the natural athletic abilities that most athletes have. This is OK since our goal is not to turn the minimally athletic child into a star. However, he may have some eye-hand coordination, perhaps not as much and not as natural as some of his athletic friends, but some. Does this mean that he can't play baseball? No. He can play baseball if he is interested in it and wants to learn the basics and is willing to practice. He may not ever be a star on his team, but he can play and have fun.

It is a rare child who does not have a smidgen of physical ability that translates into some movement or ability necessary for a sport. Try to identify the areas of his physical ability, however minuscule. See if these abilities correlate with any sports he may be interested in. (The fact sheets in Part 2 can help you and your child find a sport that's right for him.)

Also, some minimally athletic children who appear generally clumsy seem to excel in one movement or skill. Sometimes these children, with good instruction, can find considerable success in a sport.

For example, I have worked with a number of children who appeared to be totally lacking in athletic ability. However, I noticed that they could run like the wind. With excellent coaching, they were able to turn this physical ability into achievement in one of the track running events. When I was a swim team coach, I had a number of kids who were very uncoordinated. However, in water, they swam like fish! Some less-coordinated children do better in certain positions. For example, if your daughter is not a natural athlete and isn't particularly quick, she may do better playing right field rather than first base. A clumsy son may find being a guard more suited to his athletic limitations than being a receiver.

Because most hitters are right-handed, they hit fewer balls to right field. Thus, right fielders often see little action. This is why a child whose fielding skills are weak is often placed in right field. The plight of the right fielder is captured by Willy Welch in his famous poem, Right Field.

Instruction/Practice

Do you know of any natural athlete or athletic star or champion who does not study the game and practice and practice? Remember Lance Armstrong? In spite of having great aerobic capacity and long thigh-bones—being a natural cyclist—he still trained year-round by doing punishing workouts and rides. He would not be the cyclist he is if he had just rested on his natural ability laurels. Competitive figure skaters practice four to six hours a day. Their coaches follow their every move and constantly instruct and comment on their performance. Clearly, natural ability alone, even if a skater has been very lucky genetically and inherited all the right physical qualities to be a star skater, is not enough to be a star or winner. The flip side is also true: children with limited natural ability can go far and achieve considerable success in sports if they work on the other ingredients necessary to be competitive. Good instruction and dedication to practicing are some of these ingredients.

"Talent only gives you the opportunity to win."

—Chad Brown, *NFL linebacker*

Why is practice so important? Workouts and practices are times when the coach or instructor and the athlete identify weaknesses, especially skill weaknesses, and use this time to make corrections and improvements.

Good workouts and practices also help to prepare the athlete or team for competition. There was a time when I testified in court quite often. My colleagues and I noticed that the lawyers who were better prepared usually won their cases. The athlete or team that is better prepared has a better chance of winning. Practice and preparation build confidence and confidence helps performance.

Another reason is muscle memory. By practicing often, muscle memory is developed. When muscle memory allows the player to make some of the basic moves almost automatically, the brain is freed up to perform other tasks. Some of these tasks might include concentrating, analyzing, or responding to one's opponents in team sports.

All outstanding athletes—players who presumably are natural athletes—practice for hours almost every day. Children who are lucky enough to have good athletic ability will still have to work hard and practice if they want to improve and take their playing ability to a higher level.

For the less athletic children, we know that good instructors or coaches and lots of practice can make up for some of the lack of genetically determined natural ability. We often hear of baseball or basketball players who do not have the natural abilities or moves of other stars. Yet, by dogged practice and motivation, they are able to compete with the stars and in some instances are considered outstanding players, if not stars. Desire, determination, and dedication can take children far in their chosen sports, no matter the level of their athletic abilities.

Think back to your own childhood. Was there a friend of yours who didn't seem that naturally athletic yet who was able to play some sport quite well? Maybe he practiced for hours and hours to reach that level of play.

Interestingly enough, when eighth graders were interviewed about their attitudes regarding their own athletic abilities, most of them indicated that they didn't have to be born with natural athletic ability to play a sport.[11] Most believed that learning a sport is an acquired skill—one that can be learned with effort and practice. So, if your child has an excellent tennis coach or instructor, and if she really practices a lot, she can overcome some of the lack of natural ability. However, she may never be a Serena Williams on the court.

Motivation/Effort/Attitude

A number of ingredients go into motivation, effort, and attitude:

- Positive attitude
- Ability and willingness to find some satisfaction in repetitious and sometimes boring drills and practices
- Pleasure at signs of improvement
- Ability to handle setbacks or losses
- Level of determination to persevere
- Mental toughness
- Competitiveness

The word *motivate* comes from Latin and it means *to move*. Parents and coaches play a role in helping to motivate and encourage a child's continued efforts to learn a sport or game and to improve his skills or performance. A good coach is one who can motivate his players to play their best. But you and the coach or instructor can and should do only so much. Most of the motivation to play, to practice, and to try hard must come from your child. Baseball "Ironman" Cal Ripken, Jr., points out that if you push your child to play sports and the motivation to play is not coming from the child, then "you're taking the enjoyment and love out."[12] If you or the coach find that you are expending great efforts to motivate your child to practice or perform, a reevaluation is in order. It may be time to stop completely or to find another sport.

A positive attitude helps in many ways. A "can-do" attitude helps players do their best. Negative thinking often becomes prophecy that comes true. Children who think they can't learn the moves of a sport are less likely to learn the moves. Athletes who don't believe that anything is possible on the playing field are less likely to succeed or produce their personal best. The mind is a very powerful thing, and a positive mind-set can make the difference between an athlete doing his best and failing. Furthermore, a negative attitude can infect other team members. Players with a positive attitude can, even if they are not the best players, often inspire others to play better. So even children lacking in natural athletic ability can create a little bit of an edge with their positive attitude.

> *"You can accomplish so much with a strong will. Just do your best. No matter what. Don't let negative thoughts creep in. Don't talk yourself out of anything."*
>
> —Rebecca Twigg,
> *Olympic cyclist and holder of several world titles*

Athletes who play in frigid weather are told to ignore the cold and just tell themselves that it's really nice outside. Many Green Bay Packers are able to do this. In spite of below-zero weather and extreme wind-chill factors, they play without long sleeves. Seeing them play in a blizzard you'd think it was 100 degrees. By not focusing on the cold weather, players can concentrate on playing well.

In a book explaining the power of the mind and mind-set, a psychologist went to Russia for a conference. He arrived in Moscow a few days early so he could take in the sights before the conference began. After being out all day, he returned to his hotel. The phone rang. He picked up the phone and listened for a few seconds. Finally, he said to the caller, "I don't speak Russian, can you speak English?" The caller replied, "Bob, this is Phil, I got in early, too." Phil had been speaking English right along, but Bob's mind-set was that he was the only English speaker to arrive early for the conference, so he concluded that the caller must be speaking Russian. An athlete's positive attitude and mind-set can give him an edge, or they can limit his perspective and performance.

Mental toughness can often trump limitations in physical ability. It is not unusual to see a pitcher, whether Major League or Little League, get trounced in the first inning and his team is down by three or four runs. This same pitcher doesn't give up, pulls himself together, settles down, and pitches near-perfect innings the rest of the game. Other pitchers might fall apart mentally and never regain their pitching control and skill in subsequent innings. The ability to focus mentally and to use the mind to overcome emotional meltdowns and to regain composure is an important ability in sports.

When an athlete has mental toughness, he doesn't allow his mind to tell him what his body can or cannot do. Mental toughness is such an important factor when playing sports that I cover it in more depth in the next chapter.

"Every single day I wake up and commit myself to becoming a better player. Some days it happens, and some days it doesn't. Sure, there are games I'm going to dominate and there are going to be games when I struggle. But it doesn't mean I give up."

—Mia Hamm, U.S. women's soccer star
and Olympic gold medalist

Competitiveness doesn't mean winning. It means the desire to do your best when competing or to see improvement in your performance under the pressure of competition. It means giving opponents a run for their money and in so doing, bringing out your best and the opponent's best. This, too, is such an important concept that another chapter is devoted to it.

Yogi Berra used to say, "Sports are 90 percent mental and the other half is physical." Notwithstanding Yogi's humorously fuzzy math, most sports require more than sheer athleticism. With good motivation, effort, and a positive attitude, most children can achieve some success whether or not they are blessed with natural athletic abilities.

Tactical/Strategic Abilities

Many sports involve the ability to analyze, problem solve, and strategize. Sometimes a lesser athlete can make up for some lack in natural abilities or physical attributes by being very good at the tactical/strategic aspects of the sport, or playing smart. Tennis and golf are good examples. It is often said that golf is more a mind game than a physical game. Certainly, mental toughness is a part of this notion. But golf involves almost continuous analyzing of the shots and decision making: the distance, the terrain, what club to use, how much muscle to put into the swing, the angles, and the slopes. A child who has patience and good analytical skills might end up playing better than a child whose physical skills are superior but who lacks patience and analytical skills. Famous golfer Bobby Jones said, "Competitive golf is played mainly on a five-and-a-half-inch course: the space between your ears."

A child who is not the most gifted athlete on the tennis court may gain some success because of his analytical skills. For example, he may observe some subtle weakness of his opponent and he may be able to exploit that weakness. He may notice that his opponent tires easily, so he deliberately tries to return the ball to the opposite side of where his opponent is. He may see that his opponent has a weak backhand and thus tries to hit his shots to his opponent's backhand. If a pitcher notices that a star hitter seems unable to hit a ball that is low and inside, that's where he will try to pitch. Outthinking your opponent is a perfectly acceptable tactic in sports.

"I'm not exceptionally fast or overly powerful. But I have a good work ethic, and I make up for it by using technique and trying to be smarter."

—Dot Richardson,
Olympic gold medal–winning softball player

Some children are naturally more cerebral and take to the more mental aspects of the sport they are playing. Also, certain sports require a more analytical approach than others. By maximizing their analytical/tactical/strategic skills and bringing them to the game, they can, to a degree, often make up for their lack of natural athletic ability.

As you can see, playing sports or games involves more than sheer athletic ability. Children who are natural athletes certainly have an edge, though that will probably not be enough to succeed. They will have to have the right attitude and show strong will and other mental attributes to achieve in their sport. Children with minimal athletic ability or few of the physical attributes associated with a particular sport can often achieve excellence through good instruction and training, practice, motivation and effort, and tactical and strategic skills. Cynthia Gorney, who coached her daughter's soccer team, said of one of the players, "The girl who swore she had been born clumsy learned to run like a yearling down the side of the field."13 Many parents have seen their uncoordinated children blossom into more than adequate athletes. Even the most ordinary athlete can occasionally perform in extraordinary ways. The worst thing parents can do is to underestimate the athletic potential of their child.

Of course, if children have natural athletic abilities they will still need to practice, show motivation, and develop their strategy and tactical skills. They can't just coast on their natural abilities alone.

Mental toughness means a lot of different things. In the next chapter I take a look at this quality or trait—a quality that can give athletes an edge in competition.

6

Mental Toughness

> Finishing the last few miles or kilometers of these races
> requires mind over matter—one's mental toughness
> keeps the body moving though it is physically trashed.

MENTAL TOUGHNESS refers to the ability to play your best under stress, pressure, or adverse circumstances. It means playing with confidence, positive thinking, concentration, and intelligence. It can mean overcoming various emotional pressures or heartaches. Sometimes it means having courage and being brave. Mental toughness is required when the pressures of performance mount and the athlete must not let the pressures have a negative impact on his performance. The athlete needs mental toughness to ignore all distractions that can interfere with his performance.

When referring to elite athletes or stars, it can also refer to "playing hurt." Curt Schilling, pitcher for the Boston Red Sox in the 2004 World Series, was called "heroic," "courageous," "unbelievably tough" when he played with a painful and seriously damaged ankle. Over and over again the TV cameras zoomed in on blood seeping through his sock while he was pitching on the mound. Without mental toughness, even an elite athlete can lose to a lesser opponent.

Figure skater Nancy Kerrigan was assaulted with a leg injury as a result a few months before the 1994 Olympics. She went on to win a silver medal. A year before the 1998 Olympic games, Alpine skier Picabo Street severely injured the ligaments in her knee. She had to endure painful rehabilitation. Then, only a week prior to the Olympic games, she crashed into a fence while skiing, losing consciousness and suffering some bruises. A week later she went on to win the gold medal in the giant slalom ski event, the Super G. After the race, she noted that the crash helped her win. "I think I needed a big crash to get my mind off my knee." (Children and adolescents, however, should not be expected to play with any serious illness or injuries.)

The Burden of Past Losses

Time and again, athletes with disappointing losses have headed into new races or games with the burden of their past hanging over them. Even so, they have managed to shake away disabling pressures to turn in some of their best performances. American speed skater Dan Jansen was the favorite to win the 500-meter and the 1,000-meter in the Calgary Olympic Games in 1988. Three hours before the event he learned that his sister had died of leukemia. He slipped and fell in both events and failed to win any medals. In the next Olympics in 1992, again the favorite and holding the world records, he did not win a medal. With disappointment dogging him, he again raced in the 1994 Olympics, but came in eighth in the 500-meter—his best event. With only the 1,000-meter race left and his Olympic career nearly over, he told himself to forget the past and "just skate." He slipped and almost fell, but he won the gold and posted a new world record.

Since his teens, Norwegian speed skater Aadne Sondral was expected to be the successor to his countryman Johann Olav Koss and own the 1,500-meter event. Amid high expectations, he finished second in the 1992 Olympic Games in Albertville, France. Two years later, at the Olympics in Lillehammer, Norway, he missed medaling with a fourth-place finish. Heading into the next Olympics in 1998 in Nagano, Japan, he had begun to wonder if he was a loser. At first, it looked as though he was again going to be denied the gold medal. A skater from the Netherlands, Jan Bos, racing before Sondral, established a new world record. Bos and others at the rink assumed that he would be the winner, thinking it unlikely that anyone, especially Sondral, would be able to top Bos's performance. Sondral knew that in order to win, he would have to break Bos's world record established just minutes before. In spite of all the pressures going into his race and the memories of his past disappointing performances, Sondral did break Bos's record and time and won the gold.[14]

Overcoming Illness or Injury

Some other athletes or teams that have been able to overcome adversity, illness, or injury and go on to win or help their team win were speed skater Bonnie Blair who experienced a slump before the 1992 Olympics; gymnast Kerri Strug who injured her ankle on her first vault in the 1996 Olympics but a few minutes later nailed her second vault to help the U.S. women's team win the team gold; cyclist Lance Armstrong who battled testicular cancer before winning his first Tour de France in 1999; and in a performance referred to as the "miracle on ice" in the 1980 Olympics, the American ice hockey team, composed mostly of former college players and facing overwhelming odds, beat a Soviet team composed of world-class professionals. Then the Americans went on to defeat Finland for the gold. Outstanding physical performances all, but mental toughness won the day!

Certain sports and event distances seem to require almost nonstop mental toughness. Marathon races, 10,000-meter races, and the Tour de France (or any long cycling race) are examples of contests in which athletes are hurting, straining to breathe, or struggling not to collapse for the better part of the race. Finishing the last few miles or kilometers of these races requires mind over matter—an athlete's mental toughness keeps the body moving though it is physically trashed. At the finish line, the winners and the losers look about the same: most either have collapsed or are near collapse.

"Just because your muscles start to protest doesn't mean you have to listen."

—Speed skater Dianne Holum, *four-time Olympic medalist and two-time gold medal winner*

Mental Toughness in Clutch Situations

There are sports in which the winners are determined by hundredths of a second. These races require total concentration, effort, and mental toughness. One stray thought, one moment of lost focus, one negative thought, and athletes can lose. They must ignore distractions and anything that could interfere with their performance.

Sometimes the pressure on an athlete increases exponentially when the stakes are particularly high: a pinch hitter at the bottom of the ninth, two outs, in a tied Game 7 of the World Series; the goalie, in a tied overtime World Cup soccer game; and a gymnast who knows he has to nail a near-perfect routine in order to win the gold medal. (We saw this situation in the 2004 Summer Olympics in Athens. American gymnast Paul Hamm stumbled after his vault, and looking like a tipsy frat boy, almost landed in the judges' laps. He went on to receive high scores in the remaining two events and won the all-around gold.) These are clutch situations where athletes cannot let the pressure get to them. Especially in team sports, opponents and fans do their best to distract the players. In noisy football stadiums, the fans may try to make a lot of noise so that the other team can't hear the signals. In basketball, the fans wave thundersticks when a player tries to make a free throw. Sometimes players "trash talk" or make gestures to try to intimidate their opponents.

Players need mental toughness when they have to play in spite of some recent tragedy that has sapped them emotionally. We have seen athletes perform well just hours after the death of a parent, a sibling, a beloved grandparent, or a best friend. Many of them often put in one of their best performances and dedicate the game or race to the deceased relative or friend.

Mental Toughness Can Give Athletes an Edge

Mental toughness gives the elite athlete an edge. Sometimes the edge can be measured in seconds, millimeters, kilograms, or tenths of a point. But that may be all that is needed to win a close race or event. Average athletes with mental toughness can sometimes beat more talented opponents who don't have this quality.

Some young elite athletes have shown an ability to master or mentally downplay the anxieties and pressures of big-time competition and turn in winning performances while beating the older, ostensibly better, and more experienced performers. Figure skating and gymnastics, two very high-pressure sports, seem to produce young gold medalists.

Nadia Comaneci, Oksana Baiul, Tara Lipinski, and Sarah Hughes are examples. Lipinski and Hughes were perceived as loose and having fun as they darted around the ice like elves.

The lack of mental toughness—the inability to deal with the pressures and stresses of the sport, or the inability to rebound after some physical or emotional adversity—has resulted in numerous rising stars retiring from their sport.

Some children seem to have this quality of mental toughness naturally. They appear to take pressure, stress, and adversity in stride. But, other children don't seem able to rise to the occasion and show mental toughness. Some personal life situations may explain why children don't show mental toughness. And some children don't have this quality but may be able to develop it with some help. Sometimes a coach or a parent can figure out the reasons for this lack by speaking with the child. After doing so and if there is no improvement, a consultation with a sports psychologist may help. (See the section "When Do You Consult With a Sports Psychologist?" in Part 3.)

Clearly, mental toughness is an important part of all competition and can give an athlete an edge, especially in close races or performances. Patricia Miranda was the lone female wrestler on the Stanford University men's wrestling team, and being on the men's team was helping her develop mental toughness. She said, "I know I give up some things by not wrestling with women, but I'm getting amazing mental toughness getting my butt kicked every day." Though she won only once in her college career, she went on to win a bronze medal at the 2004 Athens Olympics in the women's 48 kg class.

Mental toughness can carry over to other areas of children's lives. It can increase confidence and feelings of competence and allows them to take on other hard situations they may have to face.

Another quality or trait that can give an athlete an edge is competitiveness, which is discussed in the next chapter.

7

Competitiveness

Competitiveness can mean different things
to different people. For some, it means
winning; for others, it means doing their best.

WINNING AT ALL COSTS is a message that permeates almost all sectors of our society: corporate, political, education, and athletic. Ours is a capitalistic and competitive society, and we tend to honor and exalt the winners and disparage the losers (though we do have an almost romantic penchant to root for the perennial underdogs, such as the Chicago Cubs and, formerly, the Boston Red Sox).

Getting the Message That Winning Is All

Thus, it is not surprising when children and teens think that competitiveness means winning or that winning at all costs is the goal of all competition. They see professional athletes play with serious injuries and boast about how a winner plays even when hurt. They hear about coaches who have been fired from their job because their teams didn't have winning seasons, or didn't make the playoffs, or didn't win States, or Nationals, or World. They overhear their parents refer to an Olympic runner as having "just" won the bronze. They see fans booing a player after he strikes out. They read about elite and star athletes using steroids and other drugs to give them a winning edge. They note that athletes who fail to win the top prize don't get the endorsements—and in some sports, the endorsements add up to more money than the athletes earn playing the game. They learn of coaches who are abusive of their players and who even cheat but who, if fired, are quickly hired by another team, school, or university. They get the idea that if you don't win, you're a loser.

We must teach that competitiveness in sports does not equal winning. Yes, an athlete with a competitive spirit may play to win—no players compete with the desire to lose. But competitiveness means a lot more than wanting or trying to win. It means doing your best against opponents who also want to do their best. Competitiveness is the sum of many ingredients: attending practices, training hard, having a positive attitude, having healthy lifestyle habits, teamwork, playing by the rules, playing your best during competition whether you are the favorite or the underdog. A child does not have to have great athletic ability to be competitive. Not giving up and giving her all is being competitive.

Admittedly, competitiveness can mean different things to different people. For some, it means winning; for others, it means doing their best.

I divided the book If Winning Were Easy, Everyone Would Do It: Motivational Quotes for Athletes, *a collection of quotations culled from the sayings of well-known athletes, coaches, and sports psychologists, into twenty-seven core categories. I found it interesting that only a handful of the quotes suggested that winning was everything or the only thing in sports. By far, most of the quotes fell into the category I titled "Doing Your Best."*

There *is* a correlation between competitiveness and winning. A child who has average athletic talent but who plays with competitiveness may win; a child who has great athletic talent but who plays without competitiveness may not win. This may explain why we often see athletes who have less athletic ability and the teams with fewer stars beat the better athletes or the better teams. This is why the slow turtle beat the much faster rabbit!

Competitiveness Helps to Bring Out Your Best

It is not enough to *want* to do well or do one's best. Athletes have to take that want and implement action to bring about their goal of doing their best. Competitiveness helps athletes go from wanting to do their best to taking the *action* required to accomplish this goal. Competitiveness helps to overcome fears of failure, anxiety, or having an off day physically. Even champions have days when they know they are not physically up to par. But they don't let themselves think, "Oh, I feel a little off today, I'm probably not going to do well." Instead, their competitiveness drives them to focus on the positive and they say, "OK, I'm still a little weak from the flu. What can I do to still do my best?" They don't line up excuses in case they lose or perform worse than expected. They look for ways to propel themselves into a mindset of doing their best. Maybe they're going to look harder for their opponents' weaknesses; maybe they're going to approach the game more tactically, using their smarts more; maybe they're going to force themselves to go after a few more balls on the court than they usually do—anything that can give them an edge.

> *"The bigger the game the better. I'm an adrenaline junkie. I feed off big crowds and noise."*
>
> —Curt Schilling,
> pitcher for two World Series championship teams

The Tougher the Competition, the Better

Athletes with that competitive drive often opt out of competitions that might provide them with easy wins. An easy win is not satisfying to them. They tend to do their best only when they are competing against athletes or teams that can and do beat them at times. There's not much of an incentive to do their best if athletes or teams know they're going to win easily. Over the years rivalries between two competitors or teams have often brought out the best in both and in the case of individual sports, led to broken Olympic, World, or championship records. Think of Pete Sampras and Andre Agassi in tennis; Brian Boitano and Brian Orser in figure skating; the U.S. Women's Soccer Team versus China; pole vaulters Stacy Dragila and Emma George; Duke versus North Carolina in men's college basketball; the Yankees against the Red Sox; or the University of Connecticut versus Tennessee in women's college basketball.

"You've got to look for tough competition.
You've got to want to beat the best."

—Grete Waitz, Norwegian runner and
winner of nine New York City Marathons

"Those who truly have the spirit of champions
are never wholly happy with an easy win.
Half the satisfaction stems from knowing it
was the time and the effort you invested
that led to your high achievement."

—Nicole Haislett, Olympic swimming champion

Competitiveness isn't just about your opponent. Yes, a fierce competitor can help bring out your best—and your best may be necessary to win. But competitiveness is about you—your ability to focus on your performance, your ability to concentrate on what you're doing, your determination to do your best, no matter what. Your opponent may win the race or competition, but you also win if you've done your best that day, that moment.

> *"Competition in its best form is a test of self.*
> *It has nothing to do with medals. The win-*
> *ner is the person who gets the most out*
> *of themselves."*
>
> —Al Oerter, *Olympic discus gold medalist*

Children and Competitiveness

Many children play with competitiveness. You can see their competitive drive in the way they practice, the passion they show when they play, their desire to play their best, and their ability to implement the behaviors necessary to bring about their best play or performance. Win or lose, they display the satisfaction of knowing that they did their best.

Other children don't appear to have this competitive drive. Sometimes it's because they have the wrong idea about what competitiveness means. If they think it means winning, there may be a number of reasons why they may hold back when they play. They may fear losing. They may fear winning. Sometimes athletes fear winning because they worry about the pressure or expectation that they feel from others (and may put on themselves) to continue to win. Each outcome may be loaded with psychological baggage.

Often, talking with such children can be helpful. By helping them to understand what playing a sport is about—having fun, improving, doing their best—they may be able to redirect their efforts from concern about winning to a desire and willingness to do their best. If they play a team sport, parents can help them understand that team members have the right to count on each other and to trust that each team member is giving his all. If players see that another player is not giving his best every moment of the game, they will lose confidence in him and may well begin to cut him out of play. The coach may also note his behavior and bench him. (Benching should not be done to punish; it should be done to give the player time to think about his behavior and/or performance and identify corrections he needs to make.)

Finally, when children don't do their best, someone needs to tell them that they are not honoring their sport. All sports have a long history of fierce competition and competitors. What makes sports engaging for most players and most fans is seeing competitors doing their best—and believing that on any given day, anyone can win.

Some of the most inspiring memories we have in sports are of athletes doing their best and in so doing, sometimes make what seem to be superhuman plays: the outfielder who chases and leaps to catch a ball "destined" to go over the wall for a home run; the basketball player who right before the final buzzer makes an "impossible" shot; the discus player who is born with a deformed nonthrowing arm yet modifies his approach to compensate for the deformity and becomes a champion; the skier who crashes early in the race, loses four seconds to the lead skiers, yet manages to pull herself together and medals; the golfer who, tied going into the eighteenth hole, tees off into the lake, recovers, and makes a difficult forty-foot putt to win the tournament; and the team that is down three games in the World Series yet never tells itself that it is not competitive and goes on to win the next four games. Not all inspiring efforts lead to a win. Sometimes such awesome performances are not enough to bring victory. But, win or lose, these athletes are winners and their efforts are long remembered.

If you and the coach have tried to work with a child who doesn't show competitiveness, see if she is interested in finding out why she doesn't seem to do her best in competition. If she expresses the desire to get further help, you may want to consult with a sports psychologist.

A number of areas that should be considered when a child is interested in playing a sport were covered in this chapter. It's time to begin to explore what sport he will play. Whether your child is a natural athlete and whether he knows for sure what sport he is interested in, it often helps first to consider some natural lead-ins to sports. In the next chapter, I offer some ideas about this.

8   Natural Lead-Ins to Sports

*After seeing a martial arts movie, does your child try
to make some of the moves she saw in the movie?*

HOW DOES A PARENT pique a child's interest in sports in a natural
and nonpressured way and help the child identify sports he might be
interested in? How do you encourage a child to play a sport who is
minimally athletic and who shows little or no interest in pursuing a
sport? What if a child is athletic but so far has shown little interest in
playing sports? Maybe a child is very athletic and wants to play but
isn't quite sure what sport to choose. Sometimes there are natural
lead-ins to an interest in sports and to the selection of a sport to play.

When a Sport Interest Is Close at Hand

It helps if children express some interest in a sport or athletic activity.
Their interest creates an opportunity for a discussion about sports and
why they are interested in this particular sport. They might have a best
friend who has signed up, or they might tell you that they can perform
some of the skills necessary for that sport and would like to learn more.
Or, "It seems like fun." Unless the reason seems totally unrealistic,
positive and supportive responses from you are important. Remember
my cousin; on the face of it, he had no basis to think that he would be
able to learn to ski. Neither did his mother.

Maybe your child will not express an interest in sports outright.
Look for indirect cues that she may be interested. Does she follow a

particular sport? Do you find that she watches a sport on TV? Does she go to soccer practices after school to watch her best friend play? Does she seem to know a lot about the sport? Has she made some offhanded comment that she wished she were more athletic so she could play soccer? After seeing a martial arts movie, does she try to make some of the movements she saw in the movie? Follow up on any such cues that might indicate an interest.

Athletic children may show great interest in playing sports, and because of their athletic skills, rarely question their ability to learn any sport. Still, they may have little idea of what sport or sports to play. In bigger cities, the choices can be overwhelming. It helps if you can winnow the choices.

Since exposure to a sport is often a good lead-in, anything you can do to bring various sports to your child's attention can be helpful. Watching sports on TV is probably one of the easiest ways to introduce a child to sports. With network coverage and cable channels dedicated to sports and sports events, just about every sport imaginable can be found, even the less popular team and individual sports. It is a rare weekend that one cannot find some of the less common sports on TV. Also, you can find magazines devoted to almost any sport. So if your child is clueless about a sport that may interest him, watching sports on TV or looking at sports magazines are good ways to begin his search for the right sport.

Most sports or athletic activities do not require great athletic skill at beginning levels. Even a clumsy or awkward child can probably learn the rudiments of a sport and improve. However, anticipate that he might see that other children get the hang of it sooner or perform much better. One of your discussion points is to prepare him for this. Emphasize that the goal for now is just to learn the basics of the sport and to enjoy participating.

Your child may show an interest in a sport that is expensive to learn. The sport may require costly equipment and/or some classes or private lessons. Try to rent the equipment at first. Look into Play It Again Sports and similar used sports goods stores if renting is impossible. Find classes or lessons that are introductory and limited in number. For example, find a skating instructor who gives ten lessons for a set fee. Skates can be rented at the rink. Before beginning, have your child agree to finish the ten lessons. If he doesn't wish to continue after those lessons, that's fine. It's important that children are taught not to expect instant success and that they give the activity a fair trial before deciding whether to continue or to quit.

Other familiar sports that can be expensive to learn are golf, tennis, and skiing. Many individual sports involve group or individual lessons and equipment. Check first with your child's school to see what kinds of sports program it offers. Keep in mind that clubs, youth groups, and community centers may offer such lessons, usually at a reduced rate. Of course, some team sports are extremely expensive and beyond the reach of most families. Polo is one example.

One reason your son may not express an interest in sports is that no sport that he has seen catches his fancy. It may be that he would benefit from learning about some less common or less visible sport such as fencing, archery, equestrian events, curling, or diving. Exposing your child to these sports takes some effort and creativity on your part. You can check out books from the library about such sports or athletic activities. Libraries also have instructional videos that show the basics of a sport. There may be contests or events of these sports held in or near your town or city. Your child may develop an interest in one of them by attending such meets or tournaments. Think about all your relatives and friends. Perhaps one of them has played or still plays one of these less familiar sports. Uncle Jack on your mother's side may have been a fencer in his youth. Maybe he'd like to show his grandniece a few of the basic moves. He also might enjoy the attention.

Some parents may be saying to themselves, "My son would never be interested in some of these sports. They're not cool." True, some kids will not be interested in a sport that none of their friends play. However, others will prefer to try a less common sport. For some of them, the anonymity these sports provide is a positive. Their friends won't see them. Other kids are individualists and they like the idea of not playing or learning a sport that everyone else plays. Kids who wouldn't play soccer in a million years may become fascinated with archery or badminton.

Minimally Athletic Children

Children without many athletic skills need help to find sports that compensate for their physical weaknesses. Some children may suffer from tunnel vision. For example, they may have terrible eye-hand coordination and thus do poorly in any sport involving catching, throwing, or hitting a ball. They rule out all sports requiring these skills and conclude that there isn't any sport for them. However, they may be decent runners and/or jumpers. They need to shift their thinking to very different categories of sports—in this case, perhaps to track and field events. Parents can help them understand that different sports require different athletic skills.

When thinking about different sports for your child, be sure to give consideration to his physical abilities and how these abilities may tie in with a particular sport. For example, usually when we say a child is minimally athletic, we are commenting on his gross-motor coordination. Seldom are we referring to his fine-motor coordination. Gross-motor coordination refers to the larger muscles that allow for movement of the arms and legs. Fine-motor coordination refers to the smaller muscles that allow for movement of, for example, the fingers. These are the muscles that allow the neurosurgeon to do delicate surgery, or your dressmaker to do intricate sewing. Let's look at both of these types of coordination for a moment.

Even if a child seems poor in gross-motor coordination, it does not rule out some sport that requires it. With practice, even the clumsiest child can show improvement. And do not underestimate the role of motivation. I have seen many kids with poor gross-motor coordination achieve some success in basketball through practice and sheer will. They manage to be good enough to play through grade school, or middle school, or, for a few, through high school. And they've enjoyed themselves and had fun.

"In life, not just in sports, if you don't try, you cannot know what you can do."

—Canadian Manon Rheaume,
the first woman to play in an NHL hockey game

Some kids who trip over everything may have very good fine-motor coordination. They may show good eye-hand coordination. Soccer and basketball may prove too frustrating for them, but they may become quite skilled in sports or activities requiring fine-motor coordination and good eye-hand coordination. Billiards and archery are sports or games where these skills are important.

Sport Choices and Temperament

A child's temperament can be another important point when considering a sport for him. Let's say your child seems always to be in motion. He may enjoy a sport that is very physical. However, maybe he is more naturally sedentary, quiet, and cerebral. A sport that isn't physical the way soccer or basketball is but requires a lot of thinking, analyzing, and strategizing might appeal to him. Golf may be the sport for him. If your child is quite aggressive, sports that are very competitive and aggressive in nature should be considered. Also, physical activities that are aggressive but have a large component of restraint and self-discipline might fill the bill. Tae kwon do or karate, popular martial arts, might be the activity of choice in this instance.

Should you encourage your child to play team sports or individual sports? It is a consideration that involves temperament but also many other factors. This is such an important question that the next chapter is devoted to it.

9 Team Sports and Individual Sports

The search for a sport your child will
enjoy may require some trial and error.

BEFORE CONSIDERING the question of team sports versus individual sports, parents should identify any biases they may have. Too many parents seek to relive their childhood sports experiences through their children. While it's understandable that a father who was a star basketball player might want his son to play basketball, basketball might not be the best sport for his child, whether he is athletic. A mother may credit her team sport experiences with her rise in the corporate world years later. Indeed, some surveys of top women executives support this mother's conclusion. She may want her daughter to gain similar benefits from playing team sports. A father may have some prejudices concerning certain sports. He may feel that some sports are not masculine enough for his son. Or a parent may have some negative feelings about his daughter being a tomboy or playing what in his opinion is an "unladylike" sport. A parent may disparage certain sports as being "too blue collar." Parents must identify their biases and then try to set them aside when helping a child decide on a sport.

If your child wants to play a sport but doesn't know whether he wants to play an individual sport or a team sport, a starting point is to look at the pros and cons of team and individual sports. It's not a matter of one being better than the other; it's a question of which one might be better for him. There are no hard and fast rules for this exploration.

The Appeal of Team Sports

Team sports require more social interaction than individual sports. Social skills are more in demand, and children playing team sports will have to develop and increase these skills for some success in these sports. For this reason, kids who are outgoing and who interact with others easily and comfortably seem to enjoy team sports. Children who tend to be retiring and quiet may find team sports rather challenging. But even kids who have poor social skills can sometimes grow in these skills and come to enjoy team sports. A parent has to be careful here. A child who is extremely shy may do better in an individual sport, at least initially.

Team sports require the ability to cooperate with others for a common goal. Children who play with other kids in a cooperative manner or who share readily usually find playing a team sport easy and satisfying. Children who have problems sharing or playing cooperatively may find playing a team sport difficult and unsatisfying. This is not to say that perhaps children like this *should* play team sports so that they can learn how to share or work cooperatively. If these children do participate in a team sport and they hog the ball or the spotlight, the other players or the coach will usually want to teach them a lesson. The coach may bench them, giving them plenty of time to consider how they need to change their game.

Sometimes team sports require more than cooperation for the sake of the team as a whole. They may require certain sacrifices on the part of the players. For example, in baseball, it is common to ask a player to bunt in order to move a runner from first to second. Bunting is not considered very glamorous, and the successful bunter is usually thrown out at first. There are many more instances when a player will be expected to do something to advance the team, not himself. A child should understand that this is a part of team sports. The legendary UCLA basketball coach John Wooden emphasized this when he said, "It's amazing how much can be accomplished if no one cares who gets the credit."

When a runner carries the ball twenty yards down the football field, he gets all the glory. But he knows he couldn't have succeeded if some of his teammates did not tackle enough of the defenders to clear a path for him. In team sports, individual achievement depends upon the support and play of teammates. So while there can be a star of a team, the star can't win a game all by himself—he needs the help of his teammates.

Most team sports involve competition against others and winning or losing. Children who show a competitive spirit in several areas of their lives will likely enjoy the competition inherent in team sports. Some children seem to shy away from competition. They probably should not be encouraged in the direction of team sports, or they should play only in noncompetitive leagues at first.

A certain kind of pressure is associated with team sports that individual sports do not reflect. If a child plays poorly or makes a stupid play in team sports, he often feels that he's let his team members down. Some children don't mind this pressure and take errors or bad play on their part in stride. However, a child who does not handle this kind of pressure may be a poor candidate for team sports. Very sensitive children, those whose feelings are easily hurt, may not hold up to this stress. Also, minimally athletic kids may feel embarrassed playing in front of their teammates and friends.

Team sports can provide the double thrill of a team winning as well as a team member making a game-winning play. Some team members can become stars, known for their exceptionally fine play within the team system. Also, some team members can play poorly, yet their team can still win. In this respect, team sports can sometimes be forgiving of some isolated instances of poor playing or when there are some weaker players on the team. The 2001 NFL Champions, the New England Patriots, were regarded as a team with no stars. They won because they played well together as a team. After two more Super Bowl wins following the 2003 and 2004 seasons, New England players still stress team playing and look down upon individual grandstanding. There are many such examples in sports—where the clear underdogs or teams with no stars manage to win because of awesome teamwork. They play together like a well-oiled machine.

> *"The team with the best athletes doesn't*
> *usually win. It's the team with the athletes*
> *who play best together."*
>
> —Lisa Fernandez,
> pitcher for the U.S. Olympic softball team that
> won gold medals in 1996, 2000, and 2004

An only child will often gravitate toward team sports. Team sports provide a ready-made family of siblings for only children. Team members can become the main social group or focus for them. Thus, the emotional desire for social connection can be met through playing team sports. However, many only children are quite comfortable engaging in solo-type activities and entertaining themselves. Such only children may prefer individual sports.

Whether the child is an only child, team members often become very close, not just when playing together. They go to school together, they socialize together, they confide in one another. They consider team members like family. Some team members end up playing together for years.

> *"We play because we love the game, we love*
> *each other, and we love to win."*
>
> —Retired U.S. soccer star Mia Hamm,
> discussing the bond between
> her teammates on the national team

If a child wants to play a team sport, you will probably be able to find a team in your city. Team sports are often more available than individual sports. Most schools offer team sports and league or division competition. City parks and recreation centers, community centers, civic clubs, religious organizations, and various youth programs such as the YMCA and YWCA have team sports leagues. Thus, depending upon where you live, there may be many more opportunities to play a team sport than an individual sport.

The Appeal of Individual Sports

Watch the runner: heading toward the finish line, calf muscles straining, breathing labored, neck veins bulging, perspiration flying off his body. Watch the gymnast: jumping higher and higher, defying gravity, suspended in the air, twisting like a pretzel. Watch the wrestler: muscles quivering, jaw tense, eyes focused, struggling for footing. Watch the skier: racing down the mountain, leaning forward almost touching the ground, in constant danger of falling. Watch the weight lifter: hoisting more than his body weight in the air, pursing lips, grunting aloud, milliseconds from collapse.

Individual sports have a purity of form and a purity of effort. They are lonely pursuits. No one is there to help. You're all on your own. When you win, you are alone in your win; when you lose, you are alone in your loss. While you may have an opponent you have to beat to win, your real opponent is yourself. You battle your negative thoughts—"This is killing me." You make decisions in tenths of a second—"Should I sprint now or wait until I'm closer to the end?" You constantly monitor your efforts—"I need to spin faster or I'll fall out of this jump." You bring about some positive thoughts even when you're about to collapse—"Just a little push here and I can win." Individual sports require the triumph of character—the willingness to seek your personal best.

> *"I don't want to give anyone an edge in my mind. Every time I walk out on the court, I have to feel I'm the best so I can compete well. A lot of times, my chief rival is just me."*
>
> —Tennis star Venus Williams

Personal best is clearer in individual sports. Whether you beat your opponent, you are always trying to better your previous time, distance, weight, or performance. You can lose your event, yet post your best time ever. You can come in second, but perhaps the winner placed first in the state last year. You can't rely on a team member to help you make a great play, or to save the day when you're having a bad day. You are the team.

It's unlikely that a young child who chooses an individual sport is fully aware of all of these factors. Depending upon the child, there may be different reasons why he might prefer an individual sport to a team sport. Minimally athletic children may be drawn to an individual sport because they don't have to worry about letting down a team or exposing their performance to thirty of their peers.

Other children may appreciate the idea of relying on themselves and being able to see their improved performance more clearly than if they played on a team.

Parents must understand the various ways individual sports differ from team sports. For many of these sports, competition with opponents is unnecessary or can even be avoided, especially at the early learning stages or levels. Children can learn to play tennis or golf without playing against anyone or keeping score. They can achieve a black belt in a martial art without ever being in a competition. Thus, many individual sports protect a child from outright competition until he is ready or wants to compete. When they do begin to compete, most young children can easily see that they are competing not just against their opponent but also against their last best record or performance.

Individual sports teach individual responsibility. Children recognize that it is their own effort in learning, practicing and performing, or competing that counts. Self-discipline is essential. Any improvement, however small, can be thrilling and satisfying. Children learn more about themselves when they play individual sports than when they play team sports. Personal pleasure and fulfillment are clear benefits and values of individual sports.

Children learn and play a number of individual sports in team settings. For example, tennis, swimming, wrestling, track, and golf are individual sports, yet many children participate in them as members of a school or a club or recreational-center team. Thus, their opponents may be teammates as well as competitors from another team. In the case of these sports, playing them can give children the benefits of an individual sport *and* the camaraderie of a team sport. It should also be noted that for some individual sports played on teams, there are also team events, such as relays, or races where, for example, overall team points or scores are recorded. For example, two schools compete at a swim meet. All the points from the individual events and the relays are added up and the team with the most points wins the meet.

There are other benefits of individual sports. Children who play an individual sport are more likely to play their sport in middle age than if they play a team sport. This is especially true in the case of tennis, golf, swimming, and skiing. Adults who played individual sports when younger also tend to be more physically fit when they are older than adults who played team sports when they were younger. There is also the injury factor: certain team sports, such as basketball and football, are grueling on aging joints and muscles. You don't see Joe Namath or Dick Butkus playing football these days. Instead, they can be seen hobbling on the golf course. Plus, it can be harder to round up enough players to form a team.

If a child is older, it will be easier to find classes or instruction in the individual sports than the team sports. For example, if your child is fifteen and wants to start playing basketball, you will find few teams for beginners in their teens. You can find summer basketball camps that do teach the basics to kids of all ages, but then after the camp there will be limited opportunities for your child to play on a team. In contrast, instruction for most individual sports is available for children of all ages, and there are more opportunities to play and even compete. So, if a child is starting late—in his teens—it is easier to take up an individual sport than a team sport.

Some children seem to blossom when they participate in an individual sport. A very hyperactive child will find certain individual sports easier to learn and to play than many team sports. These children are easily distracted, especially when there are too many stimuli. Team sports are overloaded with stimuli: not only does a child have to concentrate on his play, he also has to keep track of his team members and opposing team members. This child may do well in an individual sport that has one-on-one or small-group instruction, and when he plays the sport, he has to focus only on himself.

Children who appear to enjoy solitary pursuits may be temperamentally better suited for individual sports than team sports.

It's important for parents to know and understand their children's temperament, strengths, and weaknesses, as well as their preferred style of interacting with people. With this information, it will be easier to guide them to a sport that will be best for them.

One of the downsides of many individual sports is that qualified and/or professional instructors are usually required to teach them. Thus, individual sports usually are more expensive than team sports, as it is necessary to find a coach or instructor and pay for individual lessons or classes. In his book, *Landing It*, Scott Hamilton recounts how his parents sold their home and bought a smaller one in order to pay for his figure skating lessons and coaches. By the time he began to enter competitions, the costs for coaching and training averaged $8,000 per year. Of course, lessons or coaching for individual sports at the beginner or low-competitive levels will not be nearly as costly. Some clubs or gyms offer scholarships.

As you can see, the decision on whether an individual sport or a team sport is best for your child can be a complicated one. Make sure to include your child when you begin to consider whether a team sport or an individual sport is best for him. Ideally, all children would have experience playing both. Since many sports are played in different seasons, it is usually possible for a child to participate in both individual and team sports. Many individual sports can be played year-round. Indeed, young kids who are at least average or above-average athletes usually prefer not to specialize in one sport and play different sports. However, it may be unrealistic to expect that minimally athletic children can learn and participate in more than one sport at a time.

The search for a sport your child will enjoy may require some trial and error. Once a sport has been identified, try to set up a trial period or introductory classes for him. When the trial period or the introductory classes are completed, no matter the athletic ability of your child, you and your child will want to discuss how it's going and whether he wants to continue now that the trial period is over. Your most important questions to ask are:

• In general, has this been a positive experience?

- Is he having fun?
- Is there some evidence, however small, that he is improving in or learning the sport?

A "yes" answer to these three questions is essential to your evaluation process and to whether he should continue to learn or play the sport. But even with "yes" as the answer to all three questions, he may decide that he doesn't want to continue with that sport or maybe even any sport. This is fine. Or he may tell you he doesn't like that sport, but he wants to try another. This is fine, too. Back to square one to begin the search for another sport to explore!

Finding the right coach or team is probably one of the most important tasks you have to do before your child begins learning or playing a sport. What do you look for and what questions do you ask? The next chapter should help you with this task.

10   Finding the Right Coach and Team

Just because a coach won a gold medal for figure
skating in the Olympics does not mean that he
is a good coach for young children or beginners.

ONCE YOU AND YOUR CHILD have identified a sport or game, you
will need to find a coach, instructor, or teacher. In very small towns,
your search and choices may be quite limited and you may have to sign
up with whoever is available. In larger towns or cities, your choices
may be overwhelming. Let's look at this search from the point of view
of team sports and individual sports.

Finding a Team Sports Coach

Your main concern is the quality of the experience your child has while
learning a sport and playing it. Gather the names of possible coaches
and teams. You will want to meet and speak with the coach individually. Ask the coach questions about his background, his experience,
and his philosophy of coaching. Some sample questions:

- Where did you learn to play? How long did you play?

- How long have you been coaching? At what levels? Do you like
  coaching minimally competitive leagues? Have you attended
  coaching clinics?

- What is your philosophy of coaching? Do you emphasize excellence over winning? How do you deal with minimally athletic kids
  on your team?

- How do you handle parents who pressure their kids to play or to win?

You also will want to observe the coach at a practice and a game. Some things to look for are:

- The personality of the coach is important. Look for a coach who is personable, warm, and nurturing (though some firmness is sometimes necessary).

- Does he show leadership qualities?

- Does the coach teach at the developmental level of the kids? Are his expectations in line with their developmental levels? Does he speak in a way that children can understand him?

- You want to find a coach who knows the basics of the game. In some instances, the coach may be a parent who has never played the game himself. Thus, he may not have the in-depth knowledge of the sport or know its finer points, but he should have a grasp of the basics.

- A coach should be able to direct not only the practices or lessons but also be able to guide players in the proper training and conditioning regimens necessary for the sport.

- Does he discipline in a manner that doesn't punish but, rather, teaches? Does he discipline in a way that encourages the kids to learn how to self-discipline?

- He should display good teaching skills, namely, the ability to explain and demonstrate the fundamentals of the sport to the players. Has he designed interesting drills to help learn these fundamentals? Does he make learning each new skill fun?

- Does he explain the logic (the "why") of each fundamental or skill?

- See if he can make corrections in a way that is constructive and positive. Any evidence of verbal abuse—yelling, screaming, cussing, or berating players—is unacceptable.

- Is he able to deal with and treat each child individually? Is he patient?

- How is he with players who appear to be minimally athletic? Does he treat them with respect? Does he go more slowly with them? This is especially important if your child is not very athletic.

- Does he encourage playing as a team?

- He should be inclusive and be able to treat all players equally, without showing favoritism.

- Does he show respect for and love of the game?

Phil Jackson, who has coached both the Chicago Bulls and the Los Angeles Lakers, is no slouch when it comes to winning; he has led these two teams to nine NBA basketball championships. However, he wrote of the importance of teamwork and the love of the game, "You guys need to get together and remember what you're doing this for. You're not doing it for the money. It may seem that way, but that's just an external reward. You're doing it for the internal rewards. You're doing it for each other and the love of the game."[15]

Many former players recall the powerful and lasting impact their middle school or high school coaches had on their lives. They felt they learned a lot about life from them. Some credit their coach with turning their lives around. You're not just picking a coach for the athletic part of your child's game; you're also picking an adult who will be a role model for him.

Next, you need to scope out any assistant coaches; make sure they work in a collaborative and seamless manner with the coach and that they also have good teaching skills. Check to see that they have positive interactions with the children.

If you can, try to speak with some of the parents of the players:

- Find out how long their child has worked with this coach.

- Ask them for their impressions of the coach.

- What do they feel are the coach's strengths and weaknesses?

- Is he a good role model? Are the coach and the assistants the kind of people they want their child to spend three to six hours a week with?

- Does their child look forward to going to practice?

- Is their child improving?

- Does their child have fun?

- Is their child dealt with fairly?

When you attend a practice and/or game, note the verbal and physical behavior of the parents. Are some parents verbally aggressive toward their own child, other team players, the coach, opponent players, other parents, and the judges or referees? Are they supportive of all the players and the coach(es)? Do they accept the calls of the referees? Observe their behavior following a win and following a loss. Pushy or ill-behaved parents can turn games into tense environments that take away all the fun.

Studies show the importance of keeping the fun in youth sports. Seven out of ten children drop out of organized sports by the age of thirteen. One of the reasons most often given is parents who push their kids so hard that the fun of playing is gone.[16] The National Alliance for Youth Sports reports that about 15 percent of youth games involve verbal or physical abuse by parents and coaches. When the Youth Sports Institute asked kids who had abandoned sports at age ten what might lure them back, their top three answers were interesting: If practices were more fun. If I could play more. If coaches understood players better.[17]

Finding the Right Team or League

If your child is quite young, just starting, or minimally athletic, it is better to find a league or team that is noncompetitive or low competitive. For these types of leagues, look at the sports programs offered by schools, parks, and recreational leagues, the YMCA and YWCA, and other civic groups or organizations. Stay away from private clubs, travel clubs, or leagues for players with advanced skills. Since your child will only be exploring a team sport, it is important to find a team that has the following as its stated values and principles:

- Learning the basics of the sport
- Friendship
- Teamwork
- Sportsmanship
- Having fun

Make sure the team accepts all children who sign up. There should be no tryouts to make the team.

You and your child should understand that at the beginner levels of most team sports, more children may want to play on the team than the team has positions for. Most children's teams and good coaches deal with this problem by making sure that every child has a chance to play. They accomplish this with the minimum-play rule. For example, in baseball, each child must play at least two or three innings of the game. The coaches do not play only the best players so that their team wins. Consequently, while some kids are much better than others at the sport, they will not necessarily play more innings or minutes than the minimally athletic children. The whole purpose is to give every player a chance to play. This value may continue all the way through high school.

Check to see if a team you're considering embraces the minimum-play rule, and for certain team sports, the *mercy rule*. (The mercy rule prevents one team from trouncing the other team. For example, a youth baseball league may have a rule that once a team leads by more than fifteen runs, the game is stopped. It's OK for young children to experience losing, but being trounced isn't a useful experience.) Don't let your child join a team or league that seems to only emphasize winning games.

Safety Issues

As you evaluate different teams or leagues, you should investigate the team or league's practice with respect to safety issues. Check to see that they require physical exams, adequate safety/protective equipment, appropriate safety rules, safe practice conditions, and safe facilities. Make sure the coach is not conducting a strenuous football practice in 100-degree weather. (If so, this is not the team, or coach, for your child.) Heatstroke can kill grown men as well as young children. Be sure you, the coach, and your child know the early signs of heatstroke and heat exhaustion as well as the steps that should be taken if any signs develop. Also, when observing a practice session, note whether the team takes breaks and if players are encouraged to drink fluids frequently. Sports drinks, like Gatorade, hydrate better than water, especially for athletes engaged in strenuous or endurance sports.[18] See if there are bathrooms nearby. At one school, students practice lacrosse in a nearby public park. In order to go to the bathroom, players have to make a mad dash to the school.

If the sports activity is outdoors, make sure players lather with plenty of sunscreen. It is not enough to do this before practice or a game; players should reapply every two hours. Be sure your children use a sunscreen with an SPF of 30 or higher.

It's also important that the coach stresses the basic movements and rules of the game. For example, in baseball, beginners should not be taught to slide either headfirst or feetfirst into bases. Injuries can occur when a runner slides into a base. Many of the rules of the game are designed to keep injuries to a minimum. If you see a coach encouraging players to play dirty—making moves such as an illegal contact in lacrosse—you do not want your child to play on his team. Yes, the referees may not catch the foul and the team scores a point, but such plays may also lead to injuries. This is bad for players and does not promote respect for the integrity of the sport.

Overuse injuries are increasingly common in youth sports. Injuries that in the past were only seen in adult athletes are now seen in athletes as young as seven. These injuries come about because of overtraining and playing too much without breaks. Overuse injuries can involve muscles, tendons, cartilage, bones, and nerves. Some of these injuries can result in permanent, career-ending damage. A good coach knows about the danger of overuse injuries and knows the proper training methods that can prevent the development of these injuries.

Watch to see if injured players are encouraged by the coach to "play hurt." Do you see injured players wave off attempts to evaluate their injuries? Do players minimize the possible seriousness of their injuries? If so, it may be that the coach subtly sends the message to his players that they must gut out injuries if they wish to play. This is not the type of coach you want for the beginner player. It is true that some very minor injuries can await treatment following the game, but without proper evaluation of all injuries, a young, growing player risks permanent damage—damage that no delayed treatment may rectify.

Before signing your child up on a team, make sure that the other players generally match up with your child in age, size, and skill level.

Injuries are more likely to occur when there are large disparities between players in these areas.

In summary, the most serious types of injuries—the ones that can cause permanent disability and/or may be life threatening—are head injuries, especially undetected or untreated concussions; broken necks; and heat-related illnesses and dehydration. Most other injuries seldom result in permanent damage, and young children usually heal quickly from the other common sport injuries: sprains, dislocations, and simple fractures.

Keep in mind that even with all these safety features present, injuries can occur. About four million children between the ages of six and sixteen end up receiving emergency-room care for sports-related injuries each year. Only couch potatoes or people asleep are free from sports injuries. A good coach, proper equipment, and compliance with common safety considerations and rules can help reduce the number and seriousness of injuries but may not eliminate them altogether.

Of course, usually the coach and the team come as a package. Just make sure that each—the coach and the team—is appropriate for your child whose main goal is to explore the sport.

Finding a Coach for an Individual Sport

Obviously, a coach or instructor of an individual sport should demonstrate some of the same qualities as a coach of a team sport. The instruction is likely to be more one-on-one or in small groups. These coaches or teachers usually have participated in the sport or activity when they were growing up. You don't often have a tennis coach who did not play tennis on a serious level at least through high school and perhaps in college and beyond. For some sports, an instructor must have achieved a certain level of competence in the activity. In many schools of tae kwon do, for example, a person cannot teach unless he has a fourth degree black belt or higher. Keep in mind, however, that a person can be a ninth degree black belt (the highest) and still be a terrible instructor. Just because a coach won a gold medal for figure skating in the Olympics does not ensure that he will be a good coach for young children or beginners. So, don't be so awed by the coach's trophies or medals that you sign your child up with him without looking for some of the qualities already mentioned.

Look for a coach who emphasizes personal improvement and skill mastery over performance or winning. Cal Ripken, Jr., observed: "Youth baseball has gotten way too serious, emphasizing winning at all costs and not teaching the right lessons . . . I'd like to reduce the pressure [on the kids] and put more emphasis on teaching skills."[19]

Some of the same safety considerations mentioned for team sports should be stressed by the instructor or coach of an individual sport. Also, certain sport-specific moves, especially in some individual sports, can cause injury. Many individual sports involve repetitive motions that can cause stress fractures and other injuries. Be sure that the coach is mindful of this problem and that he is knowledgeable about and/or insists on regular stretching every day, not just before a practice or game (and knows when it is appropriate to stretch immediately prior to athletic performance), proper warming up exercises, many breaks during practice, and other training methods that help reduce the likelihood of these types of injuries.

Since individual sports don't have some of the fun of team sports built into them, the instructor of an individual sport has to have a special knack for making lessons or practices fun. Make sure you speak with the instructor, speak to parents of students of the instructor, and make sure you observe a lesson. See if the instructor shows all the important qualities of a teacher of a sport and can make learning fun, too. Yes, you want your child to learn and show improvement and grow in mastery. But you also want the experience to be pleasurable.

As much as possible, try to involve your child in this process. Ask for his impressions after he meets the coach or teacher. Try to find out what he thought about the practice or lesson or game you attended. By researching the coaches or instructors and evaluating the teams or facilities available, you and your child should be able to make a good decision.

Never forget that this whole process is about your child. It's not about you! And, this process may have to be repeated a number of times. Children may need to try several coaches or teams before they discover the right one for them.

Let's learn about starter classes and no- and low-competition programs that are appropriate for children just beginning to play sports. And let's see how many of the common-sense factors mentioned in this chapter were present on a real-life, low-competition swim team.

11 Looking at Starter, No-, and Low-Competition Programs

> By the second or third summer, I could see
> significant improvement among those who
> could barely swim when they first began.

FOR VERY YOUNG CHILDREN, parents should look for sports programs that might be best described as starter or sports-readiness programs. These programs focus mainly on the basic movements of a particular sport. For baseball, learning how to throw a ball, catch a ball, and how to bat are the only skills taught and practiced. An actual game may not ever be played. There is no competition. Such programs offer a fun learning experience and an atmosphere wherein there is little or no failure.

Once you know the sport your young child might want to learn, canvass your community to find out whether some organization offers this type of introductory program. A starting place is the Start Smart Sports Development Program. The National Alliance for Youth Sports (NAYS) sponsors general sports development programs for children three to five years old, as well as sport-specific programs for Start Smart basketball, soccer, baseball, and golf. The Start Smart program for golf is for kids five to seven. All classes are once a week for six weeks. While parent involvement is mandatory, trained coaches and instructors conduct the classes. NAYS partners with YMCA/YWCAs, parks and recreation centers, police athletic leagues, and many other community-based organizations to offer Start Smart programs throughout the country. Check with NAYS (www.nays.org or 1-800-729-2057) to see if any Start Smart programs are available in your community. If there are none, speak with a local recreation agency director about contacting NAYS and starting a Start Smart program.

If no Start Smart programs are available in your communities, or if your child is interested in a non–Start Smart sport, use the Yellow Pages, speak with your neighbors, or call the various community-based youth programs to find beginner-level programs or classes in the sport of your child's choice. YMCAs and YWCAs, Boys and Girls Clubs, and recreation centers usually offer such programs for various sports.

If your child is six or older and if you can't find starter or readiness programs, try to find some no-competition or low-competition team or program that emphasizes the teaching of the basics of a sport with little emphasis on competition or winning. Look for a program or team that has many of the features mentioned in the previous chapter.

Low-Competition Teams

What does a low-competition team actually look like? To give you an idea, let's look at a real-life, low-competition team.

During graduate school, I was the swim team coach for a local community center. This team trained only in the summer months when the kids were out of school.

We began in June, practices were held five mornings a week, and they lasted one and a half hours. The children ranged in age from six to eighteen. Anyone could join. Practice sessions involved heavy-duty teaching of the basics of each of the four strokes and working on starts and turns. The workouts involved sprints and longer distances. Meets with other community centers were held once a week, beginning in July. Swimmers raced by age group (six and under, seven- and eight-year-olds, nine- and ten-year-olds, etc.) and, of course, by stroke and distance.

Many of the parents watched the practices and workouts and served as timers and judges for the meets. The parents became friends. After a meet, I was thrown into the pool, and we all went to have ice cream or pizza, depending upon the time of the meet.

All the kids swam because they wanted to. Winning was not emphasized because this team was a member of a minimally competitive league. What *was* emphasized was developing competent swimmers,

swimmers who learned to swim easily and efficiently and for fun. The hope was that all the children would continue to swim in their adult years and experience joy and satisfaction.

Many of the kids on the team made lasting friendships with one another. Some went on to swim on their high school swim teams. A handful swam for their college teams. A few continued to swim in a master's program, a swim program for good adult swimmers. About one-fifth of master's program swimmers choose to swim competitively.

Were there some good athletes on the swim team? Yes, there were. But most were minimally athletic to average athletes who learned to swim very well and had lots of fun at the same time. Many of them became good enough to occasionally win a first-, second-, or third-place ribbon. By the second or third summer, I often saw significant improvement among those who could barely swim when they first began. A number of the minimally athletic kids went on to become accomplished swimmers. The better swimmers invariably helped the other swimmers. I still see some of my former swim team members from time to time. They tell me that the swim team was the highlight of their childhood summers.

This swim team had all of the ingredients of a good experience:

- A coach who knew the basics and could teach them to each child

- A low-competition atmosphere

- Infrequent swim meets with other teams at a comparable level

- Every child swam

- Supportive parental involvement

- Emphasis on learning to swim well and having fun; little emphasis on winning

Many teams, leagues, and classes are designed to promote exploratory learning and/or participation in a sport or athletic skill. Once you begin looking for the starter classes, the right league or team, or instructor for your child, you may be pleasantly surprised by how many choices you have.

Some parents may be chomping at the bit, ready to plunge in and teach their children the basics. Should parents do this? The next chapter takes up this important question.

"Should I Teach My Child the Basics?"

> When I was a swim team coach, I spent considerable
> time correcting bad habits, habits that had
> gone uncorrected by parents or former instructors.

SHOULD A PARENT teach her child the basics? This is actually a complicated question. An associated question is "Can I teach my child the basics?" Whether to take on the task of teaching your child the basics of a sport or game he has chosen to try is a question requiring a number of considerations.

Your Relationship with Your Child

Do you and your child have an easygoing relationship? Does she take instruction from you comfortably, without tension or tugs-of-war? How does she respond when you make corrections or give constructive criticism?

Your Teaching Style

Are you able to teach in a way that is fun? Are you able to break down moves into simple units? Are you patient? Do you become frustrated easily? Are you able to be positive?

How Well Do You Know the Sport or Game You Will Be Teaching?

Most parents are not Olympic athletes, nor have they played a sport on a college or professional level. Yet many are able to teach their children the basics of a sport or perhaps even coach a sport. Many parents teach their children how to swim, throw a ball, shoot a basket, or ride a bike without ever having competed in any of these sports.

If children are fairly athletic, they can usually teach themselves the basic moves of a sport, or pick up the basic moves quickly with the guidance of a parent, instructor, or coach. In this case, even if their parents know little about the sport, it is probably OK for them to teach their children the basics. Athletic children tend to have positive experiences when they are learning a sport.

However, for minimally athletic children, the stakes are a little higher; the potential for frustration and failure is greater. It is for this reason that I believe that parents of minimally athletic children should know a little more about the sport if they plan to teach the basics to their children.

When learning a sport or physical movement, a child experiences frustration when her form is not correct. For example, I would see a child who was trying to swim move her arms in such a way that she was having to work harder to move a few yards and was becoming exhausted. By making a minor correction in her stroke, she was able to swim more efficiently without becoming tired. Before the correction, swimming was not a positive experience; after the correction, she was swimming faster and with less effort and more enjoyment. When I was a swim coach, all the kids knew how to swim before they joined the team. However, I spent considerable time correcting bad stroke techniques and other bad habits, habits that had gone uncorrected by parents or former instructors.

In short, we don't want any child to quit a sport before he has barely begun because of too much frustration and too few rewards. So, I suggest that you teach your child the basics of a sport only if you know enough about the sport to teach those basics correctly. Besides knowing the basics, it would be helpful if the parent also knows some basic coaching techniques. Some organizations teach parents how to be volunteer coaches. (One such program offers a course you can take online, and information about it can be found in the Other Resources section in the back of this book.) In short, we want children to have positive experiences so that they will be motivated to continue playing or participating in the sport.

If your relationship with your child is a good one, if your teaching style is appropriate, and if you know enough about the techniques or basic movements of the sport to teach them correctly and efficiently, then go ahead and begin. If you don't have all three of these ingredients, I suggest that you consider finding an instructor or coach.

Let's say that you have taught the basics to your child and he is interested in going beyond them to the next level and/or participating in some organized league or team. At this point, unless you've had some experience coaching, it's best to transfer him to the care of an experienced or professional instructor or coach. Assuming that you got him off to a good start, now is the time for the pros, or knowledgeable volunteer parent coaches, to take over.

Now that your child is ready to join a team or start to compete, you need to teach him about sportsmanship, and you will have to be a good role model for appropriate behavior—win or lose. Because parents are emotionally involved when they attend their children's practices or games, showing sportsmanlike behavior can be tough at times. The next chapter will help you with this.

13 Parents and Sportsmanship

*You don't want your child to quit a sport—
a sport he may be enjoying—because of you.*

GOOD SPORTSMANSHIP has been a growing concern in this country. It used to be that we associated poor sportsmanship, especially fan violence, with European and South American soccer games. (In the 1950s, some stadiums in South America were built with moats around the playing fields that prevented rioting fans from storming the fields.) We've read of hundreds of fans erupting in destructive, angry, and violent behavior—behavior that resulted in many deaths.

Increase in Sports Violence in the United States

More recently in the United States, we have seen a significant increase not only in the disorderly, provocative, and violent behavior of fans, but also in the inappropriate and violent behavior of players. Consider some of the following incidents:

- At a Detroit Pistons–Indiana Pacers basketball game in 2004, a beer-tossing fan set off a violent and out-of-control scene with Goliath-sized players punching out fans.

- A Clemson–South Carolina football game had players of both university teams swinging at each other. So many players were involved that it took almost a battalion of state policemen to break up the melee. The constant replay of the Pistons–Pacers game was cited by some as an inciting factor for the Clemson–South Carolina scene.

- Baseball pitcher Frank Francisco was charged with assault after heaving a chair at a heckler during an Oakland–Texas game.

- Home fans at professional football and basketball games are encouraged to distract opposing players at key moments when concentration is required. The waving of towels and thundersticks when an opposing player is trying to make his free throws is a good example.

Some referees and umpires have expressed concern for their own safety at these games. They fear getting hurt when attempting to stop these player-fan altercations. This increasing lack of civility seems centered on professional, and to some degree, collegiate team sports. Because many children look to professional players as role models, it is important that professional sports clean up its act.

Violence and Poor Sportsmanship in Youth Sports

But violence and poor sportsmanship is not limited to the fields of collegiate and professional sports. This problem has trickled down into youth sports. Obnoxious, bullying, and violent parents have contributed to the deterioration in sportsmanship and to an increasing number of children who leave their sport(s) because of their parents' behavior at practices or games. In 2000, most of us recoiled when hearing about a hockey parent pummeling another parent to death right at the rink. Angry parents, venting their wrath at other parents, coaches, referees, and, yes, their own children, make many of their children cringe.

Good sportsmanship pertains to fans (including relatives and friends of players), players, coaches, officials (referees, judges, and umpires), and league or organization officials. Coaches are not immune from poor sportsmanship. You'd think that coaches have enough on their plate to focus on without exhibiting poor behavior. Yet in many cases coaches lose it. A coach of an Illinois high school basketball team was recently fired after he drew up a play that had a player throw the ball at a heckler. The Temple University men's basketball coach ordered one of his players to play rough, resulting in a broken arm of an opposing player. The coach was suspended for the rest of the season by the president of the university. Coaches have been known to run on the field or court and yell at and push officials. As a parent of a youth athlete, you have an important role to play when it comes to sportsmanship. You are accountable for your behavior during games, you have some say as to your child's behavior, and you have some say as to the behavior of coaches and officials.

Keeping Your Cool When Your Child Is Playing

Being a supportive parent of a child who is exploring a team or individual sport is not always easy. The buzz of victory, though temporary, can be quite seductive. The thrill of seeing your child win or being the star is always exciting. Seeing a child lose is difficult, and witnessing a team lose game after game isn't much fun. Watching a child play poorly can be a painful experience for a parent. "It is tougher emotionally to watch my kids in sports than it was to play in the World Series," said Jim Sundberg, a former Kansas City Royals player.

Sundberg's observation sparks the question of "Why?" Why do many fans, including parents, act like maniacs? While there are many reasons and combinations of reasons that probably are accurate, anthropologists provide an interesting insight when they suggest that fan attachment to their favorite teams harks back to tribal days. Back then, you always fought for your tribe. So our modern-day athletes, especially Olympians (they represent our country) and professional athletes (they represent our city), are seen as our tribal warriors. If they win, we win. (Interestingly, elite athletes are expected to have a "warrior mentality.")

How does this apply to parents of youth athletes? Who better represents our tribe than our children? It's not necessarily that we need to see them or their teams win (though for some parents this is their main objective)—it's more that we want to see them do well. When our child plays his heart out and he or his team still loses, we feel his pain.

If he's hurt on the field, of course we hurt. And if he's injured because of an illegal play of an opponent, even the calmest parent might become a little riled. Tribal behavior is infectious.

Social psychology students at Arizona State University decided to study team identification after the ASU football team won and lost games. They found that after winning a game, the number of fans wearing the school colors rose 30 to 40 percent.[20]

Parental behavior has become such a concern that a number of youth leagues have instituted parent training or classes prior to the start of the season. Parents are taught the importance of sportsmanship and the dos and don'ts of appropriate behavior during practices and games. They must sign a code of conduct that often includes the penalty of being banned from attending practices or games if they break the rules.

Parents often start with good intentions and resolutions of being supportive of their child's efforts and backing the coaches and the referees. Sometimes, though, parents can be so carried away with winning that they become overinvolved with their child's practices and performance. Also, parents who were former athletes may find themselves trying to relive past athletic accomplishments through their children. The exhilaration of a child's success in sports sometimes fills emotional needs unmet since their glory days of the past.

Such parents may find it difficult to be objective. In truth, this is hard for many parents. They can become judgmental and critical, and some even become abusive of their kids, other players, the coaches, and the referees or judges. They are obnoxious and often embarrass their children by their behavior.

When asked if they had ever seen a parent be verbally abusive during a game, 87.6 percent of the respondents replied yes.

When asked if they have ever seen a coach being verbally abusive during a game, 90.4 percent of the respondents replied yes.

When volunteer coaches were asked what was the most difficult part of their job, 69 percent of them said it was dealing with the parents.[21]

In 2004, Houston Astros' pitcher Roger Clemens spit sunflower seeds at an umpire. Was this during a major-league baseball game? Nope. In this case, Clemens was not the pitcher—he was the parent, attending his son's Little League baseball game. He disagreed with the umpire over his call at second base. Clemens's ten-year-old son was the second baseman. Because of his behavior, the umpire ejected Clemens from the game. This is an example of how an otherwise good sportsman when *he* is the performing athlete lost his cool when the performing athlete was *his child*.

A reporter who accompanied a hockey travel team of eleven-year-old boys for a weekend of games wrote the following:

"But if you travel for the weekend with a team as accomplished as the Royals, what you see—aside from some exciting hockey—are parents on a balance beam, intent on supporting their children but always in danger of slipping off into self-interest and allowing their children's dreams to become their own.

"Understandable as it is that they are excited by their sons' skills and triumphs, many of the Royals' parents openly admitted that the excitement could skew their judgment and that they struggled with the line between serious support of the Royals and going overboard."[22]

One of the parents, also an assistant coach of the Royals, was quoted in this article as observing that when you watch these boys play, because they're so good, you find yourself treating them "like a miniature professional team." Then the parents have to remind themselves that the players are "only 11 years old."

When parents act poorly, some children start playing for their parents rather than for themselves. Cal Ripken, Jr., famous shortstop for the Baltimore Orioles, emphasized how important it is for parents to let their kids enjoy the sport and not to stress winning: "I hope my kids, Rachel and Ryan, will have the same approach. For them, I'm not concerned with winning. I want them to build on a bedrock of love for their sports and self-discovery."[23]

At one time good sportsmanship was focused primarily on how players conducted themselves upon losing. Now, however, in highly competitive leagues and especially at the professional level of sports, we often see the winners display poor sportsmanship. Of course, winners have a right to be happy and jubilant, but we've seen professional football players strut, prance, and dance twenty to thirty yards *before* reaching the end zone. Other boorish and showboating antics occur in other sports. Unfortunately, children sometimes copy these behaviors. Good sportsmanship means behaving well when one wins, when one loses, and when one disagrees with a call.

Parents and Good Sportsmanship

You have probably read about parents of stars (as well as ordinary athletes) who pressured their children and were overinvolved with their day-to-day training, coaching, and game performances. Some stars have had parents who have been appropriately supportive. Julie Foudy, a soccer player and member of the teams that won the 1999 Women's World Cup and the 2004 Olympics, praised her parents. "My parents were the type who didn't know what position I played. If they knew what number jersey I had on, that was a bonus. They were very laid back, but very supportive. . . . So I get concerned when I see that [parental pressure] sometimes because the poor kids just burn out at an early age."[24]

While parents don't have to be as laid back as Foudy's, they do need to be mindful of their support roles. They need to display good sportsmanship. They need to be there at the down times and the up times. They don't want to lose sight of the goals: having their kids learn a sport or athletic skill, participate in the sport, and have fun.

How do parents accomplish these goals? They work on maintaining a supportive and helpful manner. Here are a few pointers:

- Remind your children of the goals: explore a sport, learn the skill(s) involved to play the sport, work at it, get better at it, and have fun.

- Praise their efforts.

- Point out improvements in their skill or performance.

- Try to focus on the positives; avoid negatives or criticisms.

During games, show sportsmanship and be a good and enthusiastic fan:

- Do not scream or yell criticisms at anyone, including your child. Never berate your child in public, and you shouldn't do it in private, either.

- Do not boo the opposing players.

- Do not boo a bad call by a referee, judge, or umpire. Show respect toward officials. (A number of youth sports referees have either retired or quit because of the verbal and physical abuse by parents and coaches.)

- Do not tell the coach how to coach.

- Do applaud good play or performances by any player or athlete. A really exciting catch in left field should be admired, even if an opposing player made it.

- Show respect to all players or participants.

- Of course, parents should refrain from any physical or emotional displays like pushing or shoving.

After games, continue to be a good sport:

- Win or lose, praise the efforts of the team.

- Win or lose, tell your child you enjoyed watching the game and watching him play.
- If you didn't see the game, don't ask "Who won?" at first. Ask "How did it go? Did you play? Did you have fun?"
- If he or his team loses, help him with defeat—it is one of the lessons of life. Remind him that his effort is what counts, that all winners lose at times, and that the sun will still come up the next morning.
- Teach him that there are lessons to be learned from losing—sometimes these lessons cannot be learned unless he has tasted defeat.
- Win or lose, tell him that you love him and does he want a cookie?

"I used to be the sorest loser, but I've learned that kind of attitude prevents you from getting anything out of a defeat."

—Hillary Wolf, *two-time Olympic judo medalist*

It's important that you insist that your child shows good sportsmanship at all workouts and before, during, and after sporting events. Make sure he is as graceful in losing as he is in winning. It's important that he shows respect to both his teammates as well as the opposing players. He should treat his coach and the officials with due respect also. If you see behavior that is unacceptable, you should be prepared to take steps to see that this does not happen again. If your interventions don't seem to work, explain to him that he is not honoring his sport by his behavior and therefore you are going to remove him from the sport. When you do this, you can always set up conditions he has to meet in order to resume playing.

Some children react to calls they don't like or poor performance with temper outbursts and/or out-of-control behavior. Depending upon the reasons behind his behavior, it may be enough to tell him that it is unacceptable and if he wants to continue playing it has to stop. However, if there are repeated incidents, he may need the help of a psychologist or a sports psychologist. (See "The Foul-Tempered Athlete" in the "Special Situations" section in Part 3.)

It's important to show respect to *all* players. It may be that your child's team or gym is inclusive and allows physically or mentally disabled children to play. It is important that you are a model of good behavior when disabled children play and that you make it clear that your child should treat his teammates appropriately. Disabled children may move more slowly, they may behave in odd ways, or they may contribute to a defeat. They need special encouragement and patience, and it's essential that they not feel ostracized or teased. Be sure to give them extra praise for their efforts and make sure that your child, as a teammate, is supportive of all disabled players.

These suggestions are not meant to be exhaustive. Parents should hold their children accountable for sportsmanlike behavior. Also, if parents want playing a sport to be a positive experience for their child, they need to maintain positive and helpful behaviors themselves. You don't want your child to quit a sport—a sport he may be enjoying—because of you. It really doesn't take much to show good sportsmanship. Try to remember at all times that your child's needs are more important than yours.

When is it time for your child to play at a higher level, or to quit a sport, or to take a break? Hard questions, but I give you some guidelines to each of these questions in the next chapter.

14   **Time for Changes**

Taking a break from a sport can be a useful and necessary step, eventually leading to the child quitting the sport, going back to it, or participating in a new sport.

AT SOME POINT in your child's participation in an athletic activity it may be a time for changes. She may continue on as she has been playing, she may ramp up her participation to a higher or more competitive level, or she may want to quit or take a break.

Playing at a Higher Level

After your child has played a sport for several years, you may find that he wants to notch up, to play the sport at a higher, more competitive level. Is this good or bad? This depends upon the reason or reasons he gives you for wanting to take his game to a higher level. A parent should discuss these reasons with him to make sure that it is something he really wants to do. A number of children will reach this point. Let's look at some of the acceptable reasons a child might give.

Appropriate Reasons

1. **"I'm much better than I was when I started."**
   Some children progress so much that continuing as beginners would be too easy for them. It would provide little or no challenge if they remained on the current team or league.

2. **"I'm bored. I need to learn more complicated moves."**
This is a variation of the previous reason. Most kids seek challenges. Once they've learned the basics of a skill or sport, they will become bored if they don't graduate to the next level.

3. **"I think I'm ready for more competition."**
The early, exploratory phase of learning a sport or skill may not have involved much competition or perhaps no competition. It is sometimes difficult to fully gauge his progress unless there is some or more competition. This is especially so in individual sports where the competition is as much against self as others. Also, most children find competition fun.

4. **"I'm really good at this."**
An athletic child may progress rapidly and need the challenge of competition to enjoy the sport and go to a higher performance level. Or, a minimally athletic child may find that he's more athletically talented than you or he had thought, especially in this sport. Also, some children appear to become more athletic as they grow older. Sometimes late bloomers turn out to be very athletic.

> *"All my life I've been a late bloomer. What's important is just that you bloom."*
>
> —PGA golfer Chip Beck

These are the most common reasons for evaluating the need for changes. At this point, the parent should make sure the child fully appreciates the ramifications of going to the next level. Doing so will often involve learning the skills or sport at a more complex level and will also increase the competition level. She may have to practice and compete more often. The importance of winning may be emphasized more. After evaluating her stated reasons, you should always emphasize that you are OK with this decision but that playing the sport at the next level must still be fun.

Poor Reasons

Your child may give you poor reasons for playing at a higher level. Some of these are:

1. **"Mike is going to play with the Falcons next season."**
   It is easy to see the appeal of this reason. Maybe Mike is one of your son's best friends. Perhaps your son has played baseball with Mike the past two years and he doesn't want to be left behind. But though Mike may be ready to move on to the next level, both in terms of skills and maturity, your son may not be ready.

2. **"You would like to see me play with the Eagles next season."**
   This reason is a clue that, despite your best efforts, your daughter may be playing more for you than for herself. You may have confused supportive involvement with overinvolvement and are reaping too much vicarious satisfaction in her participation in a sport. You will need to look at this carefully and sort things out with yourself and with her.

3. **"This level is for sissies."**
   Beginning levels of sports, especially those with few or no competitive opportunities, may not feel aggressive or elite enough for some children. They may feel that playing sports at beginning or minimally competitive levels don't count.

These are all poor reasons for going to the next or more advanced levels of a sport. When your child first began playing a sport, you may have done a good job explaining what the goals were for playing sports. Over time, other ideas or notions may have crept into his head. If you hear one of these poor reasons, or others equally lame, it's time to review the original goals.

Quitting the Sport

If your child is quite young and has just begun playing a team sport or has just started individual sports lessons, he may want to quit after a few games or sessions and switch to another sport. This is perfectly acceptable as trying a variety of sports makes sense at a young age. Try to have him complete the time signed up for or the block of sessions you have already paid for, but after that, let him quit and look into another sport.

After playing a sport or game for a year or two (or more), your child may indicate that she wants to drop out of the sport entirely. She may have good reasons to support this decision. Parents should listen carefully to their children's desire to quit a sport. Keep in mind that a child, especially a very young child, may not always be able to articulate a clear reason.

Some of the more common reasons are:

1. **"I'm not interested anymore."**
   Your child first began playing a sport because he was interested in playing it. He may have enjoyed it and had fun for a year or two. He's at a different developmental level now and may have lost interest in the sport.

2. **"I have too many other things I like to do."**
   It may be that, along with piano lessons and the young children's theater group, your daughter's interest in sports has waned. Her interest in other activities may have become stronger than her interest in sports.

3. **"I have too many activities; I want to give up soccer."**
   Your child may feel overprogrammed and has decided that he needs to reduce how much is on his plate. At this point, he may like his other activities more than soccer.

4. **"I'm not having fun anymore."**
   When a child isn't having fun, one of the main reasons to participate in a sport in the first place is gone. However, some discussion should follow to make sure that the lack of fun isn't due to something that can be changed. Would a different coach or team make a difference?

5. **"I don't want to compete anymore."**
   It may be that for any number of reasons, a child no longer enjoys playing or wants to compete. Sometimes a league or a particular team has become too competitive and the pressure to

win has crept into the games. Perhaps he feels too much stress. Or maybe he doesn't want to compete against friends. Check with your child to understand his reasons; sometimes a change of team or coach might be needed. But really listen. It's possible that he no longer finds competing fun. Changing the team, coach, or even sport isn't the answer and won't change his mind.

The older the child, the trickier quitting becomes. If the child has been playing on a team for several years, he has probably learned the importance of commitment to the sport and to the team. We want him to honor his commitments. Even if his reasons are sound, he should be encouraged to continue until the end of the semester or the season or until a replacement has been found for him. At that point he can quit.

You need to take into consideration the child's age, how long he's been playing, what kind of player he is, his current interests, any circumstances in his life that bear on whether he should quit, and his reasons for quitting. You also should take into consideration the understanding you had with him when he originally signed up for a sport. For example, if he signed up originally because he wanted to explore the sport or play for a while, he didn't sign up for life. If you pressure him to continue when he has some perfectly good reasons for quitting, you will be breaking your early agreements with your child. You may also be violating some of your initial reasons for encouraging the child to play some sport.

That said, it is perfectly OK, depending upon some of the reasons given, to see if your child might be interested in some other sport. Maybe he is burned out or tired of soccer after five years but maybe now he would be interested in trying another sport. Mike began tae kwon do when he was five. By the time he was nine he had his black belt. Having achieved this level, he lost interest, and most of his friends were playing team sports. He announced to his parents that he wanted to quit tae kwon do, and he started playing basketball. He was quite good at basketball and eventually played varsity for his high school team. Though he has graduated from college, many of his best friends are his high school teammates.

Taking a Break

Sometimes a child doesn't necessarily want to quit a sport but wants to take a break. Or maybe he isn't sure he wants to continue and wants to take a break in order to test his feelings. Unfortunately, he may not quite know how to present his wishes and they may come out as "I want to quit." So when a child seems to be saying he wants to quit, parents should tease out his reasons and feelings in a nonthreatening way. It may turn out that he didn't realize that there was a middle position or choice available—he can take an open-ended break from the sport. A wise parent will suggest and support such a break. Again, there should be an understanding that he does not have to return to the sport if, after the break, he decides that he really wants to quit.

I've encouraged many kids and their parents to think about taking a break when I've sensed that the child seems less interested or burned out. Depending upon the sport, professional athletes often have a three- to six-month break between seasons. Some kids play sports or take lessons year-round, with occasional breaks of a week or two. It's not surprising that after playing several years without enough breaks, kids may need to pause for a complete break from the sport.

These breaks should be complete or near-complete absences from participating in the sport. During the break, a number of different observations are possible:

- The child may find himself missing playing or practicing. In this instance, he may decide to return to the sport.

- The child may realize that he doesn't miss the sport and it's time to quit.

- The child may realize that he wants a different coach, or a different league, et cetera. In other words, it's not so much that he wants to quit the sport, but that he wants some change.

- The child may decide that he's through with the sport, but he misses the physical activity. He may want to explore some new sport or athletic activity.

Taking a break from a sport can be a useful and necessary step, eventually leading to a player quitting the sport, going back to it, or participating in a new sport. Whenever a child begins to talk about notching up or dropping out of a sport, he may have many valid reasons. He deserves a respectful and supportive discussion. During discussions about quitting or taking a break, keep in mind that you are not arguing a case before the U.S. Supreme Court. You are talking with your young child or teenager. You should be calm and gentle. Your conversation may require getting below the surface of his stated reasons. Even if he does end up quitting sports entirely, at least he got a taste of sports and he enjoyed himself for a period of time. The activity fulfilled the original goals and expectations that the two of you agreed to. He may grow up and play the sport recreationally or, if he doesn't play, he may become an enthusiastic and knowledgeable fan.

The next section of this book contains fact sheets on fifty-one sports and instructions on how to use them. Good luck!

PART 2

Guide to Sports

Conceptualizing Sports

BEFORE TAKING a detailed look at fifty-one sports, it's important to learn some different ways to conceptualize sports. Parents and children need to have some system or method to place sports into different categories—something a little more sophisticated than just individual sports and team sports. This will help both of you as you evaluate various sports to determine which one(s) might be best for your child.

A number of sports experts have offered different classification systems. None are right or wrong. Four are presented here.

Classification System 1: Level of Physical Involvement and Contact

This classification system was put forward by William Strong, a pediatric cardiologist. It helps you understand the degree of physical involvement and contact involved in sports:

Strenuous (contact)
Football, ice hockey, lacrosse (especially boys), rugby, wrestling, diving

Strenuous (limited contact)
Basketball, field hockey, lacrosse (girls), soccer, volleyball

Strenuous (no contact)
Cross-country running, gymnastics, skiing, swimming, tennis, track and field

Moderately strenuous (no contact)
Badminton, baseball (limited contact), golf, table tennis, equestrian riding

Nonstrenuous (no contact)
Archery, bowling, shooting

This system allows you to consider whether your child has the capacity for or interest in sports that have a high degree of physical involvement and contact. Some children may not be emotionally ready for a strenuous sport. They may be fearful of physical contact or getting hurt. Other children may have some physical conditions or limitations that make playing a strenuous sport inadvisable. A child who has asthma should consult his doctor before pursuing a strenuous sport. (Although swimmer Amy Van Dyken, an asthmatic athlete in a strenuous sport, won a gold medal in the 2000 Olympics.) A willowy-built and lightweight child probably should think twice about playing a high-contact, strenuous sport. An overweight child probably should not begin playing a very strenuous, high-contact sport. Keep in mind, though, for very young players, the rules of many sports often limit the amount of contact allowed. Also, very young players often engage in a less strenuous or contact form of the sport. For example, diving is classified as a strenuous contact sport. Potentially all divers could hit the springboard and hurt themselves. However, the really dangerous contact part of diving is when adult 10-meter platform divers enter the water at velocities approaching 40 mph. If the diver hits the water a little off, sprained wrists, torn shoulder joints, broken thumbs, wrenched backs, and persistent headaches can result. Young children seldom learn platform diving (they begin with 3-meter springboard diving) so they should not suffer the type of impact injuries that are possible in platform diving.

Classification System 2: Degree of Contact
Sports psychologists Rainer Martens and Vern Seefeldt developed what looks like a simpler version of the first classification system. They divide sports into three categories and recommend the minimum age for each:

Collision
Football, ice hockey, lacrosse (especially boys), rugby—ten years of age

Contact
Basketball, soccer, baseball, wrestling—eight years of age

Noncontact
Swimming, tennis, track and field, badminton, golf, gymnastics, archery, bowling—six years of age

Notice that neither of these two classification systems considers whether a sport is a team sport or an individual sport. As you can see, in the second system, Martens and Seefeldt suggest that involvement in collision sports is not appropriate for children under ten. Contact sports are suitable for children eight and over. They recommend that children be at least six for any noncontact sports.

Classification System 3: Open and Closed System Sports
Pediatricians Michael Nelson and Barry Goldberg offer a classification system that looks at the complexity level of sports—some sports have more variables and demand more decision making than other sports.

Closed System Sports
With closed system sports the activity conditions are fairly stable or constant. There are not a lot of decisions to make while playing closed system sports. Walking, running, and swimming are examples. Let's look at swimming. In a swimming event, the goal is to traverse the pool as fast as possible. The swimmer does not have to make decisions such as judging the speed of the ball (as in batting in baseball), or deciding which teammate to throw or pass the ball to or where (as in baseball as basketball), or deciding whether to shoot or pass (as in basketball). Another way to think about closed system sports is to consider the number of variables—closed system sports are characterized as having fewer variables to learn, master, or consider than open system sports. Other closed system sports include gymnastics, diving, bowling, archery, and most track and field events. Generally, the closed system sports tend to be individual sports.

Open System Sports

These sports require a number of decisions, and the activity conditions may be constantly changing. More complexity, decision making, and strategizing are required in these sports. Open system sports include basketball, baseball, lacrosse, ice hockey, soccer, and volleyball, and are generally mostly team sports.

What are the implications of the last system for picking the right sport for your child? Generally speaking, very young children do better in closed system sports than open ones. Until age ten, many children find it difficult to coordinate their eyes, arms, and legs with their brains. Thus children under ten do best when they only have to focus on the basic skills required in the closed sports, like running and swimming. They don't have to worry about executing the fundamental moves of the sport *and* navigating the various mental decisions that are required for open system sports. If a child is under ten and wants to play an open system sport, slower sports like baseball and soccer are better choices.

Besides age, in what other ways might you apply the concept of closed and open system sports to your child? A child who has a serious attention deficit disorder would probably best begin with a closed system sport. A child who is not very well coordinated would probably do best with a closed system sport so that he can concentrate on learning the fundamental moves of the sport without having to also learn and make the various types of decisions necessary when playing an open system sport.

Classification System 4: Aesthetic, Weight-Class, and Endurance Sports

This classification system applies mainly to individual sports.

Aesthetic Sports

These are usually judged sports with a strong subjective element to the scoring or judging. Grace and smoothness of movements are part of the sport. Aesthetic sports include gymnastics, diving, and figure skating.

Weight-Class Sports

For these sports, the events and competition are divided by various weight classifications. An athlete competes on the basis of her weight. Because of this, small, lighter kids are on an equal footing with their opponents. Some of these sports include rowing, boxing, wrestling, and some of the martial arts.

Endurance Sports

Endurance sports typically require long, sustained physical effort. Skiing, cycling, tennis, and long-distance races in swimming and certain track events are examples of endurance sports.[25]

These four classification systems are intended to give parents and children some different ways to think about the many sports that your child may want to try. You may pick the system that makes the most sense to you, or you may want to use elements of all four. You may also want to incorporate some other considerations into the classification system(s) you use. For example, if your child has never run well and is not particularly quick on his feet, you may want to eliminate sports that require running or being quick-footed. Thus, you eliminate running sports (certain track sports), tennis, and soccer. You do give consideration to sports like golf, archery, and swimming.

Here are some other concepts you may want to use in addition to these classification systems.

I think of some sports as being mainly, though not solely, *technique-driven sports*. At the higher levels of performance, all sports require good technique. But some sports require fairly good technique early on to even be able to perform some of the basic movements of the sport. A beginner swimmer can have poor technique but he can swim, he will not hurt himself, and he may even occasionally win a race. A beginner gymnast will generally be unable to do certain routines without attention to technique, and without good technique, may hurt himself. Golf is another technique-driven sport. It requires strength and power but with only strength and power and poor technique, many balls will end up in the lake or bunker. Diving also requires strength and power but without good technique there will be a lot of belly flops. An impatient child may not have the right temperament to learn a sport that requires precise technique in order to satisfactorily perform even the most elementary moves or routines of that sport.

While mentioned earlier, it's important to remember that many sports are characterized as being either *gross-motor sports* or *fine-motor sports*. Gross muscle movements are generally movements of the arms and legs. So sports that depend mostly on arm and leg movements or coordination are gross-motor sports. Some examples include running, cycling, diving, and skiing. Fine muscle movements are generally movements of the eyes and the hands and fingers. So some sports that depend mostly on eye-hand movements or coordination are fine-motor sports. Some examples are archery, billiards, and shooting. Obviously there are far more gross-motor sports than fine-motor sports, though some sports require both. Remember to consider what your child's gross-motor and fine-motor strengths or weaknesses are when looking for a sport for him.

Using a classification system along with some other concepts can help you narrow the choices once you've identified a group of sports that fit your child. For example, he may show a special knack for all sports involving balls. He probably has good hand-eye coordination. But there is a huge difference between lacrosse and golf. Boy's lacrosse is an extremely strenuous contact sport but golf isn't. Whichever system(s) you choose, do not use them rigidly. They are meant to be helpful starting places, ways of thinking about different sports, not absolute rules that dictate what sport your child should pick.

Researching Sports

IT'S TIME TO LOOK more closely at a number of sports and learn some of the basic features of each and how these elements may match some of a child's abilities, natural preferences and interests, physical build, and emotional makeup. Remember, these are only guidelines on how to match up the sport with your child. This is not an exact science but rather taking some basics of each sport and making judgments about how these correspond to some of your child's abilities and inclinations. Even if you find a good match, it won't work if a child isn't interested.

Involve your child in as much of this research as her age, reading level, and comprehension will allow. Explain any information she can't follow or understand herself. For example, a six-year-old child may not be able to read a book, but you can tell her what you've learned. In most instances, materials and resources in the next section are geared to children. Invite questions from your child to see how well she understands the information about a particular sport that you and she are exploring.

For each sport or family of athletic events, you will find the following:

1. **Basic Abilities.**

It will help if your child has some of the abilities or physical traits mentioned. However, some children appear to have none of them and still accomplish modest success in the sport. Some of the training or instruction in the sport will go toward developing or increasing some of these abilities. You will note that I sometimes use the word *strength* and sometimes *power*. They are not used interchangeably. A person who can lift a box weighing one hundred pounds is considered to be stronger (has more muscle strength) than a person who can't. A person who can push a three-hundred-pound bookcase over an inch is considered stronger (has more muscle strength) than a person who can't. For our purposes, power is the combination of strength and speed or acceleration (how quickly muscle fibers fire) often over distance (how far a person moves or how far a person can move an object). Some sports are mainly strength sports, others are mainly power sports, and still others require significant amounts of both. A boxer with strength but little or no speed will probably be floored if matched with a boxer who is just as strong but who can combine his strength with speed (power). Technique can affect power. For example, a golfer who hits the ball with a bad swing (poor technique) may not hit the ball very far. The bad swing can result in little or no power, and power in this sport is necessary for distance—how far the ball travels. (Of course, some bad swings can have power but little accuracy.) In this section, the words *stamina* and *endurance* are used interchangeably. Stamina is the resistance to fatigue. It is especially important in strenuous sports (lacrosse) and long-distance events (marathon).

2. Other Elements.

This section covers the type of or need for coaching or instruction and how much practice is expected of a beginning or low-competitive participant. While some parents are able to teach the basics of a sport to their children, beyond the basics it's important for children to learn from experienced instructors or coaches, especially if the child is not a natural athlete. They are more knowledgeable concerning safety considerations, and they are more likely to identify a child's bad habits or techniques and correct them before they become too entrenched. They are also more knowledgeable about the right kind of training and conditioning that is required for the sport. (Coaches can be volunteer coaches as long as they are knowledgeable and experienced.)

3. **Events.**

I will not name all of the events. I also note how the rules and time periods of the games for beginners may differ from regulation games or formal competition. The events presented for each sport involve competition on some level. Remember, though, that children can learn and play many competitive sports without ever competing. For many of these sports, I will note some of the modified versions or rules of the sport when kids are playing it. For example, youth baseball leagues commonly play only six innings, not nine. In youth basketball, the baskets are usually set lower than for adult play and the periods are shorter. When very young children play soccer, offside rules are seldom taught or enforced.

4. **Safety Issues.**

This section includes common injuries and equipment or gear required for safety. For some sports, perhaps the most important safety equipment will be the helmet. Make sure you buy the right helmet—one that is sport-specific and one that is not too big. Of course, some sports are safer than others. However, no matter the sport, every parent and child should understand that there is always the potential for injury.

5. **Miscellany.**

Factors such as how the sport is judged or scored and whether the sport is a team or individual sport are covered here. I may indicate that a sport is an individual sport but played mostly on teams or within a team context. The typical costs involved are also listed. Parents should always investigate renting equipment to reduce initial costs. This is very important, especially if your child wants to learn a sport that requires expensive equipment. Also, for the more expensive sports, look for special, introductory classes that are often bargains. Some youth sports programs have scholarships available for children who may not be able to afford them otherwise.

6. **Related Sports.**

Related sports also covered in this section of the book will be identified in **_bold italics_**.

7. **Your Child and (name of sport).**

The common physical abilities and psychological traits associated with a particular sport will be listed. This is where you might be able to match your child with a sport that fits best with his strengths and weaknesses as well as his interests and emotional makeup.

8. **More Information.**

Resources may include associations, books, movies, teaching videos, and Web sites. Even though I've noted each movie's rating, be sure to preview the movie first for its appropriateness for your child. Amateur and/or youth resources will be emphasized, though for some sports the professional association for the sport is mentioned. Book authors' names will be in parentheses.

9. **Did You Know?**

This section will include interesting historical and other facts about the sport.

None of the material in each section is intended to be exhaustive. Nor have I attempted to cover every sport ever played. I've included many well-known sports because your child is more likely to have some familiarity with them and you are more likely to find introductory lessons or beginner teams in your area for these sports. But, because of a number of reasons, your child may prefer to look into a sport that is off the beaten track, little known. Thus, I have also included a number of these sports for your consideration and exploration. However, finding venues that house such sports close to where you live and finding teams and/or instructors for some of these sports may prove to be a challenge. Extreme sports—sports that involve some daredevil-like risk taking—are increasingly popular, especially with teenagers. Some of them are snowboarding, freestyle skiing, and ice climbing. A couple of these sports are presented in this section.

Fact Sheets

Individual Sports

ALPINE SKIING

Basic Abilities

Skiing requires general physical fitness, including strength, especially leg strength. Tight control of body movements and balance and concentration are important.

Other Elements

Ski lessons help with the basic techniques, but coaching is required if the skier wants to compete. Practice is necessary for improvement. Many people take up skiing and never compete, even though they may become quite competent skiers.

Events

The main events in Alpine skiing are downhill, slalom (the skier must maneuver around gates), and the super slalom (fewer gates and not as steep as the slalom).

Safety Issues

At beginner levels, this sport is relatively safe because beginners do not go very fast, they are unlikely to run into trees at high speeds, and they don't have far to fall if they are young. Even so, a helmetless five-year-old skier died when he crashed into a tree at a Colorado ski resort. As skiers pick up speed, the potential for serious falls increases, along with the risk of injury. Broken bones are possible. Make sure that instructors emphasize good technique and safety, for example, controlled speed.

Miscellany

Judges monitor that the skier stays within the course and gates. Time alone establishes the winner. Skiing is an individual sport; however, if competition is desired, skiers often join a team. Costs: lessons, skis, and other gear (helmet, boots, poles, goggles, suit, gloves, warm clothing, and thermal underwear). Ski lift tickets are usually included with the cost of lessons or team or club membership; if not, many ski areas discount these tickets for children. Also, a number of ski programs have beginner lessons for children and an all-inclusive fee that includes ski rental, lessons, and lunch for the day. If ski slopes are miles away, a parent should factor in travel expenses. Without some special deals, skiing is considered an expensive sport.

Related Sports

Snowboarding, freestyle skiing, ski jumping, speed skiing, and cross-country skiing

Your Child and Alpine Skiing

Does your child have quick reflexes? Does she like to go fast? Is she coordinated? Does she tolerate cold weather?

More Information

Web site: www.discoversnow.com
Video: *The Fundamentals of Downhill Skiing* (Best Film & Video Corp.)
Books: *A Basic Guide to Skiing and Snowboarding* (U.S. Olympic Committee); *The Basic Essentials of Alpine Skiing* (Carol Poster)

Did You Know?

The earliest knowledge we have of skiing is from cave drawings from Eastern Russia dating from between 7000 and 5000 BC. The men on skis were probably hunters. The modern form of skiing developed in Norway.

* * *

In 1911 Norwegian polar explorer Roald Amundsen skied and used sleds pulled by dogs to reach the South Pole.

ARCHERY

Basic Abilities

Archery is a sport that requires upper-body strength, excellent eye-hand coordination, concentration, and very good, precise technique.

Other Elements

Lessons and training are important; repetitive practice is an essential part of learning the sport. Archery is a precision, fine-motor sport.

Events

Beginners shoot at short distances, and competition usually requires shooting a specific number of arrows at several different distances.

Safety Issues

A shooting range laid out safely is essential. Pulled and sprained muscles and repetitive motion injuries are possible.

Miscellany

Judges monitor for rule compliance. Each archer fills out his own scorecard, which is verified by scorers. Although archery is an individual sport, some events are team events, for example, three archers versus three other archers. Costs: lessons, bow, quiver, arrows, and membership at range.

Related Sports

Field archery

Your Child and Archery

Archery is a fairly solitary sport, though it is often offered in schools and camps. Does your child enjoy solitary play? Can she focus in on minute details? Does she have good eye-hand coordination? Has she shown interest in other target sports, like darts?

More Information

Web site: United States National Archery Association,
            www.usarchery.org
Books: *Archery: Know The Sport* (Donald W. Campbell);
            Archery Is For Me (Art Thomas); *Better Archery for Boys & Girls* (George Sullivan); *Archery: Steps to Success* (Kathleen M. Haywood and Catherine F. Lewis)

Did You Know?

Using bows and arrows for hunting goes back thousands of years. In the twelfth to fifteenth centuries, English and Scottish kings employed archers as soldiers. However, they had to ban golf, bowling, and football because so many of their archers were abandoning archery practice to play those sports.

* * *

In the 1992 Olympics, Antonio Rebollo of the Spanish archery team shot a flaming arrow to ignite the Olympic torch in the opening ceremony.

* * *

Do you remember the story of William Tell—the story of the Swiss patriot and archer who shot the apple placed on his son's head? Historians doubt that this ever happened and even question whether there was a William Tell. The August 2004 issue of *Smithsonian Magazine* presents this debate.

BILLIARDS

Basic Abilities

It helps to have good eye-hand coordination; controlled movement of arms, hands, and fingers; and the ability to analyze shots.

Other Elements

While a child can learn to play billiards on his own, lessons are necessary to become adept at the basic techniques and the finer points of the game. A great deal of practice/playing games is important so that the player can encounter as many of the various combinations and permutations that occur, while knowing that these combinations are virtually infinite. This is a fine-motor sport.

Events

Though variations of billiards exist, the basic features of most involve playing on a pool table with one cue ball and fifteen numbered balls. This is called pocket billiards or pool. Players play anywhere from three to seventeen games, depending on the event. The player who sinks all of his balls first is the winner.

Safety Issues

While billiards is a fairly safe sport, injuring fingers and repetitive motion injuries are possible.

Miscellany

In high-level competition, judges monitor for fouls. Otherwise, billiards is a nonjudged sport and an individual sport. Costs: billiard table, cues and balls, and lessons. Membership in pool clubs or halls is common for competition. In the past, pool halls were not regarded as child-friendly environments by many parents. More recently, there has been an attempt to make playing billiards more family friendly. Some clubs and halls have newly built areas for pool playing that encourage playing by all family members.

Related Sports

None

Your Child and Billiards

Billiards is an accuracy and precision sport. Does your child have good fine-motor skills? Is your child mathematical, and does he like to analyze situations? Is he calm? Does he have high frustration tolerance?

More Information

Videos: *Billiards for All Age Groups; BCA's How to Play Pool Right*

Books: *Sports: The Complete Visual Reference* (François Fortin); *Willie Mosconi on Pocket Billiards* (Willie Mosconi)

Did You Know?

Though the origins of this sport are unclear, it may have originated in China. We do know that a billiard table was built for King Louis XI of France in the 1400s.

* * *

Willy Mosconi, former world champion in billiards, learned to play when he was young by using potatoes and a broomstick.

BOWLING

Basic Abilities

Balance, control of body, and upper-body strength are useful for a person who wants to participate in bowling.

Other Elements

Some lessons and practice are required for excellence or competition.

Events

This sport is played casually at the beginner level. Points are determined by how many pins are knocked down, and the bowler who has the highest points at the end of ten frames (one game) wins that game.

Safety Issues

Bowling is a safe sport. Children should be guided in the choice of the correct ball weight for their size and strength. Slipping and falling may cause minor injuries, and some muscle strain is possible.

Miscellany

Winners are determined by score/points. While bowling is an individual sport, it is often played on teams. Costs: ball, bowling shoes, initial lessons, and bowling alley charges, though balls and shoes are always available for rent. Increasingly, new bowling centers are built to be more family friendly.

Related Sports

Lawn bowling and bocce

Your Child and Bowling

Does your child have good balance? Is she fairly calm? Does she have good body control? Bowling is a social sport, usually played with others. Does your child enjoy casual group situations?

More Information

Video: *Teaching Kids Bowling* (Westcom Productions Incorporated)
Books: *Bowling for Beginners* (Don Nace and Bruce Curtis);
            Sports: The Complete Visual Reference (François Fortin);
            Bowling Basics: A Step by Step Approach (Gerald P. Carlson
            and E. Harold Blackwell)

Did You Know?

Artifacts dating from 3200 BC show that a primitive form of this game was played in Egypt.

BOXING

Basic Abilities

Quickness, strength, stamina, and cardiovascular fitness are assets for boxers.

Other Elements

Instruction is important for learning techniques and safe moves. Practices once or twice a week are common for beginners.

Events

Boxing matches between two opponents consist of a certain number of rounds. A referee ensures that rules are followed, and judges score the match based upon punches landed successfully on the opponent. The boxer awarded the most points wins the match. While still a sport played mainly by boys and men, adolescent girls and women are showing an interest in this sport, and they are participating in boxing events for girls and women.

Safety Issues

Boxing brings up a number of safety concerns, so much so that some people contend that boxing is not a safe sport for children *or* adults. The chief concern involves the possibility of brain damage because of repeated blows to the head. Broken noses and jaws are also possible. These risks can be reduced if boxing is learned *only* for conditioning and if there is no sparring (boxing with a partner or opponent). If there is no sparring, the risk of head injuries is eliminated. Look for a boxing program where basic boxing skills and moves are taught and physical contact is avoided by only working out with punching bags and shadow boxing. For more advanced youth, some programs allow light sparring with considerable oversight.

Miscellany

While what constitutes a point in boxing is clearly stated, it is a judged sport and an element of subjectivity is involved. It is an individual sport, though often one participates on a team. Costs: gloves, instruction, and training, with most boxing gyms providing other gear. If sparring takes place, headgear is mandatory.

Related Sports
Kickboxing

Your Child and Boxing
Is your child quick on his feet? Does he like to exercise, run, and jump rope? If he is going to learn to spar with partners or opponents, is he fearless in terms of physical contact? (In two recent fights between junior welterweights, a total of 2,747 punches were thrown.)

More Information
Web site: US Boxing, www.usaboxing.org
Video: *Boxerobics: The Ultimate Conditioning Program*
           (Advanced Fitness Education)
Books: *Fitness Boxing* (Frank Kurzel); *Fighting Fit: Boxing
           Workouts, Techniques and Sparring* (Doug Werner
           and Alan Lachica)
Movies: *Rocky* (PG); *Million Dollar Baby* (PG-13)

Did You Know?
The ancient Greeks believed that fistfighting was one of the games played by the gods on Mount Olympus. There is a reference to boxing in Homer's epic *The Iliad*. As practiced in ancient Greece, it was a brutal sport, often leading to death.

CYCLING

Basic Abilities
Good cyclists have excellent aerobic and anaerobic ability and conditioning. Strong leg muscles and considerable physical endurance are necessary.

Other Elements

Almost all children learn to ride bikes on their own or with parents teaching them. To enter cycling races, however, requires instruction and training in the technical skills of cycling. Training and conditioning several days a week are important.

Events

Different kinds of cycling include road racing and track racing. The events vary, depending on the type of cycling. All events have certain distances or stages and, generally, the cyclist with the fastest time wins.

Safety Issues

Minor injuries from just riding a bike include pulled muscles and sprains. More serious injuries can occur if the cyclist falls or crashes. The Centers for Disease Control (CDC) estimates that 330,000 children from ages five to fourteen are injured while riding their bikes. Emergency rooms treat almost 140,000 children every year for head injuries suffered while bicycling. Helmets can prevent up to 85 percent of such head injuries and therefore should be mandatory gear. Broken arms, legs, and shoulders can occur with falls.

Miscellany

Cycling is a timed sport with judges along the course. It is an individual sport, though many cyclists ride for teams. Costs: instruction and/or coaching, bike, suits/uniforms, shoes, gloves, and helmets. Largely because of the success of Lance Armstrong in the Tour de France, interest in cycling has increased in the United States. Consequently, there are more opportunities to obtain good instruction and find tracks than in the past. Bicycling is not an impact sport (unless you crash), and it can be enjoyed for a lifetime.

Related Sports

Triathlon and BMX (Bicycle Motocross)

Your Child and Cycling

Does your child enjoy riding her bike? Does she like to ride fast and long distances? Does she have long and strong legs? Does she use good judgment when she rides, that is, does she go only as fast as her skills call for?

More Information

Video: *The Fundamentals of Bicycle Touring* (Elliot Bay Film Company)

Books: *Cycling in Action* (John Crossingham); *Sports: The Complete Visual Reference* (François Fortin); *Lance Armstrong* (Sandra Donovan); *It's Not About My Bike: My Journey Back to Life* (Lance Armstrong)

Movie: *Breaking Away* (PG)

Did You Know?

Leonardo da Vinci drew the first sketch of a pedal bike, although it was not actually built at the time. The first pedal bike was built four hundred years later.

DISCUS

Basic Abilities

Good discus throwers usually have strong muscles, especially in the arms, shoulders, and back; good concentration; as well as height.

Other Elements

Learning the proper technique is essential, and good instruction and coaching are required. Discus throwers must practice several times a week to improve their performance and their conditioning.

Events

Discus events consist of each thrower making a set number of attempts. The competitor with the longest throw wins.

Safety Issues

Pulled muscles, sprains, dislocations, and repetitive motion injuries are possible.

Miscellany

Judges determine the success of the throw or if a foul is committed. They measure the distance of each throw. Discus is an individual sport, though competitors are often members of a track and field team. Costs: coaching fees, track and field team fees, discus, uniform, and shoes.

Related Sports

Hammer, shot put, and decathlon

Your Child and Discus

Since some whirling around is necessary for this sport, can your child do this without becoming dizzy or disoriented? Does he have muscle strength? Does he like to throw things long distances?

More Information

Videos: *Run Faster, Jump Higher, Throw Farther: How to Win at Track and Field* (Sabin); *Track & Field, Part III—Throwing Events* (Human Kinetics); *Discus Throw Drills* (Sports Nation Video)

Books: *Fundamentals of Track and Field*, 2nd ed. (Gerry Carr); *The Young Track and Field Athlete* (Colin Jackson)

Did You Know?

Many of today's sports had their start as utilitarian endeavors such as transportation or hunting. Sometimes the military incorporated the activity for its purposes or for training. In order to lighten their load, ancient warriors would throw their shields across rivers before crossing them. Somewhere along the line, warriors turned this action into a game of "Who can throw his shield the farthest?"

DIVING

Basic Abilities

It helps for divers to have good body control, strength and power, excellent technique, and grace.

Other Elements

Diving is a highly coached sport. To attain technical competence, considerable practice is necessary, with a great deal of repetition.

Events

High dive (10-meter platform); springboard (3-meter). Dives have different degrees of difficulty, and beginners will learn the easiest dives first. For competition, a diver will perform anywhere from four to six different dives.

Safety Issues

The water must be deep enough to prevent the diver from hitting bottom; most common injuries occur when a diver hits the springboard or platform during the dive, or when the diver hits the water at high impact and the body is not aligned correctly upon entry. Head injuries are possible. Beginner divers generally do not learn platform diving.

Miscellany

This is a judged sport. Judges determine points, and the points are multiplied by the degree of difficulty of a particular dive. Diving is an individual sport, though most often it is performed on a team. Costs: swimsuit, lessons/coaches, membership in a club or swim center.

Related Sports

Synchronized diving

Your Child and Diving

Diving is a very technical and precise sport. Beginners will work only on 3-meter springboards, so a dive takes all of a couple of seconds.

Does your child seek out or enjoy repetitive activity without showing boredom? Does she like to jump on the trampoline? (This is a part of diving training.) Is she graceful in her body movements? It's important that she doesn't become dizzy or queasy when her body is in motion.

More Information

Book: *Dive Right In* (Robert Hirschfeld)
Movie: *Breaking the Surface: The Greg Louganis Story* (no rating)

Did You Know?

We have evidence that people dived as early as the fourth century BC and that the Vikings dived twelve centuries later.

EQUESTRIAN JUMPING

Basic Abilities

A rider must have patience and a firm, yet gentle way with her horse. Excellent concentration is essential.

Other Elements

Instruction is necessary to learn proper riding and the technical skills to teach the horse to jump. Considerable practice is necessary, both for the horse and the rider, but especially to foster a good relationship between the horse and the rider.

Events

A course requires that horse and rider jump over a number of different types of obstacles. Judges evaluate how well the horse jumps, and this includes the approach, the actual jump, and the landing.

Safety Issues

Falling or being thrown by one's horse are the main safety concerns. Broken bones and serious head and spine injuries are possible.

Miscellany

This is a judged sport, so there is a degree of subjectivity. It is an individual sport. Costs: all equestrian sports are quite expensive. Many participants own their own horses and must maintain the upkeep and health of the horse. Instruction and outfits are additional costs. Membership in an equestrian club is common and expensive.

Related Sports

Dressage and polo

Your Child and Equestrian Jumping

Does your child love horses? Does she like to ride horses? Is she patient when working with horses? Can she concentrate?

More Information

Web site: United States Pony Club, www.pony.org
Video: *Today's Horse for Today's Kids*
               (American Production Services)
Book: *Improve Your Riding Skills* (Carolyn Henderson)

Did You Know?

Many equestrian sports, including jumping, began as recreational pastimes and for hunting. The military also used these sports for training.

FENCING

Basic Abilities

Good fencers usually exhibit controlled body movements, precise technique, grace, quickness, and stamina.

Other Elements

Fencing requires technical instruction. Considerable training and practice are necessary to master even the basic elements.

Events

Fencing matches consist of two opponents touching certain body targets on one's opponent with a foil (the name for a fencing sword). Electric monitors establish whether a target has been hit. Referees and judges watch for rule compliance. There are several different forms of fencing depending upon the type of sword used, though use of the foil is the most common.

Safety Issues

Repetitive motion injuries and pulled and strained muscles are some of the most common injuries.

Miscellany

Though fencing is a judged event, points are awarded via electronic sensors. It is an individual sport often played on teams. Costs: instruction, foil (or épée or saber), and outfits. Membership in a fencing club may be necessary.

Related Sports

None

Your Child and Fencing

Since fencing is not a common sport, it is unlikely that any of your child's friends take fencing instruction. Does your child like to make quick, controlled body movements? Does he like to engage in swordplay (though fencing does not consist of the freestyle motions of swordplay)? Is he graceful?

More Information

Video: *Fencing. Vol. 1: Fundamentals—Basic Beginner Training* (Videoactive Company)

Books: *A Beginner's Guide to Traditional and Sport Fencing* (Doug Werner); *The Art and Science of Fencing* (Nick Evangelista); *The Woman Fencer* (Nick and Anita Evangelista)

Did You Know?

Ancient Egyptian art shows fencers wearing masks. Fencing with swords was a form of combat in ancient times. The Germans developed fencing as a sport in the fourteenth century. It became widespread by the sixteenth century. In Europe, fencing duels took place to settle disputes of honor, but most countries outlawed them by the nineteenth century. Thereafter, fencing became an organized sport.

FIGURE SKATING

Basic Abilities

This sport demands body control, precise technique, concentration, flexibility, physical strength, and balance. Figure skaters must be performers, skating to the audience and to the judges. They also need to be expressive and creative.

Other Elements

This is a highly coached sport with a very intense and trusting relationship between the coach and skater. Considerable practice is necessary to learn the various techniques and, once learned, further practice and repetition are required to nail down each move.

Events

Competition involves a short program of a few minutes with a specified number of technical elements, and a long program, often called the free program, with no technical elements required. Both programs are performed to music selected by the skater and coach. Of course, children can learn to figure skate without intending to compete.

Safety Issues

Good coaching and good ice conditions reduce the risk of injury. Even with a good coach and optimal ice conditions, injuries are possible, including pulled muscles; sprains; arm, ankle, and leg fractures; and head injuries. Beginners often wear knee, elbow, and wrist pads, as well as a helmet.

Miscellany

Judges determine the scores or points for each skater. This is a highly judged sport, and factors extraneous to the actual performance sometimes influence certain judges. A young skater should be aware of and be able to handle the subjective element in judging this sport. This is an individual sport, though it is often performed on a team or club. Costs: skates, costume, lessons/coaching, and membership in a skating club.

Related Sports

Speed skating, in-line skating, pairs skating, and ice dancing

Your Child and Figure Skating

Does your child have a sense of balance? Can she roller-skate? Can she twirl around without getting dizzy? Is she physically flexible? Does she take instructions well? How's her frustration tolerance? Does she handle stress well? Is she graceful?

More Information

Web site: United States Figure Skating Association (competitive skating), www.usfsa.com

Video: *Eazee Skating* (Donna Ashton-Good)

Books: *Magic on Ice* (Patty Cranston); *The Young Ice Skater* (Peter Morrissey); *Ice Skating* (Peter Morrissey); *Born to Skate: The Michelle Kwan Story* (Edward Z. Epstein); *Sarah Hughes: Golden Girl* (Nancy Krulik); *Landing It: My Life On and Off the Ice* (Scott Hamilton)

Movies: *Nutcracker on Ice* (intended for children); *Artistry on Ice* (no rating)

Did You Know?

Skates made of animal bones date from 800 BC.

* * *

Though skating was born in Europe, figure skating as we know it today began in the United States.

FREESTYLE SKIING

Basic Abilities

Leg and torso strength, endurance, concentration, and good body control especially in the air are all abilities required for freestyle skiing. Some creative skills are necessary to choreograph acrobatic moves.

Other Elements

Generally, freestyle skiers learn Alpine skiing before they progress to freestyle skiing. Lessons are essential for a good foundation in the technical skills of skiing. Trampoline training is an important component of practicing freestyle skiing.

Events

There are three types of freestyle skiing—moguls, aerials, and ballet.

Safety Issues

Young beginners do not make the kind of moves that can lead to serious injuries. As the skier progresses and performs more difficult routines, more serious injuries are possible, including sprains, head injuries (though helmets are worn), dislocations, and broken bones.

Miscellany

This is a judged sport with the judges awarding points. Though some of the scoring is based upon certain objective criteria, the rest is based on form and creativity considerations. Freestyle skiing is an individual sport, though skiers are often on teams. Costs: skis, helmets, goggles, warm skiwear, lessons, and coaching. Lessons are available at ski clubs and many ski resorts.

Related Sports
Alpine skiing and *snowboarding*

Your Child and Freestyle Skiing

Does your child like to do somersaults and back flips? Does she have good balance? Is she creative? Does she have strong legs? Does she have nerves of steel?

More Information

Books: *The Encyclopedia of the Winter Olympics* (John Wukovits); *A Basic Guide to Skiing and Snowboarding* (U.S. Olympic Committee); *The Winter Olympics* (Larry Dane Brimmer); *Sports: The Complete Visual Reference* (François Fortin)

Did You Know?

This sport is a mix of Alpine skiing and acrobatics. It began in the 1960s, was recognized as a sport in 1979, and is now an Olympic sport.

GOLF

Basic Abilities

Golf requires considerable control, both physical and mental, proper technique, coordination, concentration, and analytical skills.

Other Elements

Instruction is needed to teach the various skills involved as well as the analytical parts of the game. Considerable practice and repetition are needed to learn the techniques.

Events

Golfers play eighteen holes, though beginner golfers usually play only a few holes. Beginner golfers rarely compete, and even more advanced golfers may not compete against others.

Safety Issues

Generally, golf is considered a safe sport, though it is possible to hit yourself with your club, get hit by another player's ball, and so on.

Lower-back and shoulder problems can occur but are unlikely with beginner players.

Miscellany

In competition, judges oversee rule compliance. Each player keeps his own score. Though an individual sport, golf is often played on a team, for example, a school team. Golf is sometimes played with two players (one team) against two other players (a second team), though there are some other variations of team playing. Costs: starter clubs, bag, and lessons. Unless included with the lessons, there may be greens fees. Since participation in golf has been flat the last few years, various golf organizations are trying to bring new players to the sport by offering more introductory lessons, reducing greens fees, and so on. Try to find programs specifically geared to children and courses that have junior golf courses. Junior courses are designed for children and are characterized by being shorter in length than most courses, perhaps only four-hole courses. Considered a lifetime sport.

Related Sports

None

Your Child and Golf

Is your child fairly calm? Does he have high frustration tolerance? Is he patient? Does he seem to prefer a slow-paced activity rather than a fast-action activity? Is he analytical? Does he pay attention to details? Is he able to listen carefully when learning? Does he like to walk? Golf is a mental game and emphasizes finesse moves over gut-strength swings. Thus, accuracy (placement and location of the ball) is often more important than the distance of shot.

More Information

Web sites: Young Golfers of America Association, www.ygaa.com;
Play Golf America, www.playgolfamerica.com

Video: *Play Better Golf, Vol. 1—The Basics*

Books: *The ABC's of Golf* (Dan Kirby); *Junior Golf* (Nick Wright);
          The Young Golfer (Richard Simmons); *Beginning Golf*
          (Bruce Curtis); *Tiger Woods* (Michael Bradley);
          Golf Annika's Way (Annika Sorenstam)

Did You Know?

The Romans brought a form of a stick-and-ball game to the British
Isles. But it was the Scots in the mid-fifteenth century who dug a
hole in the ground and made getting the ball into the hole the goal
of the game.

GYMNASTICS

Basic Abilities

To be a gymnast, it is desirable to have flexibility, coordination, concentration, control, gracefulness, power, and stamina.

Other Elements

Gymnastics requires instruction and coaching, and considerable practice is necessary to achieve proper technique.

Events

Floor exercise, vault, horizontal bar, uneven parallel bars, pommel
horse, parallel bars, rings, and balance beam. While many events are individual, there are also team competitions in this sport.

Safety Issues

This can be a high-injury sport, with sprained ankles, pulled muscles,
and stress fractures as the most common. Lower-back injuries are
possible. A number of these injuries are the result of overuse. At very
competitive levels, the emphasis on slenderness can lead to eating disorders such as anorexia and bulimia. To limit injuries, a good coach
who emphasizes conditioning and teaches proper techniques is essential. Safe equipment and practice areas are necessary for proper training and safety.

Miscellany

This is a point-system sport, and a panel of judges awards the points. Thus, a subjective element is involved. Even though it is an individual sport, it is usually taught and played in a group/team setting. Costs: apparel, lessons, and sometimes club fees.

Related Sports

Trampoline and cheerleading

Your Child and Gymnastics

Is your child flexible and limber? Does she enjoy doing cartwheels, handstands, and walking across one-inch-wide fences? Is she graceful? How's her balance? Is she small and light? Does she show an interest in watching gymnastics on TV, and does she turn herself into a pretzel while watching? Once she progresses beyond the beginner's level, she will need to be able to handle the pressure of performing increasingly difficult and technical routines.

More Information

Check your local YMCA/YWCA for programs/classes.

Web sites: Wendy Hilliard Foundation, www.wendyontheweb.org; USA Gymnastics (national youth gymnastics organization), www.usa-gymnastics.org

Videos: *Kids of Degrassi Street* (WGBH Video); *Pad Drills* (TMW Media Group)

Books: *The Young Gymnast* (Joan Jackman); *Landing On My Feet* (Kerri Strug); *Fundamental Gymnastics* (Linda Wallenberg Bragg); *The Gymnastics Book: The Young Performer's Guide* (Elfi Schlegel)

Did You Know?

Ancient drawings from 5000 BC Egypt show that acrobats performed for the pharaohs and Egyptian nobility.

HAMMER

Basic Abilities

Hammer throwing is a general strength and technique-driven sport. It also calls for steady balance and coordination.

Other Elements

Instruction and coaching are necessary to teach the technical skills of this sport, as well as to guide the thrower's conditioning. Practices several times a week are common.

Events

Hammer throwing meets take place in a protected throwing area. Each thrower usually is allowed a set number of throws. The competitor with the longest throw wins.

Safety Issues

Pulled muscles and muscle strains are common. Shoulder dislocations and back injuries can occur. Proper conditioning is essential, not just for performance, but also for safety.

Miscellany

Judges oversee each attempt and rule on whether the throw is fair or foul. They are also in charge of measuring each throw. Though often played on track and field teams, hammer is an individual event. Costs: team fees, which may or may not include coaching fees, hammer, suit, and shoes.

Related Sports

Discus, shot put, heptathlon, and decathlon

Your Child and Hammer

As with discus throwing, a hammer thrower must whirl around before releasing the hammer. When at the amusement park, can your child ride on the whirling rides without becoming ill? Is he strong? Does he like to practice things over and over again? How's his balance? Height helps.

More Information

Videos: *Run Faster, Jump Higher, Throw Farther: How to Win at Track and Field* (Sabin); *Track & Field, Part III—Throwing Events* (Human Kinetics)

Books: *Fundamentals of Track and Field*, 2nd ed. (Gerry Carr); *Sports: The Complete Visual Reference* (François Fortin)

Did You Know?

This sport probably began with the English and Scottish sport of throwing sledgehammers. The sport's name is now a misnomer as it consists of throwing a ball weighing sixteen pounds attached to a four-foot wire.

HIGH JUMP

Basic Abilities

Strong leg muscles, quickness, and flexibility are important for high jumpers.

Other Elements

Coaches teach the technical elements of this sport. A high jumper can expect to practice several times a week. The trampoline is part of the training.

Events

Generally, a bar is set at a qualifying height. All jumpers must clear that height in order to proceed. Then the bar is raised little by little. The jumper with the highest jump wins.

Safety Issues

A landing cushion protects jumpers when they fall over the bar. However, injuries are still possible and can include pulled muscles and sprains, and broken arms, wrists, and legs.

Miscellany

Judges oversee the competition and rule compliance. They monitor the bar heights and determine if the jumper has made the jump successfully. High jump is a track and field event and often performed with a team, but it is an individual sport. Costs: team fees, possible coaching fees, uniform, and shoes.

Related Sports

Long jump, triple jump, pole vault, heptathlon, and decathlon

Your Child and High Jump

Does your child like to bounce on the trampoline? Does she like to jump up? Does she have strong legs? Can she run short distances? Height helps.

More Information

Videos: *Run Faster, Jump Higher, Throw Farther: How to Win at Track and Field* (Sabin); *Track & Field, Part II—Jumping Events* (Human Kinetics); *Becoming a Champion High Jumper* (Sports Nation Video)

Books: *Fundamentals of Track and Field,* 2nd ed. (Gerry Carr); *The Young Track and Field Athlete* (Colin Jackson)

Did You Know?

We know that some of the earliest records of high jump date from Africa. The Celts also were known to have high jump competitions. It became an official event in 1840 in Great Britain.

* * *

American Walt Davis contracted polio when he was eight, and by the time he was eleven he could barely walk. In the 1952 Helsinki Olympics he won the gold in high jump.

HURDLES

Basic Abilities

Speed, quickness, leg and back muscle strength, stamina, concentration, good rhythm, and good coordination are important abilities for the athlete competing in hurdles.

Other Elements

Hurdles require an extra skill besides running—the ability to jump over a hurdle. Learning the technical skills for hurdles requires instruction and coaching. Runners train several times a week.

Events

As with running meets, hurdles includes sprint and long-distance events. Some hurdles competitions include the 100-meter, 400-meter, 800-meter, and 1,500-meter.

Safety Issues

Safety issues are the same as for running: ankle sprains, pulled muscles, shin splints, and leg and foot fractures. Because of the possibility of falls, broken arms and wrists can occur. Good running shoes are important for safety as well as for performance.

Miscellany

All runners race against the clock. Judges monitor the track and races for rule infractions such as racers stepping out of their lanes. Hurdles is an individual sport, though it is often performed with a track and field team. Costs: team fees can be nominal if the sport is a part of a school track and field program, but costs will include shoes and uniforms.

Related Sports

Running, steeplechase, heptathlon, and decathlon

Your Child and Hurdles

Do you see your child successfully jumping over obstacles that are a foot or more high? Does he like to run? Does he have good stamina? Long legs help.

More Information

Videos: *Run Faster, Jump Higher, Throw Farther: How to Win at Track and Field* (Sabin); *Track & Field, Part I—Running Events* (Human Kinetics); *Becoming a Champion Hurdler* (Sports Nation Video)

Books: *Fundamentals of Track and Field,* 2nd ed. (Gerry Carr); *The Young Track and Field Athlete* (Colin Jackson)

Did You Know?

While we think of the ancient Greeks as the developers of many of the running events, they did not hold races with obstacles. Competitions with hurdles started in Great Britain in the early 1800s.

IN-LINE SKATING

Basic Abilities

Balance and coordination are important abilities for in-line skating. Strong leg muscles are important also.

Other Elements

Children who have learned how to roller-skate can usually shift to in-line skating fairly easily and without formal instruction. To become better or to prepare for competitive in-line skating, participants often rely on coaching. As with most sports, practice is important for competition.

Events

The several forms of in-line skating include speed skating, which involves skating around a track. There are contests for different distances and individual as well as team (relay) events. The skater(s) with the fastest time wins. Acrobatic skating, on the other hand, is a judged sport. Skaters are judged on their technical performances.

Safety Issues

Falling and collisions are possible in this sport, and injuries can result. In addition, pulled and strained muscles are possible, as well as arm and hand fractures. Skaters should wear helmets, wrist guards, and elbow and knee pads.

Miscellany

Speed skating is a timed sport. Because acrobatic skating is a judged sport, there is an element of subjectivity involved. In-line skating is an individual sport, though there can be team events. Costs: skates, helmets, protective padding, outfits, and instruction, as well as possible skating club membership fees.

Related Sports

Skateboarding

Your Child and In-line Skating

Does your child enjoy roller-skating? Does she have good balance? Does she seem to like to go fast or to do some acrobatic maneuvers when she roller-skates?

More Information

Web sites: www.inlinelinks.com; Skate FAQs, www.skatefaq.com; International Inline Skating Association, www.iisa.org

Video: *Skating Fit: The Complete In-line Skating Workout* (ABA)

Books: *In-Line Skating Basics* (Jeff Savage); *In-Line Skating* (Dawn Irwin); *Get Rolling: The Beginner's Guide to In-line Skating* (Liz Miller)

Did You Know?

In-line skating is a more recent sport. Though roller skates were developed over two hundred years ago, in-line skating (skates with the rollers in a straight line) was developed in the United States in the 1980s.

JAVELIN

Basic Abilities

Those who want to participate in javelin should have strong muscles (especially strong arms), steady running ability, and power.

Other Elements

The ancient spear throwers probably didn't have coaches, but students of javelin throwing must have instruction, since technical skills as well as conditioning are necessary to throw a javelin a competitive distance. Considerable practice and training are required. Expect practices several times a week.

Events

Javelin events usually consist of a set number of attempts (throws). The thrower with the longest throw wins.

Safety Issues

Tendinitis, shoulder dislocations, pulled muscles, elbow injuries, and repetitive motion injuries are among those suffered by javelin throwers.

Miscellany

Judges monitor the competition, call valid throws as well as fouls, and measure the distances. Javelin is an individual track and field event, although usually performed on a team. Costs: nominal if the person is a member of a school track and field team, though sometimes there are individual coaching fees. Possible costs include the javelin, uniform, and shoes.

Related Sports

Heptathlon and decathlon

Your Child and Javelin

Does your child like to run? Does she like to throw things (balls, sticks, etc.) into the air and see how far she can throw them? Is she coordinated? Does she have a sense of balance?

More Information

Videos: *Run Faster, Jump Higher, Throw Farther: How to Win at Track and Field* (Sabin); *Track & Field, Part III—Throwing Events* (Human Kinetics); *Javelin Throw Drills* (Sports Nation Video)

Books: *Fundamentals of Track and Field*, 2nd ed. (Gerry Carr); *The Young Track and Field Athlete* (Colin Jackson)

Did You Know?

The early form of the javelin was a spear, and it was used for hunting wild game and for killing enemy soldiers. For years javelin events were held in the same venue as other track and field activities. In the 1980s, participants began throwing the javelin so far that the safety of track athletes was in peril. Eventually the javelin was redesigned so that it could not be thrown as far.

KAYAKING

Basic Abilities

Kayaking requires the ability to swim, strength (especially upper body), power, and endurance.

Other Elements

Kayak instructors teach the technical skills that are required. Practice and aerobic conditioning are essential.

Events

Competitive kayaking includes flat-water racing and white-water racing. Flat-water racing takes place over a water course (a facility that looks like a long swimming pool). Different events have different distances. White-water courses are either natural or artificial, laid out, and laced with gates the kayaker must negotiate. While the winner is determined by the clock, how a racer manages the gates can result in penalties with a set number of seconds subtracted from his total time.

Judges determine the penalties. Of course, not all kayakers compete; many enjoy kayaking in rivers or seas just for recreational enjoyment.

Safety Issues

Crashes can cause injuries. Safety gear, especially helmets and life jackets, are mandatory. Perhaps the safest form is recreational flat-water kayaking since there are no rapids for the beginner to navigate. A child can always graduate to white-water kayaking if he reaches the level of skill required for this type of kayaking. Even with life jackets, children need to be comfortable in the water and be able to take care of themselves should they end up in turbulent water over their head. Except for crashes, the most common injury—shoulder dislocation—is caused by poor technique; the second most common type of injury is overuse syndrome of the shoulder, elbow, and wrist—also due to poor technique.

Miscellany

Judges in white-water kayaking determine rule compliance and penalties. Winners in each type of kayaking are determined by the clock. Kayaking is an individual sport, though there are team events. Your child can take up kayaking and chose never to participate in competitions. Costs: instruction, kayak, paddle, helmet, life jacket, and possible course costs. Beginner classes will often be in swimming pools, ponds, or calm lakes, rivers, or streams. Because kayaks can be quite expensive, for example, recreational kayaks can cost around $400 to $500, look for programs that rent kayaks. Those that offer half-day and all-day instruction are often the best for the money and allow for a lot of practice. Make sure the program is geared toward children and promotes safety.

Related Sports

Canoeing and sailing

Your Child and Kayaking

Does your child like the water (as kayaks can capsize)? Is he strong (as he needs to be able to right the kayak if it overturns)? Does he like boats? Does he know how to swim? (While he'll have a life jacket on, he will have to be able to swim in case of capsizing or being thrown out of the kayak.)

More Information

Video: *Kayaking Basics* (Vernal Productions)
Books: *Whitewater Kayaking* (Jeremy Evans); *Kayaking* (Julie Bach)

Did You Know?

Canoes and kayaks were invented more than six thousand years ago and were used for transportation and hunting. In the 1800s, kayaks were used in different sports.

LONG JUMP

Basic Abilities

Strong legs, flexibility, coordination, and running ability are basic assets for participants in this sport.

Other Elements

Like most track and field sports, long jump requires learning very specific skills, such as approach run, takeoff, flight, and landing. Coaches teach these skills and conduct training and practices, usually several times a week.

Events

Competitors usually make a set number of attempts—often three. The competitor with the longest jump wins.

Safety Issues

Pulled muscles, muscle sprains, twisted ankles, and foot fractures are possible.

Miscellany

Judges determine fouls involved with takeoffs and landings; they also verify the distances of each jump. Long jumping is an individual sport, though usually competitors perform as members of a track and field team. Costs: team fees, possible coaching fees, uniforms, and shoes.

Related Sports

Triple jump, high jump, heptathlon, and decathlon

Your Child and Long Jump

Can your child run short distances? Does she have strong leg muscles? Does she like to take running jumps? Being tall and thin is helpful.

More Information

Videos: *Run Faster, Jump Higher, Throw Farther: How to Win at Track and Field* (Sabin); *Track & Field, Part II—Jumping Events* (Human Kinetics); *Becoming a Champion Long Jumper* (Sports Nation Video)

Books: *Fundamentals of Track and Field,* 2nd ed. (Gerry Carr); *The Young Track and Field Athlete* (Colin Jackson); *The Man Who Could Fly* (Bob Beamon)

Did You Know?

Long jump was a part of Celtic games over four thousand years ago. The first recorded long jump was in 708 BC in ancient Greece.

* * *

One of the greatest long jumpers was Jesse Owens. In the 1936 Berlin Olympic Games, he won four gold medals, including one for the long jump. Because Owens was African American, Hitler refused to shake his hand. Owens set the world record for the long jump at these games, and it held for over twenty-five years.

LUGE

Basic Abilities

The sport of luge calls for quick reflexes, power, and nerves of steel.

Other Elements

Coaching and instruction are necessary to learn the technical skills—starting, steering, braking, and so forth. Considerable practice is required.

Events

A luge is a type of sled that is designed to go very fast. Luge has singles and doubles events. A race consists of going down a luge track of a specific distance. The shortest time across one or more runs establishes the winner.

Safety Issues

Luge racing can be quite dangerous because of the high speeds. While beginners generally do not attain the velocities of more advanced competitors, there is still the potential for moderate speed and out-of-control crashes. Helmets are mandatory. Pulled muscles and broken arms and legs are possible if a crash occurs.

Miscellany

While judges monitor the course, racers with the fastest times win. This is an individual sport, though there is a doubles event. Costs: if you find a luge track near you, you will have to pay for instruction, and perhaps membership fees to use the track and luge. Buy or rent your own suits, helmets, shoes, and gloves.

Related Sports

Bobsledding and *skeleton*

Your Child and Luge

Does your child like to sled down hills? Luge racing is like sledding except that racers lie on their backs and race feet first. Is he strong? Does he have quick reflexes and body control? Does he like to go fast?

More Information

Books: *Bobsledding and the Luge* (Larry Dane Brimmer);
            The Sport of Luge (Piotr Rogowski)

Did You Know?

The history of sledding dates from the 1480s in Norway. The first international competition was held in Switzerland in 1883. While most of the terms and language of this sport are German, luge is the French word for sled. When whizzing down the track, luge athletes become virtual flying machines and can hit speeds in excess of 90 mph.

POLE VAULT

Basic Abilities

Pole vaulters' performances are enhanced by quickness, flexibility, speed, strong legs, strong shoulder and abdominal muscles, and good balance.

Other Elements

Pole vaulting requires very sound technical skills. Coaches teach these skills and oversee proper conditioning and practices. Practices are often held several times a week.

Events

The crossbars are set at some initial height that most competitors can clear. After each round, the crossbar is raised. The competitor who clears the crossbar at the greatest height wins.

Safety Issues

Without very good technical skills and training, a competitor may experience serious injuries. Insist on helmets and adequate padding in landing and surrounding areas. Injuries can include sprains, dislocations, and broken bones.

Miscellany

Judges set the crossbars, determine whether an attempt is successful, and verify the crossbar heights and eventual winning height and competitor. Pole vaulting is a track and field event and an individual sport, though competitors usually play on a team. Costs: team fees, possible coaching fees, uniform, poles, and shoes.

Related Sports

High jump and decathlon

Your Child and Pole Vault

Can your child sprint? Does he enjoy jumping on the trampoline? Does he have upper-body strength?

More Information

Videos: *Run Faster, Jump Higher, Throw Farther: How to Win at Track and Field* (Sabin); *Track & Field, Part II—Jumping Events* (Human Kinetics); *Becoming a Champion Pole Vaulter* (Sports Nation Video)

Books: *Fundamentals of Track and Field*, 2nd ed. (Gerry Carr); *The Young Track and Field Athlete* (Colin Jackson)

Did You Know?

Vaulting probably started in Europe as a means for crossing water canals. Poles have been made with different materials over the years— wood, bamboo, aluminum, and finally, fiberglass.

* * *

In the 1936 Berlin Olympics, an American won the event. Two Japanese vaulters should have squared off to determine who would win the silver and who would win the bronze. However, the team's manager refused to let them compete against one another. Instead, after the games, the silver and bronze medals were cut in half and welded together. A half-silver and half-bronze medal was then given to each of the two Japanese vaulters.

RUNNING

Basic Abilities

Basic abilities vary somewhat depending upon whether the runner is a sprinter or a distance runner. Sprinters need to be fast on their feet and powerful. Distance runners must have very strong leg muscles, endurance, great aerobic ability and conditioning, and the ability to make tactical decisions during a race.

Other Elements

All children can run, and some can run quite fast with little or no formal instruction. However, to be competitive, coaching is necessary in order to learn some technical skills, improve form, and to learn proper conditioning methods. Most track teams meet several times a week to practice.

Events

Some pure running events include 100-meter (winners in this event are considered the fastest runners in the world), 200-meter, 400-meter, cross-country, and marathon (the longest running race, 26.2 miles). The 100- and 200-meter races are considered sprints; the others cannot be run at full speed after the start gun is fired.

Safety Issues

Ankle sprains, knee injuries, pulled hamstrings, shin splints, and leg and foot fractures are possible. Good running shoes are essential for safety as well as for performance. The running track or area must be in good condition.

Miscellany

While judges and referees monitor the track and races, runners race against the clock. Running is an individual sport, though there are team relays. Running is usually performed in a track and field team. Costs: membership fees or association costs if a private club or team; nominal costs if a civic team or public school team. Additional costs include good running shoes.

Related Sports

Hurdles, steeplechase, race walking, heptathlon, and decathlon

Your Child and Running

Does your child like to run? Does she have good stamina? Is she quick on her feet? Does she hold up well when in pain or out of breath?

More Information

Videos: *Run Faster, Jump Higher, Throw Farther: How to Win at Track and Field* (Sabin); *Track & Field, Part I—Running Events* (Human Kinetics)

Books: *Fundamentals of Track and Field,* 2nd ed. (Gerry Carr); *The Young Track and Field Athlete* (Colin Jackson); *Wilma* (Wilma Rudolph)

Movies: *Chariots of Fire* (PG); *Endurance* (G)

Did You Know?

Running is a sport that dates from antiquity. Some running events took place in Egypt more than four thousand years ago.

* * *

The marathon is the longest running race. It was originally 40 kilometers. But in 1908, the British Olympic committee extended it by an extra 385 yards because they wanted the race to go from Windsor Castle to the Olympic stadium in London. Thus the modern marathon is 42.195 kilometers, or 26.2 miles, long.

SHOOTING

Basic Abilities

Good eye-hand coordination, excellent concentration, controlled body movements, and upper-body strength are assets for this sport.

Other Elements

The beginner thinks all she has to do is get ready, aim, and fire. She will soon see that there is more to shooting than meets the eye. Instruction and training are necessary to gain competence. Practice, by repeating the same movements over and over again, is necessary. This is a precision, fine-motor sport.

Events

Various events use different kinds of firearms. Different types of shooting include skeet shooting (involving a moving clay pigeon catapulted into the air), trap shooting, and so on. This is a target sport, so points or winning is based upon hitting targets. Competition involves a number of rounds and total points gained.

Safety Issues

The shooting ranges should be designed with safety features. In this sport there is a high risk for hearing loss or eye injuries if ear protectors and goggles are not used. Repetitive motion injuries are possible.

Miscellany

Judges oversee rule compliance. Officials establish winners objectively by looking at the targets or counting the number of clay pigeons that were hit. This is an individual sport. Costs: guns, ear protectors, goggles, telescopic sights, lessons, and shooting range fees.

Related Sports

Biathlon

Your Child and Shooting

Shooting is a very controlled-motion sport. If your child prefers lots of freestyle, large body movements, this is perhaps not the sport for him. Does he have good eye-hand coordination? Does he like precisionlike movements as well as details? This is not a high novelty sport. If your child needs a lot of variety, shooting may not be the right sport for him.

More Information

Book: *Sports: The Complete Visual Reference* (François Fortin)

Did You Know?

The original shooting sports were with bows, arrows, and spears, primarily for hunting and war. With the development of firearms, guns were an additional means of hunting and a weapon of war. Shooting with firearms became more of a sport in the 1800s.

SHOT PUT

Basic Abilities

Shot put requires strength, especially of arm, back, and abdominal muscles, good balance, and coordination.

Other Elements

Coaching is necessary to learn proper techniques and proper conditioning. Considerable practice, with many throws a week, is necessary. Shot-putters should expect to practice several times a week.

Events

Events take place in a shot put area, called a fan, with each competitor allowed a set number of attempts. The person with the longest throw is the winner.

Safety Issues

Dislocations, sprains, and pulled muscles can occur.

Miscellany

Judges rule on whether the throws are fair or foul and whether the thrower's position is fair or foul. They measure the distance of each throw. Costs: team fees, possible coaching fees, shot put, uniform, and shoes.

Related Sports

Hammer, discus, heptathlon, and decathlon

Your Child and Shot Put

Does your child have good balance? Is she strong? Height helps.

More Information

Videos: *Run Faster, Jump Higher, Throw Farther: How to Win at Track and Field* (Sabin); *Track & Field, Part III—Throwing Events* (Human Kinetics); *Becoming a Champion Shot Putter* (Sports Nation Video)

Books: *Fundamentals of Track and Field*, 2nd ed. (Gerry Carr); *The Young Track and Field Athlete* (Colin Jackson)

Did You Know?

The ancient Greeks threw stones during war. Shot putting probably was an offshoot of stone throwing. In the fourteenth century, iron balls replaced stones, though today the balls are usually made of bronze. In formal competition, the balls weigh about 16 pounds for men and 8.8 pounds for women.

SKELETON

Basic Abilities

Quick reflexes and powerful legs are assets for those who participate in this sport.

Other Elements

Coaching is required to learn the basic skills and techniques of skeleton, and regular practice several times a week is important.

Events

Events are conducted on an ice-covered track; skeleton uses the same tracks as bobsledding and luge. Tracks have some straight and some curved sections. Racers lie on the skeleton (a special type of sled) on their stomachs, head first, with their faces just inches from the ice. Competitors race against the clock.

Safety Issues

While beginners do not go as fast as more advanced racers, the potential for injuries still exists. Injuries can range from pulled muscles to broken limbs, shoulder bruises, and head and facial cuts. Helmets are mandatory.

Miscellany

Skeleton is a timed race, but officials monitor the race as well as inspect the track. Skeleton is an individual sport, though racers may be members of a team. Costs: coaching and instruction, fees for the use of track, skeleton, helmet, shoes, and gloves. Presently there are not many skeleton tracks in the United States.

Related Sports

Luge and *bobsledding*

Your Child and Skeleton

If your child likes to go fast on her sled, skeleton may be the sport for her. Does she have strong legs, and is she quick on her feet? Is she fearless?

More Information

Web sites: United States Bobsled and Skeleton Federation, www.usbobsledandskeleton.org; Skeleton Sledding, www.capital.net/~phuston/skeleton.html; Christopher Soule, www.soule-man.com

Book: *Sports: The Complete Visual Reference* (François Fortin)

Did You Know?

With their chin just inches from the ice, sliders reach speeds around 85 mph. The gravitational forces can exceed 5Gs. Skeleton was invented by an Englishman in 1892.

SNOWBOARDING

Basic Abilities

It helps to have good balance and coordination for snowboarding. Overall strength is important.

Other Elements

Learning to snowboard will go faster with lessons. For competition, considerable practice is required. Many people snowboard just for fun and never enter competitions.

Events

There are two types of snowboarding. Half-pipe is an example of a freestyle snowboarding event. Alpine snowboarding includes slalom events. Snowboarding became an Olympic sport in 1998.

Safety Issues

Young beginners tend not to build up too much speed, so injuries are few and minor. Wrist injuries and sprains are most common. Collisions with other snowboarders and trees can cause more serious injuries.

Miscellany

Some boarding events, like the slaloms, are races against the clock. Others, like the half-pipe, are judged events—judges award points based upon style, height, and the difficulty of the aerial tricks performed. Snowboarding is an individual sport. Costs: lessons, board, helmet, bindings, boots, wrist guards, knee pads, gloves, goggles, and warm and waterproof clothes. Lessons generally are a half day or full day and are available at most ski areas or resorts. Some resorts offer a series of four to eight lessons.

Related Sports

Alpine skiing, freestyle skiing, and *skateboarding*

Your Child and Snowboarding

Is your child coordinated with good balance? Does he have good muscle strength, concentration, and fast reflexes? Is he OK about falling (even good snowboarders fall often)? Does he like to be out in the cold?

More Information

Web site: www.ussnowboard.com

Books: *The Young Snowboarder* (Bryan Iguchi); *Beginning Snowboarding* (Julie Jensen); *A Basic Guide to Skiing and Snowboarding* (U.S. Olympic Committee); *To the Edge and Back* (Chris Klug); *Snowboarding Skills: The Back-To-Basics Essentials for All Levels* (Cindy Kleh)

Did You Know?

This is one of the more modern sports. It may have early roots in children's play. They built something similar to today's snowboards by taking barrel staves and riding them sideways down snow-covered hills. As we know it today, an early form of snowboarding started in the 1960s when skis were tied together to create a surfboard. The first competitions took place in Vermont in the 1970s.

* * *

Chris Klug won a bronze medal in the 2000 Olympics, eighteen months after he received a liver transplant. He's written a book about his life.

SPEED SKATING

Basic Abilities

Short-distance speed skaters have to make quick starts and have strong leg muscles. For the longer events, skaters need endurance, good aerobic capacity, general physical strength, and powerful legs.

Other Elements

Lessons are recommended in order to learn the most efficient and effective techniques. To compete, coaches are necessary to direct training. Considerable practice and training are required to compete at the high levels of this sport.

Events

Some of the events include 500-meter, 1,500-meter, 5,000-meter, 10,000-meter (men only), and relays. There are two different types of rinks: short track and long track.

Safety Issues

Skaters skate on ice at high speeds. Injuries can occur because of falling or collisions (which in turn cause falling). Injuries can be quite minor, sprains and cuts, or more serious, broken bones and head injuries.

Miscellany

Speed skating is a timed sport, and the fastest skater wins. Judges make sure that the rules are followed, especially noting if a competitor slides into or obstructs another skater. This may result in disqualification. Except for the relay events, speed skating is an individual sport. Costs: skates, helmets, knee pads, shin guards, and membership in a skating club.

Related Sports

In-line skating, figure skating, and *ice hockey*

Your Child and Speed Skating

Can your child skate? Does he like to go fast? Does he have strong legs? Does he like the cold?

More Information

Web sites: U.S. Speedskating, www.usspeedskating.org; Winter Sports Page, www.wintersports.org

Books: *The Encyclopedia of the Winter Olympics* (John Wukovits); *Speed Skating* (Larry Dane Brimmer); *Bonnie Blair: Power on Ice* (Wendy Daly); *A Winning Edge* (Bonnie Blair); *Full Circle: An Autobiography* (Dan Jansen)

Did You Know?

Speed skating was the first of three forms of skating—speed skating, figure skating, and hockey—to develop into a sport. The first speed skaters who raced were the Dutch in the 1500s. By the 1700s, speed skating had spread all over Europe. The first modern speed skating competition took place in Norway in 1863.

SQUASH

Basic Abilities

It helps to have quickness, speed, power, stamina, good eye-hand coordination, and good tactical abilities.

Other Elements

Instruction is necessary to learn the game and its technical skills. A player must practice several times a week to improve his game.

Events

Squash can be played on a squash court either as a singles game or a doubles game. In competition, a referee or judge calls the scores.

Safety Issues

Strained and pulled muscles are common, as well as soreness in shoulders and elbows. Repetitive motion injuries can occur.

Miscellany

Squash is an individual racket sport, and it combines some of the features of tennis, racquetball, and badminton. It also has a doubles event and is sometimes played on teams. Referees and judges call the scores.

Costs: instruction, racket, shoes, and protective goggles. Membership in an athletic club that has squash courts is common.

Related Sports

Tennis, badminton, and racquetball

Your Child and Squash

Does your child have good eye-hand coordination? Does he move around quickly on his feet? Does he have good stamina?

More Information

Books: *Learn Squash and Racquetball in a Weekend* (Jahangir Khan); *Sports: The Complete Visual Reference* (François Fortin); *Squash: A History of the Game* (James Zug)

Did You Know?

This seems to have been an English sport originally. It came to the United States some time in the late 1800s, and it was played at many of the colleges and universities in the eastern United States, though it enjoys more widespread popularity today.

STEEPLECHASE

Basic Abilities

The steeplechase combines running, hurdling, and, to some extent, long-jump abilities. Running speed, quickness, general strength, good rhythm and coordination, endurance, and cardiovascular fitness are desirable.

Other Elements

Coaching is necessary to learn proper technical skills and style and proper conditioning methods. Considerable practice and conditioning are essential. Participants should expect to train several times a week.

Events

Events can be of varying distances for beginners, though advanced runners train for the 3,000-meter race. Steeplechase races consist of several laps around a track filled with hurdles and water jumps. Official steeplechase events are for men only, though this tradition may change in the future.

Safety Issues

Possible injuries to athletes include ankle sprains, shin splints, pulled muscles, and leg, foot, and arm fractures. Proper shoes are important for foot safety as well as for performance.

Miscellany

Steeplechase is a timed event. Judges oversee the track and race and call rule infractions. Steeplechase is an individual sport, though competitors are usually members of a track and field team. Costs: nominal if a part of a school track and field program; shoes and uniforms. This is not a common sport in this country, though some schools have track and field coaches who can teach this sport.

Related Sports

Running, hurdles, heptathlon, and decathlon

Your Child and Steeplechase

Does your child like to run and jump over obstacles? Does he run fast? Does he have good stamina? This is not a common sport.

More Information

Books: *Fundamentals of Track and Field,* 2nd ed. (Gerry Carr); *Sports: The Complete Visual Reference* (François Fortin)

Did You Know?

Students at Oxford University turned steeplechase, which was originally a horse race with obstacles, into a running race consisting of running, hurdling, and jumping over water.

SWIMMING

Basic Abilities
Strength of arm and thigh muscles, quickness, and endurance are important abilities for swimmers.

Other Elements
Swim coaches map out workouts for each swimmer and direct proper conditioning training. Practices run from one to two hours a day, three to five times a week.

Events
Races range from 50 meters to 1,500 meters, races for each of four strokes, individual medley (all four strokes), and relays with four team members.

Safety Issues
Swimming is one of the safest sports, though leg and shoulder strains can occur. Injuries around the pool (slipping on decks) are possible if swimmers are not careful or if they run on wet decks. If swimming outdoors, sunscreen is mandatory (SPF 30 or higher).

Miscellany
Winners are determined by the stopwatch or electronic clock (touch pads). This is an individual sport, though children usually swim on teams and there are some team events (relays). Costs: swimsuit, cap, goggles, and lessons/coaching; sometimes club fees or membership fees. Some swim teams only meet in the summer, usually in outdoor pools. Considered a lifetime sport and a great cardio form of exercise.

Related Sports
Synchronized swimming

Your Child and Swimming

Is your child comfortable in the water? Does she like to swim? Is she drownproof? Does she seem ready to focus on practices and give up just playing and splashing in the water?

More Information

Check your local or nearest YMCA/YWCA for programs and classes.
Web sites: Find the nearest Y, www.ymca.net; Swiminfo,
    www.swiminfo.com; USA Swimming, www.usswim.org;
    Total Immersion Swimming, www.totalimmersion.net;
    Amateur Athletic Union, www.aausports.org; Guide to
    pools, www.swimmersguide.com

Video: *Art of Swimming; Excellence in Stroke Technique*
    (1-800-352-7946)

Books: *Teaching Swimming Fundamentals* (YMCA of the USA);
    Teach Your Child How to Swim (Usborne Book Staff);
    The Young Swimmer (Jeff Rouse); *Swimming: Steps to
    Success* (David Thomas); *The Winning Stroke* (Matt
    Christopher); *Beneath the Surface* (Michael Phelps)

Did You Know?

Drawings six thousand years old show men swimming in the Kebir desert.

* * *

Plato once declared that anyone who could not swim lacked the proper education.

TABLE TENNIS

Basic Abilities

Good table tennis players usually exhibit quickness, excellent eye-hand coordination, stamina, and excellent technique.

Other Elements

Most people are able to play table tennis (also called Ping-Pong) at beginner levels without professional instruction. To achieve higher levels of skill, instruction and considerable time spent playing are important.

Events

While there are some variations, usually the player who reaches the score of twenty-one first wins the game. Generally, matches are played either in the best of two out of three or three out of five twenty-one-point games, and players compete in either singles or doubles matches.

Safety Issues

Though table tennis is quite safe, muscle strain and repetitive motion injuries are possible.

Miscellany

In formal competition, an umpire calls the points as well as out-of-bounds balls. This is an individual sport, though it can be played on teams. Costs: racket, balls, table, and instruction.

Related Sports
Tennis

Your Child and Table Tennis

Can your child move quickly? Does he have good eye-hand coordination? Does he have good stamina?

More Information

Video: *Modern Table Tennis 101* (Alpha Productions)
Books: *Table Tennis: Steps To Success* (Larry Hodges);
          Sports: The Complete Visual Reference (François Fortin)

Did You Know?

Ping-Pong gets its name from the sound the balls make when they bounce on the table.

* * *

Table tennis seems to have originated from the medieval game of tennis. It was popular in England in the 1800s. Eventually it spread to Japan, China, and Korea, where it became quite popular. Many of the best players in the world have come from those Pacific Rim countries. More than thirty million are competitive players of this sport.

TAE KWON DO

Basic Abilities

Tae kwon do (a Korean term, which translates as "the way of hand and foot") is a martial art and requires students to have excellent reflexes, excellent technique and form, controlled but quick body movements, stamina, and mental control.

Other Elements

A beginner does not pick up tae kwon do on his own. He learns from an instructor who is usually a fourth- or fifth-degree black belt or higher. The instructor's ability to teach children is more important than his title or rank. The training is sometimes formal, with a master-student relationship, though instruction is usually in classes. There are different schools or styles of tae kwon do, but at the beginner level, lessons near home and with a good instructor are more important than the particular style taught. In order to achieve increased levels of competence, a student must progress through different belt colors or levels leading to the black belt. Children typically attend classes from one to three times a week. Expect to see classes with students at varying levels learning together. This gives the less advanced students an appreciation for what they are working to achieve and allows students at higher belt levels to help the students at lower belt levels. Children as young as six or seven can begin to learn tae kwon do. Like all martial arts, tae kwon do emphasizes physical fitness, self-defense, and self-discipline.

Events

A student of tae kwon do can progress without entering any competitive events or tournaments. For all belt levels, students are tested mainly on form, though some very controlled sparring may be required as students advance. Breaking bricks or wood are parts of the test for the higher belt levels. Students at higher belt levels may choose to enter meets. Some of these competitions involve being judged on one's techniques and forms. Others involve sparring between two opponents.

Safety Issues

Instructors monitor for correct form and technique, thus reducing the risk of injury. Injuries are uncommon at the beginner levels. Even so, injuries ranging from pulled and strained muscles to broken toes, fingers, arms, and legs can occur. Participants wear protective gear when sparring.

Miscellany

This sport is learned only through formal lessons or training with accomplished instructors. It is an individual sport. Costs: instruction and uniform; membership at a martial arts gym or studio is sometimes necessary. Look for introductory classes with a student/teacher ratio of ten to one or less. Both tae kwon do and karate (another martial art) enjoy increasing popularity in the United States so locating classes should be relatively easy.

Related Sports

Other martial arts offered in this country include karate, judo, aikido, kung fu, jujitsu, and kickboxing.

Your Child and Tae Kwon Do

This is a very disciplined sport, with no room for free-form movements. Does your child like to make controlled body movements? Can she tolerate lots of repetition as movements are practiced over and over again? Does she like to express herself through body movements? Can she learn from adults? Can she listen carefully? Is she patient? Make sure your child understands that tae kwon do, as well as the other martial arts, is not learned for the purpose of being aggressive.

More Information

Web site: The Tae Kwon Do Network, www.tkd.net

Videos: *Beginner Taekwondo Video* by Sang H. Kim; *Black Belt*
           Poomse, Vol. 1, by Sang H. Kim (TurtlePress.com)

Books: *Parents' Guide to Martial Arts* (Debra M. Fritsch);
           The Composite Guide to Martial Arts (Ann Gaines);
           Taekwondo (Paul Collins); *The Young Martial Arts*
           Enthusiast (David Mitchell); *Martial Arts Training*
           Diary for Kids (Art Brisacher)

Movies: *Karate Kid* (Parts 1, 2, and 3—PG)

Did You Know?

Tae kwon do is one of many martial arts. Wall paintings dating from 50 BC suggest that it originated in Korea, though some believe that it may have been founded in China or Japan. In more modern times, the development of the sport has taken place in Korea. Modern tae kwon do has been influenced by other martial arts, especially Japanese karate. Korean police and military are trained in tae kwon do. Tae kwon do emphasizes mental strength and seeks to develop character, instilling such values as loyalty and honor.

TENNIS

Basic Abilities

To be good at this sport, a player needs to be quick on his feet, have excellent eye-hand coordination, overall strength and power, and good concentration as well as analytical and tactical skills.

Other Elements

Tennis lessons are sufficient when the participant plays only for enjoyment. Lessons and coaching will help if the player is going to compete. Lessons and practice several times a week are necessary for competition.

Events

Tennis is usually played in singles and doubles matches. Usually the best of three or five sets determines the winner.

Safety Issues

Because of repetitive motion, tennis elbow is common. Sprained ankles, pulled muscles, and shoulder and knee injuries are possible. At the beginner levels, these injuries are less likely.

Miscellany

The winner of the match or game is determined by the scores. Tennis is an individual sport, though it is often played on teams. Costs: racket, shoes, lessons/coaching, and sometimes club membership or fees. Most public tennis courts are free. Participation in tennis has fallen off in the last decade or so. Because of this, various tennis organizations are trying to encourage more people to take up the sport by making more introductory lessons available to beginners. Try to find such programs in your community.

Related Sports

Racquetball, *squash,* and badminton

Your Child and Tennis

Does your child like to analyze things? Does he like to plan? Is he visually detailed and observant? Does he like to run around? Is he quick? Does he have good eye-hand coordination?

More Information

Teenie Tennis, 206-881-1446
Web sites: United States Tennis Association, www.usta.com;
           Tennis Welcome Center, www.tenniswelcomecenter.com
Videos: *Let's Play Tennis* (Buena Vista Home Entertainment);
         Teaching Kids Tennis (Westcom Productions Incorporated)
Books: *Tennis for Kids* (Reggie Vasquez); *Tennis Play the Game*
         (Simon Lee); *Smart Tennis: How to Play and Win the*

Mental Game (John Murray); *Tennis Ace* (Matt Christopher); *Venus & Serena Williams* (Virginia Aronson)

Did You Know?

Evidence of various forms of ball games can be traced to ancient Egypt as early as the 1500s BC. Using bare hands, people were playing a form of today's game in the twelfth century in France. Christian monks played this game in the monasteries; it was so popular among the monks that the early Church considered banning the sport.

TRIPLE JUMP

Basic Abilities

Triple jumpers need to have strong leg muscles, running ability, speed, power, and coordination.

Other Elements

Coaching is necessary to learn the technical skills of this sport. The coach develops the conditioning workouts, and practices take place several times a week.

Events

Each competitor is allowed several attempts; the competitor with the longest jump wins.

Safety Issues

Pulled muscles, various sprains, dislocations, and foot fractures can occur.

Miscellany

Judges oversee each jump and call fouls. They measure the distances and verify those distances. Triple jumping is a track and field event and is performed on teams, though it is an individual sport. Costs: team fees, possible coaching fees, uniform, and shoes.

Related Sports

High jump and **long jump**

Your Child and Triple Jump

Does your child like to run and make long jumps? Is she a good sprinter? Is she quick? Being tall and thin helps.

More Information

Videos: *Run Faster, Jump Higher, Throw Farther: How to Win at Track and Field* (Sabin); *Track & Field, Part II—Jumping Events* (Human Kinetics); *Becoming a Champion Triple Jumper* (Sports Nation Video)

Books: *Fundamentals of Track and Field*, 2nd ed. (Gerry Carr); *The Young Track and Field Athlete* (Colin Jackson)

Did You Know?

Some historians believe that the triple jump developed from the children's game of hopscotch.

WEIGHT LIFTING

Basic Abilities

Weight lifting requires muscle strength, especially in the arms, legs, and back. Certain types of lifts require power also.

Other Elements

Instruction is essential to learn proper lifting techniques. Practices several times a week are necessary. Considerable conditioning is important.

Events

Events are classified by weight of the lifter and involve a certain number of lifts, different lift weights, and different types of lifts.

Safety Issues

Some people question how safe it is for young children to lift weights. It is best not to begin this sport before the age of twelve or thirteen. Even then, it is important that the child has a good instructor who will supervise closely and proceed with caution. Ask your child's pediatrician about his views. Common injuries include pulled and strained muscles and dislocated shoulders.

Miscellany

Referees rule on whether a lift is successful. The winner is the competitor who lifts the heaviest weights. Weight lifting is an individual sport, though it is often played on teams. Costs: instructor, gym fees, outfits, shoes, various support belts, and related equipment.

Related Sports

Powerlifting

Your Child and Weight Lifting

Is your child strong? Is he beefy, with lots of muscle mass? Does he like to work out and lift weights?

More Information

Books: *Weightlifting* (Bob Knotts); *Sports: The Complete Visual Reference* (François Fortin)

Did You Know?

Man has lifted weights from the earliest times as a test of strength. Though popular for years in Europe and other countries in the world, it became increasingly popular in the United States in the 1900s. It became a regular part of the Olympic program in 1920, and it is standing room only when the world's strongest athletes compete in this event.

WRESTLING

Basic Abilities

Wrestling calls for strength, flexibility, coordination, and balance.

Other Elements

Wrestling involves very specific moves. Instruction is necessary to learn these moves. Conditioning and considerable practice are necessary.

Events

Matches or meets consist of two opponents wrestling in a specific area. Periods last from two to three minutes. Points are awarded based upon pinning one's opponent on the mat. Wrestling is now a sport for girls and women, and women's wrestling was one of the thirty-two Olympic sports at the 2004 summer games in Athens.

Safety Issues

Since wrestling is a controlled combat sport, no inappropriate aggression is allowed. Injuries, though, are possible, such as pulled muscles, sprains, and strains.

Miscellany

Referees and judges control the matches and award the points. Wrestling is an individual sport, though players usually play on a team. Costs: this is an inexpensive sport, but costs may include uniform and coaching fees, unless one participates on a school team. There are no equipment costs.

Related Sports

Greco-Roman wrestling

Your Child and Wrestling

Does your child seem to enjoy casual forms of wrestling with siblings or friends? Is he flexible and coordinated? Does he have good balance? Does he enjoy tumbling on the floor?

More Information

Video: *The Winning Edge, Volume 1—Beginner Wrestling Video*
Books: *Wrestling for Beginners* (Tom Jarman); *Sports: The
            Complete Visual Reference* (François Fortin)

Did You Know?

One of the oldest sports that we know of, wrestling can be traced to a cave drawing found in France that dates back fifteen thousand years! Bas-reliefs (a type of sculpture) found in ancient Egypt and Babylonia show wrestlers using some of the same holds that are seen today.

Fact Sheets

Team Sports

BASEBALL

Basic Abilities
Important abilities include quickness, speed, good reflexes, and good general coordination as well as good eye-hand coordination.

Other Elements
Coaching helps beginners to learn basic skills and the fundamentals of the game. Practices take place at least once a week and sometimes two or three times a week.

Events
The team that scores the most runs wins the game. Games consist of six innings to nine innings, depending upon level and league. In beginning leagues, sometimes there is a time limit, so if it is reached before the full number of innings is played, the team that is ahead at that point wins.

Safety Issues
Being hit by the ball, either as a batter or a fielder, can cause various injuries, including serious head injuries. Little League elbow (especially for pitchers), leg and foot sprains, and pulled hamstrings may occur. Even so, baseball is a relatively safe sport. Sliding headfirst into a base can result in head injuries and should be discouraged by the coach. Helmets are mandatory for batters and base runners. If your young child

is learning to pitch, be sure that his coach does not allow him to throw too many pitches (Little League elbow can result) or encourage him to throw curveballs or sliders. Otherwise, he will be at risk for various arm injuries since his growth plates haven't fully matured.

Miscellany

Umpires call the game—strikes, balls, and fouls—and they enforce the rules. Baseball is a team sport. Costs: team or league fees, uniforms, and gloves. The club or team usually provides helmets. Baseball is an inexpensive sport, and leagues and teams for children eight and over are numerous. Little League baseball teams are found in many cities. More than 2.5 million kids are playing Little League baseball.

Related Sports

T-ball, softball, and *cricket*

Your Child and Baseball

Does your child like to throw and catch baseballs? How is his eye-hand coordination? Does he like to run? Is he patient? Baseball is a slow game. It is one of the few sports where there is no penalty for delay of the game, and there can be long periods of inactivity.

More Information

Web site: Little League Baseball, www.littleleague.org

Videos: *Arthur Makes the Team* (Random House Home Video); *Dealing with Disappointment* (Live Wire Video Publishers); *Little League's Official How-to-Play Baseball* (Master Vision); *Teaching Kids Baseball* (Westcom Productions Incorporated)

Books: *My Baseball Book* (Gail Gibbons); *The Visual Dictionary of Baseball* (James Buckley and James Buckley, Jr.); *The Young Baseball Player* (Ian Smyth); *Fundamental Baseball* (Don Geng); *Hank Aaron: Brave in Every Way* (Peter Golenbock); *Choosing Up Sides* (John H. Ritter); *The Boy Who Saved Baseball* (John H. Ritter); *Honus & Me* (Dan Gutman); *Playing Right Field* (Willy Welch);

Baseball (Julie Jensen); Baseball Oddities: Bizarre Plays
and Other Funny Stuff (Wayne Stewart)

Movies: A League of Their Own (PG); Angels in the Outfield (PG);
Rookie of the Year (PG); Eight Men Out (PG);
The Sandlot (PG)

Did You Know?

Evidence that a primitive form of baseball was played in antiquity comes from ancient Egyptian pyramid inscriptions and temple reliefs depicting pharaohs batting balls and priests playing a game involving catching balls. The modern version of baseball was developed in the northeastern United States in the early nineteenth century and is believed to have borrowed elements from other ball games, such as rounders and cricket.

* * *

Have you seen catchers, with all their padding on, chase down foul balls? In the early years of baseball, there were two catchers—one to catch the ball thrown by the pitcher and the other to field foul balls.

* * *

Most team sports have the same distance specifications for the fields of play. For example, all football fields are the same distance. However, baseball allows variations in the distance from home plate to the far outfield walls in ballparks.

BASKETBALL

Basic Abilities

Basketball players have excellent coordination, quickness, power, and stamina, as well as good skills with the fundamental moves of the game. Each player plays offense and defense.

Other Elements

Good coaching and instruction to really learn the basic moves is important. Practices once or twice a week are necessary for improvement.

Events

Games usually have four quarters. With young players, the length of each quarter varies, depending upon the league. Some beginner leagues have only two periods, each perhaps ten minutes long. Unlike many of the sports listed in these fact sheets, basketball was invented here in the United States, in the 1890s.

Safety Issues

For boys and girls ages ten to fourteen, basketball has one of the highest injury rates of all sports. Potential for minor injuries includes sprained ankles, pulled muscles, and hand and finger sprains. A collision between two players can cause more serious injuries.

Miscellany

Judges and referees control the game; they call fouls and other rule infractions. Costs: coaching, nominal fees for beginner leagues and clubs, shoes, and uniforms. Basketball is an inexpensive sport, and many youth leagues are available for children eight and over.

Related Sports

None

Your Child and Basketball

Being taller than one's peers is a plus. Does your child like to throw and catch a large ball? Is he quick on his feet? Does he like to run? Does he really like to play cooperatively, since teamwork is very important in basketball?

More Information

Web sites: Biddy Basketball International, www.biddybb.com; Harlem Globetrotters, www.harlemglobetrotters.com

Video: *The Basics: Basketball Fundamentals Training* (Gilbert Creative)

Books: *My Basketball Book* (Gail Gibbons); *Kids' Book of Basketball* (Skip Berry); *Basketball in Action* (John Crossingham); *The Outside Shot* (Walter Dean Myers);

The Basket Counts (Arnold Adoff); *Johnny Long Legs*
(Matt Christopher); *Jump! From the Life of Michael
Jordan* (Floyd Cooper)

Movies: *Space Jam* (PG); *Hoop Dreams* (PG-13); *Hoosiers* (PG-13);
Love and Basketball (PG-13); *Coach Carter* (PG-13)

Did You Know?

Basketball is one of the few sports invented in modern times. A Canadian, James Naismith, developed the game in 1891 when teaching in the United States. The first game was so slow that the score was 1–0. Originally the game was played with a soccer ball, though shortly thereafter, that ball was replaced by what we know today as a basketball. It caught on quickly, and by 1900 college students and professional teams were playing basketball.

BOBSLEDDING

Basic Abilities

Bobsledding requires participants to have strength (especially strong leg muscles), quick reflexes, and stamina.

Other Elements

Technical aspects of this sport are taught by instructors or coaches, and considerable training and practice are required to develop the technical skills and to meld as a team.

Events

Events include two-person and four-person bobsledding. The teams go down a track or course that consists of straight sections and curves. Depending upon the level, winning teams are determined by best times over one or more runs. Fastest times are determined by the clock.

Safety Issues

Crashes can cause serious injuries, including head and facial injuries. Pulled leg muscles can occur.

Miscellany

Generally, this is a coached sport. Costs: bobsledding is an expensive sport, and costs may include membership at a facility that has bob-sledding tracks. Additional costs include bobsled, uniform, helmet, and shoes.

Related Sports

Luge and *skeleton*

Your Child and Bobsledding

Is your child quick on her feet? Does she have good reflexes? Is she fear-less? Sledding at high speeds on an icy track is not for the fainthearted.

More Information

Web site: United States Bobsled and Skeleton Federation,
           www.usbobsledandskeleton.org
Books: *Bobsledding and the Luge* (Larry Dane Brimmer);
           Sports: The Complete Visual Reference (François Fortin)

Did You Know?

This sport is an offspring of tobogganing and was developed by American and English vacationers in St. Moritz, Switzerland, in the late 1800s. Originally several wooden sleds were tied together with a board. Like many other sports, it has gone hi-tech. Today bobsleds are made out of fiberglass and metal.

* * *

Early bobsledders bobbed their heads back and forth, believing that this helped to increase their speed. This is not true, but the name of the sport came from this idea and stuck.

CRICKET

Basic Abilities

Speed, quickness, and stamina are important abilities for playing cricket.

Other Elements

Coaches teach and train players in the basic skills and techniques. Considerable practice and training are necessary to learn and play this game. Expect practices at least once or twice a week.

Events

Cricket games are played a certain number of innings and time periods, depending on the league or level. Regulation cricket matches can take up to five days! Beginner level cricket games will, of course, be much shorter. The team that scores the most runs wins.

Safety Issues

Sprained and pulled muscles can occur.

Miscellany

This is a coached team sport. Cricket is not a common sport in this country, so locating a cricket league and coach may not be easy, depending upon where you live. Costs: may include membership on a team or in a league, uniform, shoes, helmet, and bats.

Related Sports

Baseball

Your Child and Cricket

Does your child like to run fast? Can he catch and throw a ball? Does the idea of playing a sport that is not very popular in this country intrigue him?

More Information

Web sites: United States of America Cricket Association,
www.usaca.org; to find cricket leagues/clubs in your state,
www.haverford.edu/library/cricket

Book: *Sports: The Complete Visual Reference* (François Fortin)

Movies: *Playing Away* (no rating); *Lagaan* (no rating)

Did You Know?

This was an English sport that spread to the various British Commonwealth countries. The first cricket clubs were established in the United
States in the 1700s, and several of the Founding Fathers were avid
cricketers, including John Adams. While still played in the United
States, its snail-like growth is because of the popularity of baseball and
the limited resources for playing the sport in this country.

* * *

Have you ever heard the phrase "sticky wicket"? It refers to a delicate
or difficult situation. It comes from cricket—when it rains, the
ground between the two wickets on the cricket field becomes very
soft and the ball bounces more unpredictably, hence fielding it becomes more difficult.

CURLING

Basic Abilities

The sport of curling requires strength in the torso and arms, good balance, accuracy in eye-hand coordination, and tactical and strategy skills.

Other Elements

Curling is played on coached teams. Practice is necessary to develop
individual skills and also to learn to play together as a team. Practices
several times a week are common.

Events

Teams win by sliding stones (heavy, round objects, less than a foot in diameter) on the ice toward the tee (target area). The stones that rest within the area of the tee or are partially in the tee area can be counted as points. The team with the most points wins the end. When a certain number of ends are played, the team with the most points wins. Although curling is played on ice, players wear certain kinds of shoes but not skates. Curling became a Winter Olympics event in 1998.

Safety Issues

Falling is possible as well as pulling arm muscles.

Miscellany

Umpires monitor to make sure play follows the rules; the umpire measures where the stones are relative to the tees and calls the scores. Costs: membership in a curling club or league, uniforms, shoes, and some equipment. Though curling's popularity has increased somewhat in the United States, there are not a lot of facilities in this country.

Related Sports

Curling is loosely similar to shuffleboard.

Your Child and Curling

Does your child have good balance, especially on ice? Does learning a very uncommon sport appeal to her? Is she cooperative with others? Is she patient? Is she analytical, as strategy and tactics are a big part of curling?

More Information

Books: *Curling: The History, the Players, the Game* (Warren Hansen); *Sports: The Complete Visual Reference* (François Fortin); *The Encyclopedia of the Winter Olympics* (John Wukovits)

Did You Know?

A primitive form of curling probably dates to prehistoric man. We think the Scots played it in the 1400s, and by the 1500s they formalized a more modern form of the game. It was also played in other parts of Europe, and a form resembling the modern game can be seen in a painting by Flemish painter Pieter Bruegel the Elder, *Hunters in the Snow* (1565). The game is very popular in Canada.

FIELD HOCKEY

Basic Abilities

Good field hockey players are quick on their feet and have good reflexes, excellent eye-hand coordination, and stamina.

Other Elements

Coaches teach this game and conduct practices, and practices take place one to three times a week, depending on the level.

Events

Games involve two periods of varying times, depending upon the level and league.

Safety Issues

Players can incur various injuries, including sprained ankles, pulled muscles, and an occasional fracture. Though contact is not a part of the rules, it occurs frequently.

Miscellany

Referees call the game, penalties, and scores. Costs: nominal if the child plays on a school team. If it is played on a recreational or private club team, there may be membership fees. Other costs include uniforms, sticks, and shoes.

Related Sports

Ice hockey

Your Child and Field Hockey

Does your child have good stamina? Is she fast? Does she like to run fast? Does she have good eye-hand coordination? Does she play well with others?

More Information

Books: *Field Hockey: Steps to Success* (Elizabeth Anders); *Sports: The Complete Visual Reference* (François Fortin)

Did You Know?

The ancient Persians and Egyptians played a game similar to today's field hockey. The more modern form of the sport was developed in England and Scotland in the 1800s. It spread to the British Commonwealth nations, and today the sport is dominated by Britain, India, and Pakistan.

FOOTBALL

Basic Abilities

Strength, speed, quickness, and stamina are needed, and depending upon the position played, throwing or catching abilities are assets for football players.

Other Elements

Players benefit from coaching and instruction to teach fundamentals and establish the game plan and strategy. Practices once or twice a week are common at beginner levels.

Events

Generally, each game lasts one hour, divided into four quarters, though times are usually shorter at beginner levels. However, football is also played informally in the backyard, with several variations such as touch football and tag football.

Safety Issues

For boys ages ten to fourteen, football has one of the highest injury rates of all sports. Minor as well as serious injuries are possible. Unless it's touch football, football is an aggressive contact sport and tackling one's opponents is a part of the game. Pulled muscles, torn knees, shoulder injuries, and broken legs, arms, and wrists are possible. Head and neck injuries can be quite serious, sometimes with spinal injuries resulting in paralysis. Helmets and protective padding are mandatory. It is important that children be matched for size and weight in this sport.

Miscellany

Judges and referees keep the game going, call the game, and enforce the rules. Costs: fees for a league or association, uniforms, helmets, and shoes. Many leagues and teams are available for boys eight and over; fewer opportunities exist for girls. Pop Warner football leagues are found in many cities, and over 225,000 children play in them. Lots of community football teams for youth are available in most locales.

Related Sports

Rugby and *soccer*

Your Child and Football

Does your child like to run, throw, and catch a football? Is he OK with aggressive physical contact?

More Information

Video: *Youth Football—Strategies for Success*
Books: *My Football Book* (Gail Gibbons); *Football in Action* (John Crossingham); *Mom, Can I Play Football?* (Jerry Norton); *Catch That Pass* (Matt Christopher); *Peyton Manning: Precision Passer* (Jeff Savage)
Movies: *The Waterboy* (PG-13); *Rudy* (PG)

Did You Know?

There is some evidence that a forerunner of football was played by the ancient Greeks. Football as we know it today was developed in the United States in the mid-1800s and was, at one time, exclusively a college sport.

ICE HOCKEY

Basic Abilities

Excellent physical condition, stamina, power, and speed are important abilities for playing ice hockey. This is one of the more physically demanding sports.

Other Elements

While many children can learn to skate on their own, learning the basics and the technical skills of hockey requires instruction and coaching. Practices are at least once a week. Ice hockey is a popular sport for boys and girls, with girls' hockey being one of the fastest-growing high school sports in this country.

Events

Games usually are played for three periods, and the times for each period vary according to the level or league.

Safety Issues

At beginner levels with young children, contact is usually prohibited, though collisions can occur accidentally. After that, in leagues that allow bodychecking, ice hockey is a rough contact sport. Players are fairly well padded, and they wear protective helmets. Even so, sprains, dislocations, pulled muscles, facial cuts, and broken bones can occur, especially if checking is allowed.

Miscellany

Referees call the game, enforce rule compliance, and rule on penalties. Costs: fees for instruction and/or team or league, uniform, skates, helmets, face masks, and sticks.

Related Sports

Field hockey

Your Child and Ice Hockey

Is your child aggressive? Does she like physical contact? Does she mind falling? Can she skate well?

More Information

Video: *Ice Hockey for Kids* (Kids World Productions)
Books: *Hockey: The Book for Kids* (Brian McFarlane); *Hockey in Action* (Niki Walker); *How Hockey Works* (Keltie Thomas); *Hockey for Kids* (Brian McFarlane); *For the Love of Hockey* (Chris McDonnell); *Mystery at Lake Placid* (Roy MacGregor); *Face-off* (Matt Christopher); *Cool As Ice* (Paul Mantell); *On the Ice With . . . Wayne Gretzky* (Matt Christopher)

Did You Know?

Ice hockey originated in Canada in the 1870s. It spread to the United States with the National Hockey League, founded in 1917. Hockey is considered the fastest of the team sports. Because it is so physically demanding, unlimited substitutions are allowed.

LACROSSE

Basic Abilities

General quickness and speed, stamina, and good eye-hand coordination are necessary skills for lacrosse players.

Other Elements

Lacrosse is a coached sport, with many technical skills and aspects. Considerable practice is necessary to learn the basics and to learn how to play as a team. Practices are held at least once or twice a week.

Events

Games are played in either two or four periods of varying lengths, depending on the league or age level.

Safety Issues

Leg, foot, and shoulder sprains are common, and foot and leg fractures are possible. Because of differing rules, there is less physical contact in girls' lacrosse than in boys'.

Miscellany

Umpires or referees call the play, determine penalties, and rule on goals. Organized lacrosse often is not offered until junior or senior high school. Lacrosse used to be primarily an Eastern prep-school sport. No more. It is the fastest growing sport in the United States, and it has become a popular sport for junior- and senior-high school students in the Midwest and West. Nationwide, more than 300,000 people play lacrosse, up from about 150,000 eleven years ago. Costs: league or association costs, uniform, stick, and helmet. Additionally, pads for boys; eye protection for girls.

Related Sports

Ice hockey, field hockey, and *soccer*

Your Child and Lacrosse

Is your child quick on his feet? Can he run almost continuously without becoming too tired? Can he play cooperatively with other children?

More Information

Web site: USLacrosse, www.uslacrosse.org, the national organization of lacrosse. Its Web site has information about the game, coaching, officiating, books, videos, and pamphlets.

Video: *Mark Millon's Offensive Wizardry* (Brainbox: Warrior)
Books: *The Composite Guide to Lacrosse* (Lois Nicholson);
           Sports: The Complete Visual Reference (François Fortin)

Did You Know?

The native peoples of North America played a game called baggatt-away. The early French priests and missionaries probably observed this game and adapted it. They called it "la crosse," as the sticks reminded them of a bishop's crozier (a cross-shaped staff). This sport is a combination of basketball, football, baseball, soccer, and hockey.

ROWING

Basic Abilities

It helps for rowers to have physical endurance; strong leg, back, and shoulder muscles; and good concentration.

Other Elements

The technical skills associated with rowing are taught by instructors and coaches. Except for one type of rowing that involves only one rower, most rowing events involve a crew of anywhere from two to eight rowers, depending upon the type and size of the boat. It's not enough to be a good individual rower; considerable training is required for a crew to learn to work together and to take orders from the coxswain.

Events

Various events have different distances, depending upon the type and size of the boat. The type and size of the boat determines the size of the crew.

Safety Issues

This is a relatively safe sport, though pulled muscles and muscle strains are common. Injuries can occur if boats collide.

Miscellany

Umpires and judges oversee races and enforce the rules. The crew that crosses the finish line first wins. Except for the individual event, most rowing races involve crews of rowers, thus, rowing is considered a team sport. Costs: membership in a rowing club or attendance at a college or university that offers rowing is necessary. Coaching costs may or may not be included. Uniforms and boats may have to be purchased.

Related Sports
Kayaking

Your Child and Rowing

Is your child comfortable and safe in the water? Can your child swim? Does he enjoy rowing when you've been out in a rowboat?

More Information

Web site: Rowing FAQ, www.ruf.rice.edu
Book: *Sports: The Complete Visual Reference* (François Fortin)

Did You Know?

Students of ancient history know that the ancient Phoenicians and Egyptians rowed for war and commerce. Rowing competitions between Oxford and Cambridge university students are famous, and northeastern colleges in the United States, especially Harvard and Yale, are known for their crew (rowing team) rivalries.

SOCCER

Basic Abilities

Soccer requires quickness, strong legs, fast reflexes, and stamina.

Other Elements

Coaching and instruction help a player to learn the basic moves and the fundamentals of the game. Practice several times a week is necessary for improvement.

Events

Soccer games consist of two periods. The times of those periods vary, depending upon the league or club. Beginner leagues commonly have twenty- or thirty-minute periods.

Safety Issues

Since contact in soccer is common, sprained ankles, pulled muscles, and knee injuries happen often. Fractures and dislocations can occur. The most serious soccer injury can be a concussion because of headers (using one's head to direct the ball). Beginners should be discouraged from making headers. Protective headgear and padding help reduce injury.

Miscellany

Judges and referees call the game for fouls and rule infractions. Costs: coaching and/or league or association fees, usually nominal for beginner levels. Shoes and uniforms are additional costs, though some leagues provide the uniforms free. Soccer is a relatively inexpensive sport in terms of equipment, and there are numerous leagues and teams for young players. About 18 million kids play in U.S. soccer leagues; 12 million of them are younger than thirteen, and 5.5 million soccer players under eighteen are girls.

Related Sports

Rugby and *football*

Your Child and Soccer

Is your child quick on her feet? Does she like to run? Does she like to dart around and zigzag when she runs? Does she have good stamina? Is she a team player?

More Information

Web sites: American Youth Soccer Organization, www.ayso.org; Soccer Association for Youth, www.saysoccer.org; www.library.thinkquest.org

Videos: *Soccer Learning Systems,* www.soccervideos.com; *Beginner: Soccer Games for Player Development,* 1-800-856-2638 or www.onlinesports.com

Books: *Kids' Book of Soccer* (Brooks Clark); *The Parent's Guide to Soccer* (Dan Woog); *The Soccer Mom Handbook* (Janet Staihar and Dick Barnes); *Beginning Soccer* (Julie Jensen); *The Young Soccer Player* (Gary Lineker); *The Captain Contest* (Matt Christopher); *In the Goal With . . . Briana Scurry* (Matt Christopher); *Winners Never Quit* (Mia Hamm)

Movie: *Switching Goals* (G)

Did You Know?

An early form of soccer was played by the ancient Greeks and Romans. The Chinese military played a game involving kicking a ball into a net around 200 BC. The English developed the more modern form of the game in the 1830s. Soccer is called football in Europe and *fútbol* in Spanish-speaking countries.

VOLLEYBALL

Basic Abilities

It is helpful to have quick reflexes, good coordination, strong arms, and to be fast on one's feet.

Other Elements

Volleyball involves considerable technique. Instruction is important to learn the basic skills, the fundamentals of the game, and the strategies. Volleyball teams practice once or twice a week in middle school, more often in high school.

Events

The first team to win twenty-five points wins the game. Games played at beginner levels may require fewer points to win. Depending on the level and/or league, a team may have to win the best of three games (or five) in order to win the match. Beach volleyball, another form of volleyball, has become increasingly popular and is frequently shown on TV. Each team has two players.

Safety Issues

Injuries are rare for young children, though jammed or broken fingers and pulled muscles are possible. Middle school children and older kids will suffer more of these injuries.

Miscellany

Referees and/or judges call the game, establish in- or out-of-bounds calls, and make other rulings. Costs: instruction with fees for club or association, uniform, and shoes. Volleyball is a low-cost sport in terms of equipment. An increasing number of middle, junior, and senior high schools have volleyball teams, especially for girls, and many recreational centers provide "drop-in" games.

Related Sports

Beach volleyball

Your Child and Volleyball

Is your child quick on her feet? Is she coordinated? Height helps.

More Information

Web site: www.usavolleyball.org
Video: *Volleyball* (Karol Video)
Books: *The Volleyball Mom's Manual: What SportsMom Thinks You'd Like to Know* (Laurel Phillips and Barbara Stahl); *Youth Volleyball: The Guide for Coaches and Parents* (Sharkie Zartman and Pat Zartman); *Fundamental Volleyball* (Julie Jensen); *Spike It* (Matt Christopher); *Gabrielle Reece* (Dynise Balcavage); *The Sand Man: An Autobiography* (Karch Kiraly)

Did You Know?

This sport was invented by American William G. Morgan in 1895. Morgan was an instructor at a YMCA in Massachusetts. He called the game "mintonette," though the name was changed to volleyball after someone observed that the players seemed to be volleying the ball back and forth over the net. Morgan blended elements of basketball, baseball, tennis, and handball.

WATER POLO

Basic Abilities

Since players are swimming or treading water during a whole game, endurance and considerable muscle strength are important. Participants must be good swimmers.

Other Elements

Water polo is a coached game, and teams practice at least once or twice a week.

Events

Generally, a game has four periods, and the time of each period is usually less for beginners. The team that has scored the most goals after four periods wins.

Safety Issues

Pulled muscles and shoulder injuries can occur. Other injuries from being hit by the ball or by another player are possible and can be serious.

Miscellany

Judges and referees call the game, enforce the rules, and rule on goals. Costs: club or association membership, swimsuits, and caps.

Related Sports

None

Your Child and Water Polo

Does your child like the water? Does he like to swim? Can he tread water for a long time without becoming too tired?

More Information

Web site: United States Water Polo, www.usawaterpolo.com

Book: *Sports: The Complete Visual Reference* (François Fortin)

Did You Know?

Water polo developed in England in the 1870s, and by the early 1900s it was popular in the United States. It is played mainly by club and college teams. No player is allowed to touch the bottom of the pool except the goalkeeper.

PART 3

Special Issues and Situations

Special Issues

IN THIS SECTION I am going to take up three areas that require some special consideration and attention: children who are overweight, children with emotional or developmental disabilities, and children who have serious medical conditions or are physically or intellectually disabled.

Overweight Children and Sports

Today, one-third of Americans are overweight or obese. Smoking-related deaths is the number one cause of preventable deaths in the United States. Obesity ranks number two. About 15 percent of children are overweight. Finding the right sport for an overweight child involves some special considerations for both the child and parent.

First, what if you don't know for sure if your child is overweight? Doctors use a measure—called the *body mass index*—to determine if a person is overweight. It is calculated simply:

$$\frac{\text{Weight in pounds}}{\text{Height in inches}^2} \times 703 = \text{Body Mass Index (BMI)}$$

Adults are considered overweight if their BMI is between 25.0 and 29.9. If the BMI is 30 and above, they are considered obese. However, for persons between the ages of two and twenty, the calculation is slightly different. Growth charts that take into account age and gender are used. Since your child's pediatrician has these charts, he can easily tell you whether your child is overweight; or you can calculate your child's BMI, then obtain his BMI-for-age by finding the appropriate growth chart on the Centers for Disease Control Web site, www.cdc.gov. A child is considered overweight if his BMI-for-age is at or greater than the 95th percentile. If his BMI-for-age is between the 85th and 95th percentile, he is considered at risk of being overweight. Any child at risk of being overweight or who is overweight should be in the care of a doctor who can deal with areas of nutrition, diet, and exercise. The goal should be to promote health, fitness, and weight loss.

Why are there so many overweight children today? Most overweight children eat too much fast food and sit around too much. Their sedentary lifestyle is because of, largely, the triumvirate of too much television, too many video games, and too much time on the computer. Twenty-five percent of children do not participate in any form of exercise. Because of this, they burn up fewer calories than they take in (eat).

Sports can play a role in helping overweight kids become healthier and fitter. One of the first things we want is for heavy children to start moving. Playing a sport can be an important first step. But the sport a child chooses makes a difference. Some sports burn more calories than others. Parents and children should be aware of this so they have realistic expectations of how certain sports can or can't help with fitness and weight loss.

I cannot emphasize enough the importance of moving and exercise. When I interviewed the mother of a child I was working with, she told me that she had lost fifty pounds in the past six months. My curiosity led me to ask her how she had accomplished this. I was prepared for her to tell me that she had stuck with some near-starvation diet for this period of time—an almost impossible feat. However, she had not changed her eating habits at all, nor had she pursued any exercise program at a gym. Instead, she said that six months before, she and her husband had bought a very run-down house with the intention of fixing it up themselves. She used to be very sedentary, but since moving into the new house, she had been stripping old wallpaper, putting up new wallpaper, priming, painting, climbing up ladders, sanding, pulling up old carpet and padding, and laying down hardwood floors. She estimated that she was in near-constant motion for five or six hours a day. Just by being active she had shed those fifty pounds!

When young kids start moving, they lose weight also. Accounts of activity programs instituted in elementary schools report that children lose weight after only a month or two.

If your child is overweight, you should make sure to consult your family physician or pediatrician before he begins a sport. The same doctor may or may not be knowledgeable enough about sports to recommend an appropriate one. If you have already identified a sport or sports your child wants to play, be sure the doctor knows of this interest and gives medical approval.

But what if your child wants to play a sport but doesn't have any idea which one he is interested in or which one would be best for him? Are there certain sports to shy away from? Are there certain sports that would be best for your overweight child?

Before looking for the right sport, keep in mind that uncomfortable situations can arise when overweight children participate in sports. I have worked with a number of young people whose weight led to discomfort and embarrassment. Parents can't always foresee these complications, but they need to be on the lookout for them and to be ready to discuss them with their children.

Sally

Sally was a high school junior. She played on her school volleyball team. While overweight, she was tall for her age, and with somewhat baggy clothes she could hide her overweight condition. However, her volleyball team picked out rather skimpy, skintight team uniforms—a tank top and tight-fitting shorts. Every time she played volleyball, Sally had to wear this uniform and her extra pounds were "out there" for all to see. She felt uncomfortable and sure that everybody was looking at her. To her credit, she did not quit the team despite her self-consciousness. This took a lot of mental toughness on her part. She showed some strength in another way. The week before the state championship playoffs, everyone on the team decided to wear the tank top with sweats to school so that the other students could quickly identify the volleyball members in classes and in the lunchroom. Sally refused. She had put up with wearing the uniform on the volleyball court but drew the line when it came to wearing part of the uniform off the court.

Bill

Bill, eleven years old, waddled when he got a hit and ran toward first base. Most of the kids on his team did not make fun of him, though other kids attending the games did. Bill could hear the taunts coming from the bleachers. He told me that a part of him almost wanted to strike out every time he was up at bat so that he wouldn't have to expose his "bowl full of Jell-O" to others. We spent a lot of time acknowledging his feelings. We also talked about how we didn't want a few kids to control whether he participated in a sport that he liked and was pretty good in. Over time, he was better able to ignore the jeering from the stands. His baseball skills also improved, and he began to command more respect for his abilities.

Tom

Tom, ten years old, was a decent swimmer who was also about twenty pounds overweight. When he swam, he wore a long T-shirt over his swim trunks. He felt less conspicuous that way. (Actually, I thought he looked *more* conspicuous.) He was interested in joining a swim team but knew that he would have to ditch the T-shirt. I began seeing him shortly after he had decided not to join the swim team. We talked about some other sports, but he felt that swimming was his best sport. I asked him how many pounds he would have to lose to feel less self-conscious in a swimsuit. Surprisingly, he said five. I told him that losing five pounds sounded quite doable compared to losing twenty. I also told him that as a former competitive swimmer and swim team coach, I had known a number of overweight swimmers. Since he really was motivated to join the swim team, he agreed to work on losing five pounds. He shed those pounds in two months, and joined the team. Six months later, he had lost the remaining fifteen pounds—he thought because of the training, having to swim over one hundred laps every practice. He went on to swim on his college swim team. I was successful working with Tom because he had been thinking that he had to lose twenty pounds. Once he realized that he only needed to lose five pounds in order to feel less self-conscious, he was able to motivate himself to lose those pounds and participate in a sport he knew he could be good at.

These are some of the more common hurdles an overweight child may have to overcome in order to participate in sports. An understanding parent who can anticipate some of these potential situations can speak with her child about them and address them as they arise. Parents can point out that all kids are teased at one time or other. (I've seen kids teased for being too fat, too thin, too tall, too short; for having curly hair, straight hair, thin hair; small feet, big feet, and on and on.) Parents can help their children develop the skills to deal with these situations. Finding a coach or instructor who has some experience working with overweight kids is important. Sometimes a therapist can help.

Once you've discussed some of these concerns with your child, and he's received medical clearance, what sports may be best for him?

The more overweight your child is, the more likely he should probably refrain from very strenuous sports at first, especially those with a lot of running, such as soccer and lacrosse. There are some exceptions to this. For example, if a strenuous sport is chosen but the lessons or team focuses mainly on learning the fundamental moves of the sport, with little competition and no overexertion allowed, then pursuing a strenuous sport may be OK. Some examples may be swimming and basketball. If your child is just learning to swim and the instructor is emphasizing form and not speed, this might be quite appropriate for the overweight child. Basketball is not contraindicated if your child is only learning the basic moves such as shooting, dribbling, and passing, and is not racing up and down the court.

If your child has his heart set on a strenuous sport that clearly is not appropriate, you can suggest beginning with one less strenuous. If over time he is healthier and loses some weight, perhaps then he can graduate to the more strenuous sport that was his first choice. It's important to have these conversations with him and to be able to compromise.

If your child is determined to play a strenuous sport and you can't find an appropriate beginner class or team, it is best to encourage him to begin with something less strenuous. Some of these include golf, bowling, and archery.

Your doctor may not approve of any participation in sports, especially any strenuous sport, if your child is extremely overweight. If he seems set upon playing a strenuous sport, find out from the doctor how many pounds he will have to lose to play. Your child may be very motivated to work on his health and weight if he is determined to play. This may be the first opening parents have found with a child who has previously resisted help with his weight. It's better when the motivation for losing weight comes from the child rather than from nagging parents. Parents should focus on the child's health and positive qualities, not solely on weight. It's important that parents let the child know that he is loved no matter what his weight is. You should emphasize good nutrition, healthy eating habits, and regular exercise. Once an overall fitness program is in place, losing weight will follow naturally.

Help set up small, reasonable goals. An unhealthy and overweight child is not going to get fit overnight. Praise him when he meets these goals.

The effort to make lifestyle changes should not be directed just toward the overweight child. It's best that the whole family makes being healthy their goal. Parents need to set an example by being physically active and eating healthily themselves. (Studies indicate that if just one parent is overweight, there is a strong likelihood that the child will be also.) Parents should be good role models for appropriate exercise and healthy eating. Keeping high-calorie junk foods out of the house is important. It's also important that parents limit how much time their children can engage in the more sedentary activities—television time, video game playing, and computer use. Support efforts to adopt higher nutritional standards at your child's school for its cafeteria and its vending machines, or pack a lunch for her.

If self-consciousness is a major concern, your child may prefer individual sports with private or small-group lessons to team sports with lots of peers looking on. However, not all individual sports are appropriate for the overweight. For gymnastics, it helps to be short and skinny. It is hard enough to hoist one's body through the air as is required for certain routines; it is nearly impossible to do this if overweight.

Once you and your child have decided upon a sport and your doctor has approved, make sure you keep close tabs on how your child is doing. If you can, attend lessons or practices to assure yourself that she is not overdoing it physically or that the coach or instructor is not demanding too much. Note whether other players or onlookers are ridiculing her in any way. If this is happening, after the practice or lesson, explore how she is feeling about what occurred. Some children are resilient and seem immune to bullying or taunting. Others take it quite hard and personally. If your child is taking it poorly, you will need to help her deal with it. It is also reasonable to speak to the instructor or coach if other team members are doing the teasing. A good coach doesn't allow this. You will have to judge how much is too much, evaluating the impact of such behavior on your child. Realistically, a few kids will always be ready to pick on overweight children. Helping your child handle name-calling is more constructive than immediately letting her quit the team. Encourage her to focus on her accomplishments and the fun she is having. Tell her that it would be a shame if she allowed a few kids to interrupt what otherwise has been a good experience for her.

Once the child does start to play a sport, especially an aerobic one, he should start to firm up and lose some weight just from the training or practices. As he becomes more proficient, he realizes that if he loses more weight he may progress more quickly. At this point he may ask for help to lose more weight. Parents should try to respond in a helpful manner and work with the family doctor or dietician to map out a fitness regimen that includes a weight loss program.

Clearly, overweight children can have positive experiences playing sports. Thoughtful and sensitive discussions need to deal with issues such as self-consciousness and health. Your child should understand that his health and weight condition might limit some of his choices in terms of the sports he can play. With open discussions, a helpful physician, and good research into the sports that may be best for him, the chances are good that your child can have a positive experience playing sports.

Children with Emotional or Developmental Disabilities

Years ago I entered a crowded elevator in a medical building. I noticed that most of the people in it were all squeezed together on one side of the elevator. I thought that strange. Then a person who was on the other side of the elevator began talking out loud to nobody in particular and seemed agitated. It became obvious to me that he was psychotic and probably had just come from seeing his doctor. Because I'm a psychologist and have worked with many psychotic patients, I was perfectly comfortable speaking with him, and I was even able to calm him down. I could hear a collective sigh of relief as the other people in the elevator began to spread out instead of being in a tight bunch at one side. I was saddened by the incident as it confirmed for me what I already knew—that many people are uncomfortable around the mentally ill.

Many emotionally disabled children want to play sports, and indeed, in many cases, playing sports may be therapeutic for them. Finding the right sport, the right team, and the right coach requires some special thought, as we don't want them to be stigmatized and reacted to like the people reacted to the man in the elevator.

Developmentally disabled children can also benefit from learning a sport. Some years ago I consulted on the case of a child from Cambodia. His mother had tried very hard to abort him. As a result, Saren was born with a number of developmental disabilities—all of which made learning very difficult for him. He arrived in this country as an infant, and when I first met him, he was still in first grade, though he was twelve years old. Saren could not perform any self-help tasks such as dressing himself or tying his shoelaces. He read on a first-grade level and was unable to do simple addition and subtraction. Because of her guilt, his mother did not push him very much, and this added to his developmental limitations. Saren's special education teachers heard about a skiing program for developmentally disabled children. With his mother's permission, he was enrolled, and he did extremely well. His success in skiing galvanized his self-esteem, and from then on he began to make progress in school. The last I heard from his mother, Saren had graduated from high school, was working in a restaurant, and aspired to be a cook some day.

The Right Team or Gym

Ideally, you want to find a team or gym that has a history of being inclusive—that has a policy that affirms the participation of all children and has some experience dealing with children who have serious emotional problems. Children with emotional problems may act out at times, display behavior that seems odd to other children and other parents, be moody, and may slow down the game or sport in some ways. Other players often show annoyance if they have not been taught by adults to have some compassion and understanding for such children.

The Right Coach

Speak with the coach about your child before enrolling him on the team or in the group lessons. Explain the specifics of your child's emotional or developmental difficulties. Tell him if your child is being treated for his problems and if he is taking any medications. Ask the coach or instructor if he has ever dealt with children with similar illnesses. Does he think your child will be accepted on the team? Evaluate the coach's responses. It is reasonable to hope that a coach will make an effort to deal with your child or explain clearly why he thinks this would not work out. However, it is not reasonable to expect the coach to have the insight, knowledge, or skills of a psychotherapist. If your child's symptoms are not under reasonable control and he will be too destructive or distracting on the team or in the gym environment, it may not be appropriate for him to play.

Let's look at some of the more common emotional problems and consider what sports might be best for kids with such problems. (Note: Parents should not use these brief descriptions to diagnose their children. Consult with a qualified professional.)

Mood Disorders

Depression

Depression is a mood disorder. A depressed child may feel sad, show diminished interest in most everyday activities, experience fatigue, have sleep and appetite problems, and have difficulty concentrating. Instead of feelings of sadness or unhappiness, some depressed children experience irritability and boredom. Sometimes depressed teens show more behavioral symptoms, like acting out, than mood symptoms. If their symptoms are severe enough, many depressed children and adolescents will be prescribed antidepressants.

What are the implications of a child having some of these symptoms? A strong exercise component associated with the training or playing of a sport can be therapeutic. Symptoms of depression often decrease with exercise. Depressed children can certainly learn to play sports; however, if one of the main symptoms for your child is poor concentration, this may have an impact on his ability to pay attention and learn the fundamentals and strategies of playing sports.

If your child is very moody and down most of the time, playing a sport with other children may help lift his spirits. Often sad kids will begin to withdraw and isolate themselves. Being with other kids and feeling connected with them can be helpful. Keep in mind that the other kids on the team or in the class may find it difficult to relate to someone who is, or seems to be, always depressed and withdrawn.

Check to see if your depressed child can handle a poor performance, or an individual or team defeat. A child already sad and moody may become more so with team defeats or personal performance disappointments. Also, depressed people tend to see certain events in a more negative light than do nondepressed people. After a performance that you may consider not his best but reasonably good, your depressed child may view the same performance as "in the toilet" or "the worst I've ever done in my whole life." This may sound dramatic or exaggerated to you, but it may be very real to him. So you can't always take his statements concerning his performance at face value.

If you can attend practices or games, this is good because you can monitor how your child is doing. If you can't, you may want to ask another parent how it went. Or, if you can't find any adult who saw the practice or game, try asking the coach. In any event, be sure to ask your child how he thought the practice or the game went. Be prepared to help with some reality checks if you sense that his view is overly negative.

What sports are best for seriously depressed children? I don't think it's possible to say that certain sports would be better or worse for them. The environment, coach, team, or other players may be more important considerations than the specific sport. Have your child pick a sport that he really wants to play. Since depressed children are often not interested in much, the fact that he is interested in playing a specific sport is a good sign and may improve his spirits. For depressed kids, I have a slight bias for sports that have interaction with or the presence of other kids. A sport with individual lessons with just the instructor and the child is not as desirable. A team or league in which there is not a lot of pressure for winning might be good for a seriously depressed child, in that there are not a lot of opportunities to feel disappointed or down. A coach or instructor who is sensitive and teaches in a positive, praising manner is important. A depressed child doesn't need a picky, critical coach who is always harping on what he is doing wrong.

Bipolar Disorder

People with this illness experience significant mood swings; they can go from feelings of depression to feelings of mania (abnormally elevated mood), sometimes in a matter of minutes, but usually these shifts in mood occur in hours or days. About 15 percent of people with bipolar illness will struggle with some psychotic thoughts or behaviors at times.

Most people with this illness, children included, take medicines that help stabilize—even out—their moods so that they do not experience extreme highs or lows.

Assuming that children with this illness are being medicated and/or their mood fluctuations are under control, they should be able to pursue any sport they wish. However, in the early stages of medication and therapy, they may experience extreme mood swings. In this instance, their moods and behavior may be unpredictable. They may not attend lessons or practices regularly, as sometimes they may feel too depressed to go to practices or games. Teammates and coaches may not be able to depend on them. If they are playing a team sport where their participation is essential—if they are one of only two catchers on the baseball team, for example—it may be necessary for the team to take steps to adjust for their illness. They may be relegated to second string, or the coach may want to bring on an extra catcher to be available in case they can't play.

It's important to discuss all of this with the coach up front so that he understands what the bipolar child is dealing with and how possible mood swings may affect the child's performance on the team.

Anxiety Disorders

A number of disorders have anxiety as the main symptom. These include overanxious disorder of childhood, panic attacks, phobias, obsessive-compulsive disorder, and post-traumatic stress disorder. Anxiety disorders are the most common mental disorders; depression is the second most common.

Overanxious Disorder of Childhood

The name of this disorder gives you a good idea of its main symptoms. The child is either anxious most of the time or becomes anxious easily and to many different situations. He displays excessive anxiety and worry. These children are sometimes called worrywarts. They are often restless, find it difficult to concentrate in stressful situations, or their mind goes blank, and they show irritability. Sometimes they experience muscle tension and sleep disturbances.

When overanxious children participate in sports, they may show signs of anxiety both physically and mentally. Before a meet, they may break out in a rash, get a headache, or be sick to their stomach. They may appear restless. Prior to a practice or game, they may worry about their performance or the performance of their team. Some overanxious children have learned to hide some of these signs. Others have not and are quite obviously stressed out and anxious.

You should tell a coach or instructor that your child is overanxious. This way he can try not to place too much pressure on him and to be watchful for practice or game situations that appear to generate too much anxiety. Look for a coach or teacher who has a calm and soothing temperament and who is patient and positive. Remember, coaches are not therapists! They cannot be expected to completely change their entire coaching style for one child.

Until you see signs that your child can cope, it is best to look for teams or individual sports with little or no competition or pressure. If a team is very competitive and goes all out to win, this may create far too much stress for the overanxious child. It's best to select a sport or team that is low key. The coach or instructor should emphasize learning the fundamentals of the sport and having fun.

Panic Attacks

Panic attacks often occur out of the blue. They are characterized by the following symptoms: shortness of breath, pounding heart, light-headedness, sweating, trembling or shaking, dizziness, nausea, fear of losing control, and fear of dying. These feelings are intense though they tend to be of short duration—in most cases lasting less than ten minutes. Some people have panic attacks with agoraphobia, meaning that they are afraid to go outside their homes. Children who have panic attacks with agoraphobia sometimes can't go to school and are homebound.

Many children who have been diagnosed with panic attacks take prescribed medications to help control them. Others with panic attacks also undergo therapy that teaches them how to relax and handle an attack if it occurs.

Unless a child's panic attacks show a pattern of appearing in specific sport environments, I think he can play any sport that interests him. The coach needs to know there is a possibility that he may have a panic attack while playing or during a practice or lesson. You should advise the coach on how to handle an attack if it does occur.

If, however, you see a pattern and your child's panic attacks seem only to occur when he is engaged in a specific sport, it might be best to withdraw him from that sport until his condition has been treated and his therapist thinks it is time to resume.

Give the coach permission to tell team members of the possibility that your child may have a panic attack so that they aren't too alarmed if it does happen. Even though your child may feel like she's dying, in fact, she's not, and we don't want the other children to think she is. I have found other players quite understanding of children who have panic attacks once they have some understanding of the condition.

Children who have panic attacks along with agoraphobia probably will not be able to leave the house to play a sport (and may not be able to go to school) until this condition is treated and there is considerable improvement. However, they can practice certain sports or activities at home—trampoline, weight lifting, and aerobic dance.

Phobias

A phobia is an irrational fear of something—animals or bugs, heights, blood, germs, flying. When in the grips of this phobia, especially when a child is near or thinking himself to be near the source of his phobia, he reacts with excessive fear and anxiety. His behavior is marked by the avoidance of the feared object or situation. For example, a person with a fear of being in elevators will avoid riding in elevators. People with a social phobia become anxious in social situations or with social contact.

Depending on the phobia, the phobic child can probably participate in any sport he wishes. For example, if a child is fearful of flying, there is no sport he can't take part in (except skydiving!). However, let's say a child is afraid of bugs. Until the condition is treated and improved, he may not be able to play a sport that is outside or in a buggy area. A child fearful of snakes may not want to play baseball if the field is very grassy and is a place where he thinks there may be snakes.

Obsessive-Compulsive Disorder

A person who is obsessive will have recurrent thoughts, impulses, or images that cause considerable anxiety and distress. These thoughts usually are not just excessive worry about real-life problems. Persons with compulsions display repetitive behaviors such as hand washing, counting, repeating words, or compulsive touching of objects.

Depending on the obsessions and/or the compulsive behavior(s), this can be one of the more disabling anxiety disorders. Children with this disorder often take medications to help control their symptoms. Parents should inform the coach of this condition, especially if symptoms are likely to occur during practices or games.

Unless a particular sport is linked to an obsession or compulsion, children with this disorder can usually play any sport of their choosing.

However, it may be that while the obsessions or compulsions are not connected with any particular sport, they will interfere with it. For example, I saw a child with a compulsion to touch doorknobs repeatedly—up to twenty-five times—before he could go through the door. If a child like him takes karate at a studio or gym that has a door leading to the locker rooms where the kids change into their uniforms, he may feel compelled to touch that doorknob repeatedly. The other kids in the class may see this behavior and think it odd. His parent will have to speak with him about how he is going to handle this. (One solution is for him to go to practice already in his uniform if the instructor will allow it.) If this becomes too much of a self-conscious or anxiety-producing situation for him, he may have to switch to another sport that doesn't have doorknobs in the practice area or learning facility. Fortunately, there are better treatments for this disorder than in the past, and medication and therapy can help reduce the compulsive behavior.

Post-Traumatic Stress Disorder (PTSD)

People with this disorder have been exposed to a traumatic event during which they experienced, witnessed, or confronted incidents that actually threatened death or serious injury to themselves or others. I've treated many children who were in car accidents wherein the child was seriously injured or someone else was seriously injured or died. Some of the New Yorkers who survived the attacks on 9/11 are now dealing with serious post-traumatic stress disorders.

The symptoms of this disorder are recurrent and intrusive memories or recollections of the event, frightening dreams (for children, repetitive play in which themes of the event are expressed), flashbacks, intense distress at exposure to situations that remind the person of the event, avoidance of stimuli associated with the event, and difficulty sleeping or concentrating.

Children who suffer from post-traumatic stress disorder can be quite disabled in their functioning. A child who lost a parent in a car accident may refuse to ride in a car again. A child who witnessed a robbery where shots were fired may not want to go into stores again. A child who survived a plane crash may not want to fly again. Unlike some of the other anxiety disorders, many post-traumatic stress disorder symptoms appear to be logical and understandable reactions to the traumatic event.

The very specific elements of the traumatic events will have to be evaluated to ascertain any possible linkage of what happened to the performance of a sport. For instance, I have treated many children who have been sexually abused. The nature of their abuse is that they were touched in inappropriate ways and against their wishes or control, usually by an adult who had power over them. Some of these children developed PTSD. One of the ways their symptoms can sometimes be triggered is by physical contact, even if it is appropriate and sometimes even if the children have given permission. Consequently, they may have a problem in a contact sport in which players often make contact with each other. Even though some contact is an expected and appropriate feature of the sport, they may recoil and react with fear and anxiety. Also, for some sports, it is not unusual for a coach to make physical contact with the child. A baseball coach might stand behind a child with a bat in his hands and guide the swing. A golf instructor might do the same. It's common for swim instructors or coaches to stand close to the child and move his arms to show him the proper stroke. With a child who has been sexually abused, a parent has to be very careful before subjecting a child to these situations. So a parent and child should probably avoid signing the child up for a contact sport if he or she has some serious PTSD symptoms related to unwanted and inappropriate touching or contact. Whatever sport is chosen, the coach needs to be aware of any situations that might alarm the child so he can be prepared in case the child does display some symptoms.

Other Disorders

Eating Disorders

The most common eating disorders are anorexia nervosa and bulimia nervosa. Adolescent girls seem most vulnerable, though we are seeing an increase in the number of men and boys diagnosed with eating disorders. People with anorexia think they are fat, even though many are actually thin, or worry that they may become fat. They eat little and lose weight. Some lose so much weight that they die. Persons who are bulimic sometimes purge (induce vomiting after eating, especially after binge eating). If they don't purge, they use some inappropriate means to lose weight such as excessive exercise or fasting. Some people are both anorexic and bulimic. Both of these eating disorders are quite serious and require special treatment with eating disorder specialists. Other eating disorders involve overeating and binge eating without purging.

Obviously, great thought should be given before allowing anorexic and bulimic children to take up any sports where being thin is a necessity or an advantage. This would just give them a ready-made excuse for maintaining their eating disorders. (A number of famous jockeys have developed eating disorders in their attempt to keep their weight down.) This means that a child with a serious eating disorder such as anorexia or bulimia should probably be discouraged from participating in gymnastics or equestrian events, and to a lesser degree, figure skating.

Another problem with anorexic or bulimic children taking up sports, especially if they are members of highly competitive teams or individual sports, is that proper nutrition and food intake is an important feature of training and competition-day readiness for many sports. Athletes often must increase their intake of carbohydrates prior to certain events for energy release. A child in the grips of anorexia or bulimia may find it almost impossible to eat properly.

Children with overeating disorders are usually overweight and may require special medical and/or psychological treatment.

Attention-Deficit/Hyperactivity Disorder

There are three types of this disorder: predominantly inattentive type (sometimes referred to as ADD); predominantly hyperactive-impulsive type (sometimes referred to as ADHD); and combined type (also sometimes referred to as ADHD). It is sometimes easier to refer to any of these as "attention-deficit disorders." Those with the inattentive type find it difficult to concentrate as they have short attention spans. Thus they often have difficulty learning. Children with either ADHD type are also hyperactive and impulsive. No matter the type, some children appear immature. Many children with this disorder take medications that help them concentrate better and medication can also help those who are hyperactive and impulsive. Psychotherapy can be an effective treatment. Famous athletes with this disorder include home run king Babe Ruth, 1976 Olympic decathlon gold medalist Bruce Jenner, and 2004 Olympic gold medalists swimming phenom Michael Phelps and runner Jeremy Wariner.

Team sports can be overwhelming for kids with attention deficit disorders. Go to a basketball game and watch the action on the court. A player has a lot to do: be ready to catch a passed ball, be ready to break open to make a shot, dribble down court, and watch out for defenders ready to block shots. All of this is happening in seconds, not minutes. In general, individual sports offer a quieter, more structured, and less chaotic environment for children with any type of this disorder. With fewer details and distractions, they are better able to take in what the coach or instructor is saying. They do not have to attend to their play and movements as well as the play and movements of opponents or teammates. Having said this, team sports that move at a slower pace might be appropriate.

Generally, when young people play soccer, the pace is slower than basketball. Baseball is a very slow game. Yes, when the ball is coming toward a fielder we're talking about seconds and not minutes, but at that moment all the fielder has to do is concentrate on fielding the ball. Football has seconds of fast action with lulls in between plays that allow players to regroup and regain their focus. The average total amount of time the ball is in play in a one-hour football game is ten to twelve minutes. You can verify this yourself by clocking from the time the ball is snapped until the play is ruled dead. In other words, there aren't long periods of fast, sustained action.

Any of the martial arts are great sports for kids with this disorder. Not only is the teaching environment quite structured, but also the instructional style is very controlled and may be authoritarian at times. At any one time, a child is learning a small set of moves and there are few distractions present to interrupt his concentration. Each new move is repeated over and over again.

Of course, many of these kids play basketball and other fast-paced sports. So a team sport that has a lot of quick action and a lot of complexity need not be ruled out automatically. This depends on the child, his motivation to play, and the severity of his attention deficit disorder. Be aware that initially he may be quite disruptive and rarely be where he should be on the field or court. Because he has difficulty concentrating, he may not follow the coach's directions very well. The coach and the child's teammates will need to be patient. Often, with medication and/or therapy, his concentration improves. With considerable repetition of instructions and movements of the game, he should show progress.

As with many disorders, the degrees of impairment vary, ranging from mild to severe. Children with the milder forms can often play team sports with no medication or therapy and become outstanding players.

Motor Skills Disorder

Children with a motor skills disorder typically show a marked impairment in the development of motor coordination. This diagnosis is made only if the coordination difficulties are not due to a medical condition, such as cerebral palsy or muscular dystrophy. Children with this diagnosis typically are clumsy and show delays in common developmental tasks such as walking, crawling, sitting, and tying shoelaces.

Children with major coordination difficulties, whether they are officially diagnosed, are often among the nonathletes. Playing a sport often seems off the radar for them. They find it difficult to picture themselves playing a sport when they see their peers playing or see sports on TV. There are many of these children, and people often call them clumsy, awkward, klutzy, or nonathletic. Even so, many children with this problem would like to play a sport if they could be convinced that it is possible they can play and not be totally embarrassed.

As I've said in earlier chapters, if they are encouraged and if you can find the right sports for these children, most can achieve some success in them.

Which sports might be best for uncoordinated children? A parent should determine whether the child's coordination deficits are gross motor or fine motor, or both.

If both, the good choices become limited, but don't give up. For one thing, most sports on the beginner levels are simplified and the expectations for performance are low. All children, no matter how poorly coordinated, can learn to swim at the beginner level. They may not look pretty in the pool, but they can learn how to swim. Bowling requires a lot of repetition of movement, and over time uncoordinated children can learn this sport. Again, they may not make graceful movements, but they can get the job done. Children can learn any martial arts on the beginning level. Golf is a good choice, especially if your uncoordinated child is analytical. Swings and putting can be practiced over and over again, and even an uncoordinated child can show improvement. Rowing is pretty much a limited-motion sport, and I've known several very awkward children who did it quite well.

When a child has only gross-motor coordination problems, look for the sports that involve primarily fine-motor skills. These include archery, billiards, and shooting.

When the coordination problems involve the fine-motor muscles but the child has good gross-muscle skills, many sports can be considered. Football, volleyball, swimming, skating, martial arts, and cycling are just a few.

Use the fact sheets in Part 2 to help you research which sports might fit in best with your child's level of clumsiness and also with his temperament.

Communication Disorders

These disorders include expressive language disorder, receptive-expressive language disorder, phonological (articulation) disorder, and stuttering. In the first two, the child has difficulty either in expressing himself or both expressing himself and understanding spoken language. The second two sometimes make it difficult for others to understand the child.

The first two can have an impact on how well the child can understand instructions and how well the child can ask questions or express himself with the coach or other players. It's necessary for a coach or instructor to be aware of your child's problems. Some of these children compensate by being very visual, so a coach who demonstrates the right moves would aid a child who sometimes has difficulty understanding language (receptive problems). If a child needs to ask questions and has difficulty expressing himself, a coach has to be patient and work with the child to understand him. Written instructions can help some of these children. I have seen children with expressive-receptive problems read books about their sports and learn the fundamental moves of their sports via the descriptions and illustrations in these books. They also can watch videos and copy the moves. Often they know the finer points of the game or sport better than their teammates or other children in their class.

Dealing with teammates or classmates may present some challenges to a child with a communication disorder. Self-consciousness and just the frustration of not being understood can, understandably, be stressful for the child. He may be expected to speak with his teammates. If he stutters or if he has trouble expressing himself clearly, he may worry that the other kids may make fun of him or reject him. In fact, I have seen this happen, but not often. More often, the other kids seem to ignore these types of problems. They are engrossed with the game or sport, getting their own moves down pat and focusing on what the coach or instructor is saying. So the few moments when a kid stutters is a minor blip that most kids take in stride. If your child is a natural athlete, his teammates may even choose him as a team leader—captain or quarterback.

Of course, some kids with communication problems will try to be inconspicuous and opt out of situations in which they would be expected to speak up. So a kid who ordinarily would be chosen as captain of his tennis team or as quarterback may pull back on his leaderships skills or reject such positions or titles. It hurts when I see a child do this, but I can understand why he does it. As this child matures and as his communication improves, or even if it doesn't improve, he may be better able to ignore how he thinks a few other kids are reacting to him and be more receptive to the idea of being a team leader.

A parent should be on the watch for his child's performance, how his communication problem is or isn't affecting his ability to learn the sport, and his relationship with the other players.

Are there any sports that are best for the child with a communication disorder? On the face of it, this child can explore any sport. Be aware, though, that if he has an expressive-receptive communication disorder and learning the sport is highly receptive-language based, that is, the coach teaches the sport via large amounts of spoken language, your child may find learning to be a challenge, though not necessarily insurmountable. Also be aware that if he has an expressive language, articulation, or stuttering problem, you might see him lean toward sports or positions where he can be the church mouse. This may be good in terms of not placing himself in positions of needing to speak, but it may not allow him to exhibit some of his strengths.

Conduct Disorder

Children with conduct disorders show behavioral problems in one or more of the following categories: aggression to people or animals, destruction of property, deceitfulness or theft, or serious violations of rules.

Most children with this disorder do not tend to last long in organized sports. If they are too aggressive and are penalized repeatedly, they may quit. If they violate the rules too much, no coach or instructor is going to continue working with them. After all, participation in sports is voluntary, so a coach can easily dismiss the child from the gym or kick him off the team. A child who distracts other players from the work at hand and wastes the coach's time on disciplining is going to be cut from the lessons or team. No coach can allow one highly disruptive child to take his attention away from coaching or for that child to intimidate other players.

Having said this, children with a more mild form of conduct disorder can sometimes find some meaning in sports participation. If they are really motivated to play, they will soon see that if they want to continue, they will have to change their behavior. Thus, involvement in sports for these children may be therapeutic.

Children with mild forms of conduct disorder may pursue any sport they are interested in. Sometimes they do better in sports with a minimal authoritarian structure or with coaches or instructors who have a more relaxed style of coaching. On the other hand, some of them do better in more authoritarian settings. Thus, a child who really wants to learn tae kwon do may do quite well even though tae kwon do instructors teach in a highly structured, somewhat authoritarian manner.

Before a child with behavioral problems joins a team or signs up for lessons, you should speak with him about the ramifications and possible consequences of his behavior. He should know that it probably will not be a matter of *if* but *when* he will be kicked out if he misbehaves. Because this is a possibility, make sure you don't put down large sums of money up front for his lessons or team.

Oppositional Defiant Disorder

Children with this disorder show at least four of the following behaviors: losing their temper, arguing with adults, actively defying requests or rules set down by adults, deliberately doing things that will annoy other people, blaming others for their own mistakes or misbehavior, being touchy or easily annoyed by others, being angry or resentful, or being spiteful or vindictive.

Oppositional children are not easy to work with, be it in the classroom, at home, on the playing field, or at the gym. These children have much in common with children with conduct disorders. If they cannot comply with the structure of the team, the rules of the game, or the instructions of the coach or instructor, they will probably be asked to leave the game, class, or sport.

It is true that some of these kids are more oppositional in one venue than in others. A child can be totally defiant at home yet be reasonably compliant on the field or in the gym. In this instance, his behavior seems directed at his parents, not others. However, many defiant children have a chip on their shoulder no matter who they are around.

If an oppositional child is really motivated to play a sport, he may be willing to work on his behavior. He will have to do so since no coach or instructor will allow his authority to be openly defied in front of others. Also, no coach will allow one kid to hassle other players, especially if the sport requires lots of cooperative teamwork. Most oppositional children have problems with their peers, as they are too confrontational and defiant. Their teammates often reject them. For this reason, individual sports perhaps hold more hope for such children, assuming they can work cooperatively with the coach. If the lessons are one-on-one there is no audience effect—a dynamic that drives some oppositional children.

So sign up your oppositional child for a sport at his peril. If he is in therapy concurrent with playing a sport, it may be that with the therapist's help he can see his choices more clearly: improve his behavior or be kicked out of a sport that he may be quite good at and is enjoying.

Some coaches and instructors are better at handling oppositional and defiant kids than others. If you are lucky enough to find such a coach, well and good. Just don't expect that all coaches will put up with or know how to deal with the defiant child.

Autism Disorder and Asperger's Disorder

Some clinicians regard autism as a spectrum disease and Asperger's Disorder (sometimes called Asperger's syndrome) as a mild form of autism. Autism is primarily an impairment in communication and the ability to interact appropriately in social situations. Thus there are significant deficits in both verbal and nonverbal skills. Many autistic children do not speak at all, or if they do speak they use words in a manner that is often unintelligible or seemingly have no meaning. They often display unusual motor behaviors or mannerisms that are abnormal in intensity or focus. Children with Asperger's Disorder will show significant impairment in social interaction, but they do better in communication and cognitive functioning than many autistic children. Asperger's Disorder seems to be more common in males.

A child with the classic autistic symptoms probably cannot sustain the communication or kind of social interaction necessary to learn and play a sport. Some treatment programs for autistic children are able, with great effort, to teach the children some basic moves, like catching and throwing a ball.

Some children with Asperger's Disorder can be found on the playing field or in the gym. You will need to find an individual-sport instructor or a team coach who knows a little about this disorder. Or you may need to educate him about it. If your child plays a team sport, he needs to understand (and probably does already) that other children may regard him as somewhat odd. Help him with ways to handle this, both in school and on the field. Many children with Asperger's Disorder have poor coordination, so it may take them longer than other children to learn a sport.

If the child has a severe form of Asperger's Disorder, he may find it easier to learn an individual sport first. This way his limited ability to interact socially will not be as taxed, as he will only have to interact with the instructor. If he shows some improvement in his ability to interact with others, he may be able to move on to a team sport if he is interested in playing one. Children with severe symptoms of Asperger's Disorder are more likely to be teased or bullied by teammates because of their very odd, and often inappropriate, behavior.

Children with a mild form of Asperger's Disorder can probably engage in any sport, including team sports. However, even with a milder form of this disorder, the coach and teammates may notice some odd behavior when interacting with these children, or they may think they are a little strange.

Self-esteem issues are important concerns with children with autism or Asperger's Disorder because other children often react to their strangeness. It is difficult for them to make friends and to feel normal. If they do have some athletic skills, they can sometimes gain some positive regard from other children who admire their ability to play the game and who then may overlook some of their odd behavior.

Substance Abuse Disorders

Usually these children are in high school, though some may be in middle school. Commonly abused substances include alcohol or drugs. Drugs can include pot, cocaine, heroin, amphetamines, inhalants, and some of the hallucinogenic drugs including Ecstasy. Some other drugs include nicotine and caffeine. Some kids may be dependent upon either alcohol or drugs, meaning that they require these substances in order to function. Others are not necessarily dependent, but they use the substance in an abusive manner (binge drinking, shooting up several times a month, smoking pot on the weekends). In this section, I am not speaking about legally prescribed drugs used as prescribed.

Space does not allow for an in-depth discussion on substance abuse. Whether it's alcohol or drugs, some reactions are common. These might include hangovers, tremors, mood disorders including depression, feeling sick, vomiting, fatigue, sleep disorders, eating disorders, flashbacks, psychotic reactions, impaired coordination, weight loss, slurred speech, blurred vision, unsteady gait, anxiety, difficulty concentrating, drowsiness, or coma. Death is possible if lethal amounts are drunk, inhaled, or ingested. In just a few weeks, four students at three different Colorado colleges died from either alcohol intoxication/poisoning or a drug/alcohol mix.

One scenario is when a child who is already active in sports begins to engage in some form of substance abuse. If there is an unaccounted-for gradual or sudden fall off in his performance, parents, coaches, or instructors should suspect substance abuse. In my experience, parents are often the very last to suspect that their child has a substance abuse problem. Once identified, the child should receive appropriate treatment. Whether he must quit the sport during treatment depends upon many factors and should be discussed with therapists and coaches. For example, if because of his substance abuse problem he cannot be counted on to attend practice or games, he should leave the sport until his attendance can be more consistent. If his play is poor or erratic, the coach may ask him to leave until he is through with treatment. How his behavior affects other players is an important consideration, and this factor alone may determine whether he should leave the sport for a period of time. Many school teams have requirements that athletes do not drink or use drugs. In these cases, any infraction may lead to an automatic ouster from the team.

Sometimes drug-related problems are associated with the company your child keeps. If you suspect that your child's teammates have encouraged drug use or are supplying drugs, it may be time to find another team or sport (with different players) or group of friends. Parents will need to talk to the coach or school officials, or even call the police if this is true.

If your child is a star player and perhaps looking good enough to obtain an athletic scholarship to college, he may be especially motivated to become alcohol- or drug-free and seek treatment.

What if your child has recently been diagnosed with a substance abuse problem and now wants to take up a sport? It is best for the child to be well into treatment before beginning. Treatment for substance abuse is intensive and requires time outside of school. In addition, there may be a certain amount of stress involved with learning and training for a sport. We don't want the newly diagnosed child to have to deal with any additional stressors when he begins treatment. After several months of treatment, given improvement, a discussion with the treating therapist is in order. He will be in a good position to determine if this is the right time for your child to embark on learning tennis or going out for lacrosse.

Nicotine and caffeine addictions can affect athletic performance. Children who are heavy smokers usually have some lung problems. Often they are short of breath, and their stamina is not good. They finish a running play in football obviously gasping for air. You will see these signs if they play any strenuous sport. This may give you or the coach an opening to explore whether the child may be ready to quit smoking. He probably knows that his smoking is limiting his performance, if only in small ways.

Athletes may find that consuming too much caffeine may affect their athletic skills. Caffeine intoxication, consuming as little as two to three cups of brewed coffee, can cause symptoms such as restlessness, nervousness, insomnia, muscle twitching, tachycardia or cardiac arrhythmia, and periods of inexhaustibility. Some of these kids go on for days without sleep, then crash. When they don't get enough good sleep, their performance may suffer, no matter the sport.

I have known a number of high school athletes who were dependent on caffeine. They drank eight or more cups of regular coffee or six or more cans of soda every day. If they tried to withdraw too quickly, they experienced some symptoms of withdrawal. Too much caffeine is not healthy, and athletes should try to limit their intake of it.

A word on doping, or illegal use of drugs to enhance sports performance. We've been hearing about professional and Olympic athletes using steroids and other performance-enhancing drugs. All Olympic medalists are tested for illegal drugs. Increasingly, various professional sports associations are implementing random testing of their athletes, with consequences if any illegal substances are found. Even now, we are seeing a number of high school students and even some middle school students using performance-enhancing drugs. Parents are often in denial when it comes to drug or steroid use by their children.

Several years ago a school district near Phoenix surveyed the athletes at three high schools. More than 20 percent said that they knew teammates or other athletes who were using steroids.

When a sports physician working with the U.S. Olympic Committee asked young athletes if they would use a drug if it would help them win an Olympic gold medal, more than half answered yes.[26]

The Centers for Disease Control indicates that between 1991 and 2003 steroid use among high school students more than doubled. In a CDC survey of 15,000 students in grades nine to twelve, more than 6 percent said that they had used steroids at least once.[27] The National Institute on Drug Abuse indicates that more than a half million eighth- and tenth-grade students, mostly boys, use steroids, some for improving their appearance, others for improving their athletic performance (www.drugabuse.gov).

It is important that parents and coaches of youth teach fair play to athletes. Children should learn that it is an insult to other players and a violation of the integrity of the game to cheat, play unfairly, or to use performance-enhancing drugs. Using performance-enhancing drugs to win and/or to set new records is cheating. Apart from questions of character, performance-enhancing drugs have side effects that are quite alarming and dangerous. In adolescents, steroid abuse can halt bone growth and cause damage to the heart, kidneys, and liver. It can also lead to impotence, shrunken testicles, lowered sperm count, and breast enlargement in male teens. In females, some of the effects include menstrual irregularities, increased body hair, loss of scalp hair, and a deepened voice. Some of these biological effects are irreversible.[28] A host of personality changes can occur, such as increased aggression, depression, and emotional volatility. Steroid use may be potentially life threatening. Also, we do not yet know the long-term effects of some of these drugs. So a child who begins using these drugs in middle school and continues, let's say, through college, will be using them for eight to twelve years.

It is understandable that an athlete may be tempted to use one of these drugs to give him an edge. This would be especially so if he wants to be a professional player or compete in the Olympics. Some Olympic races or events are won in hundredths of a second or just a couple of kilograms. Additionally, the salaries in many professional sports are astronomical. The endorsement monies that are offered to Olympic gold medalists exceed those offered to bronze medalists. So it may be easy for some athletes to rationalize the need to take these drugs.

Parents can help youth athletes learn to value their performance in sports—performance that comes from natural ability, good training habits, determination, and hard work. Coaches and parents can teach that fair competition and the challenge of competition is one of the biggest highs in life. Michael Phelps, the swimming star of the 2004 Olympics in Athens, purposefully signed up for an event he knew his opponent, Ian Thorpe, would probably win. He did this because he thought it would make for an awesome race. For Phelps, fair competition and a hard-fought race trumped being in an easy-to-win race. He wanted a race that would push him to bring out his best, even if it meant losing (which he ultimately did). This is the value we want to instill in our children and young athletes.

Children with Medical Conditions or Physical or Intellectual Disabilities

Many physically disabled or intellectually disabled children or children with serious medical conditions are able to play sports—both team and individual sports. Depending upon their disabilities or limitations and depending upon the resources available in your community, they may be able to play in mainstream leagues or competition or in leagues or competitions designed for the disabled.

No matter the physical or mental disability, I believe that most children can participate in sports. You should encourage them to do so for a number of reasons. Physical fitness is important for all children, not just the physically able. A child paralyzed from the waist down still needs to be active from the waist up for his health and fitness and to avoid needless muscle atrophy. Also, many physically disabled children were natural athletes before their disabling injuries or illnesses, so depending upon the nature of their disabilities, they may be able to continue to compete in mainstream teams or individual competition. Others might find Paralympic competition or the Special Olympics more appropriate athletic venues given their disabilities.

Perhaps as important as the physical benefits are the psychological and emotional benefits a child will gain from playing sports. Too often a child with physical disabilities concludes that she cannot play sports like other kids. This can increase her sense of loss and isolation and result in lowered self-esteem and little self-confidence. Athletics can give physically disabled children a chance to prove that they are like everyone else and boost their feelings about themselves. For these reasons, any interest on their part should be encouraged, and with some research you can find the appropriate team or venue with expert instructors and coaches to help identify the right sport for them and to teach that sport's basics.

"What I represent is just achieving what you want to do in life. It's a matter of your attitude. Some people have a negative attitude, and that's their disability."

—Marla Runyon,
U.S. Olympic runner who is legally blind

Besides mainstream youth sport leagues, let's look at some of the other avenues available. Paralympics are for athletes who have serious physical disabilities. Some of the disability groups represented include amputees, blind or visually impaired athletes, athletes with cerebral palsy, athletes with spinal cord injuries, and athletes who are affected by a range of other disabilities such as those from multiple sclerosis or dwarfism. While the Paralympic Games are held once every four years, Paralympic sports and competition are usually conducted year-round.

Paralympic wheelchair sports include basketball, fencing, power-lifting, and judo. Another Paralympic sport is wheelchair rugby, invented in the 1970s. It is played four on four on a basketball court, and players score goals when they cross the line with the ball. It became an official Paralympic sport at the 2000 Olympic games. USA teams have won gold medals twice—once in 1996 in Atlanta when it was a demonstration sport, and once in 2000. Paralympic skiing events take place with competitors on special skis, even though they are missing one or two legs. New Paralympic sports may evolve as new equipment is developed to help more physically disabled athletes participate in sports.

"I compete because I love to compete. I love to win but there's a bigger picture. I go out and give it my best."

—Rick Draney,
a top-ranked wheelchair tennis player

Your child's particular disability and its severity may determine whether he will find the Paralympics best for him or, instead, a league or team made up of other children like himself. For example, there are special teams just for the legally blind or the deaf and hearing-impaired. There is a school for the deaf in Riverside, California, whose football team had a winning season in 2004, playing against mainstream (hearing) teams. Players on this team do not necessarily see themselves as handicapped; they just can't hear.

For kids with more severe disabilities, mainstream leagues or teams or mainstream individual sports may not offer them the best chance to learn or compete in the sport. There are exceptions: I've known several teens with prostheses who played baseball and golf. I knew of a swimmer who lost her leg in a car accident and was able to compete without her prosthesis through high school. After that, she participated in Paralympic sports. If you think your child's physical disabilities are such that she would find more satisfaction in Paralympic competitions, there are several books that can help her learn more about Paralympic sports and competing on this level.

Some other associations or organizations for physically disabled children are United States Association of Blind Athletes, Wheelchair Sports USA, National Disability Sports Alliance, Disabled Sports USA, Dwarf Athletic Association of America, and the March of Dimes. All the professionals and volunteers associated with these organizations as well as with the Paralympic sports know how to specially outfit or rig wheelchairs, skis, bikes, and other equipment to make it possible for the disabled to participate. One snowboard instructor said that for just about *any* physical disability, he can figure out a way to rig the equipment so that the athlete can compete.

Whatever the disability, parents of physically disabled children should be careful about predetermining at what level their children can play. And, parents shouldn't allow their children to limit their visions of what they can do just because of their physical disabilities. Jim Abbott pitched in the major leagues with one arm. Hal Connolly won the gold medal in the hammer event in 1956. His left arm was withered because of an accident at birth. If at all possible, try to explore mainstream sports first. If they don't work out or seem inappropriate for your child, only then look for teams or leagues that are just for the disabled.

You've probably heard about the Special Olympics. Eunice Kennedy Shriver (one of John F. Kennedy's sisters) founded it in 1968. More than one million children and adults with intellectual disabilities participate in year-round sports training and athletic competition and other related programming. Special Olympics programs take place in 150 countries with more than 200 programs. There is no cost to participate.

To be eligible, a child must be at least eight years of age and identified by an agency or professional as having some intellectual disabilities or cognitive delays. Not all participants compete; some may only train and play. Instructors are often former star athletes or Olympians.

Special Olympics participants take the athlete oath: "Let me win. But if I cannot win, let me be brave in the attempt."

In October 2004, President George W. Bush signed Special Olympics legislation that had unanimous bipartisan support. This legislation provides $15 million per year for five years to fund the growth of Special Olympics programs.

Ask your child what sports he is interested in playing. Make an assessment of his physical skills and how these skills correlate with his stated interests. Evaluate the role his intellectual disabilities may play in his ability to learn and understand the basic moves of the sport. Special Olympics instructors and coaches have specialized training in helping with this process. Some children choose just to learn and play the sport; others may choose to compete. There is no pressure either way. Find out if Special Olympics programs are available in your area. The Special Olympics Web site—www.specialolympics.org—can help you locate any programs near you.

In the rest of this section, I will focus on the kind of physical disabilities that allow most children to pursue mainstream sports, leagues, teams, and lessons. Some of what follows may seem obvious to some parents of children with these physical disabilities; however, I hope it will provide some helpful information or insight.

The Deaf and Hearing-Impaired

Many deaf and hearing-impaired athletes play in all sports, with a few reaching the highest levels of their game—Amateur Athletic Union record holders, collegiate players, and professional players. When he was seventeen months old, baseball player Curtis Pride was diagnosed as 95 percent deaf. He played for the Montreal Expos and the Detroit Tigers. In 1993 he was the fifth deaf baseball player to have played in the major leagues.

As parents of deaf and hearing-impaired children know, most of their children do a good job of reading lips. This enables even profoundly deaf children to understand 70 percent or better of what the coach or instructor is saying. Learning an individual or team sport is certainly possible for most of them. A coach or teacher would have to make sure she is looking directly at the child so that the child can read her lips. The same goes for the other players or teammates. Of course, at times the action and the position/location of the coach will preclude the child's ability to read lips. Here your child will have to rely on hand signals and/or visual sighting. If the child must speak, others may have to listen carefully to understand him since often a deaf or severely hearing-impaired child is unable to speak clearly.

When observing deaf and hearing-impaired children play, most people are unaware of these impairments unless they knew beforehand, heard them speak, or saw them signing.

Teammates or other players are usually quite comfortable playing or learning with hearing-impaired peers. They usually admire them and value their contributions to the team or sport. Most teammates work cooperatively with them.

Parents of deaf children should realize that when their children play sports, they have to work hard to find ways to compensate and in doing so they can experience considerable stress. Compensating can cause deaf children to become cranky and tired. Also, when a deaf or hearing-impaired child realizes that he is missing some of the communication that is part of the game or sport, he may feel bad or stressed, especially if he misses some critical piece of information. He can become easily frustrated and needs understanding and support.

If you have a deaf or hearing-impaired child, you can let him play just about any sport he is interested in. Just be aware that some sports require more communication (receptive and/or expressive) than others and thus may make for more stressful sports to pursue. Watch to see how well your child seems to be handling the stress that comes with a particular sport, team, or coach. Remember that sports are games and that playing them should be fun. There is good stress and bad stress. Make sure there is not too much bad stress and that your child is enjoying himself.

The Blind and Visually Impaired

This group includes children who are blind or visually impaired. Finding the right sport for your partially visually impaired child requires that you take into account her interests and identify a sport whose elements are such that she can play safely and be reasonably competitive if she wants to compete.

Many visually impaired children can see shapes and even colors pretty well. With aiming devices some can even participate in sports generally requiring good eyesight, such as shooting and archery. Visually impaired children can certainly learn many sports and even be able to compete in most of them. For example, all can learn to swim, and most are able to compete. Some of the more common sports/events that partially sighted persons participate in include Alpine skiing, football, judo, and bowling.

If your child is blind, his options are greatly reduced when it comes to playing in mainstream sports leagues, teams, and gyms. He can learn some sports, like swimming, but he may not be able to engage in the sport on a competitive level. My sense is that generally speaking, individual sports hold more potential than team sports. I have heard about blind wrestlers, equestrian riders, and weight lifters. Erik Weihenmayer was the first and only blind man to climb Mount Everest. (To accomplish this he required considerable escort help from sighted climbers, including sherpas.) He has since undertaken to teach six blind Tibetan schoolchildren to climb areas near Mount Everest.

Considerable research would be necessary to evaluate your child's sports options in mainstream sports leagues, teams, and gyms. For special resources, check with the International Blind Sports Association or other organizations that serve the blind or visually impaired in your community.

During a question-and-answer session,
Erik Weihenmayer said:
"I've been climbing since I was 16 years old. That was my first love, rock and ice climbing, because I could feel my way up the pattern of the rock. There wasn't any ball that was flying through the air that was gonna hit me in the face."
Asked if being near a drop-off was frightening:
"It's an overwhelming and pretty scary sound, but I'm not looking, you know, thousands of feet down, so I'm not as freaked out as somebody looking down into some scary crevasse."[29]

Diabetes

Over 18 million Americans have diabetes; 206,000 of them are twenty and under. There are two kinds of diabetes, Type 1 and Type 2. Type 1 is more serious, and about 5 to 10 percent of people have Type 1; about 90 to 95 percent have Type 2. About one in every five to six hundred children have Type 1 diabetes. The number of children being diagnosed with Type 2 has increased dramatically because of, it is thought, the fact that more and more children are sedentary and overweight. While less serious than Type 1 diabetes, *untreated* Type 2 can be just as serious. Diabetes contributes to the death of more than 190,000 Americans per year.

There is also an alarming increase in the number of children being diagnosed with "pre-diabetes." Here, their blood glucose levels are elevated but not high enough to be diagnosed with diabetes. Those who do not exercise and who continue to overeat are at higher risk for developing Type 2 diabetes. About 41 million Americans have pre-diabetes. Sports and exercise can make it less likely that your child will develop this disease.

If your child already has been diagnosed with diabetes, his doctor has probably educated both of you on the basic treatment regimen: medication, diet, and exercise. People with Type 1 diabetes have bodies that make little or no insulin. Children with Type 1 diabetes usually require daily insulin injections. In Type 2 diabetes, the pancreas does not make enough insulin to keep the blood glucose levels normal. Those with Type 2 diabetes may be able to regulate their blood sugar levels through diet and exercise alone. Others have to take two or more oral medications that do two or more of the following: lower blood glucose levels, increase insulin sensitivity, and delay absorption of glucose from the gut. Some Type 2 diabetics require *no* medications after they lose weight and increase their activity. Thus they have a great incentive to exercise and participate in sports.

Whether your child has Type 1 or Type 2 diabetes, sports participation and exercise can be an important part of his treatment. In terms of playing sports, you should always obtain his physician's approval. What are some of the considerations before a child with diabetes selects and plays a sport?

Newly diagnosed children often become depressed and/or angry. They now have a serious medical condition that makes them different from other kids. They have to test their blood glucose levels numerous times during the day. They may have to give themselves, or if very young have adults administer, insulin shots. They have to maintain a strict diet and keep close track of what they eat—especially how much protein and how many carbohydrates. They will need to pick up their activity level if they have been inactive. When depressed or angry about their disease, some kids become noncompliant with their treatment and often end up back in the hospital numerous times, sometimes close to death. When I was a consultant to inpatient pediatrics, I saw many diabetic children whose attending doctors worried that they were depressed and wished to die because of their diabetes. Since being in private practice, I've had a number of diabetic children referred to me for the same reason.

Being involved with sports can help children feel as though they are still like most other children. However, newly diagnosed children often have wildly fluctuating blood glucose levels, at least in the early stages of treatment. It may take weeks or months before, working with their doctors, they find the right medications, the right dosages, and the right diet to control their blood glucose levels. Therefore, playing sports during this initial phase of treatment may not be a good idea.

In the early stages of learning how to manage his diabetes, a child may benefit from attending a sports camp or clinic just for diabetics. Here, doctors, nurses, and other volunteers help the child learn more about managing his diabetes while participating in sports. Your pediatrician should be able to tell you about these resources.

Once blood glucose levels have stabilized for a period of time, your child has shown good compliance with treatment, and has mastered the required diet, he can begin to seriously consider playing sports.

Generally, he can take up any sport, but some considerations are in order. Make sure that the sport allows time for him to periodically check his blood glucose levels. Blood glucose levels tend to drop during workouts, and extremely low blood glucose levels can be as dangerous as high levels. Sports with few time-outs (marathons) may be poor choices for the diabetic. He needs to be responsible enough to check his blood glucose levels at appropriate times and also to have his medications with him in case he needs to take them during practices or games. (Check to make sure that he's not so embarrassed in front of peers that he fails to do these things.) It's important that adults be around in case he develops symptoms requiring him to be taken to the emergency room. If you are not going to be at practices regularly, make sure the coaches and other adults know your child has diabetes and that they can identify the early signs of diabetic coma and insulin shock and know what the proper responses are. See to it that the coach or instructor is cooperative and makes it easy for your child to excuse himself to check his glucose levels or to take his medications. The key to playing healthily is for your child to really understand his illness and to be able to implement and manage his treatment program knowledgeably.

A number of athletic stars have diabetes. Swimmer Gary Hall, Jr., won gold medals in the 2000 and 2004 Olympics. Jim "Catfish" Hunter played baseball in the major leagues. Arthur Ashe was a famous tennis player. Boxer Sugar Ray Robinson had diabetes.

Asthma

Asthma is a serious illness, one that can lead to death if it is not controlled with medications and appropriate lifestyle adjustments. Controlling it takes considerable vigilance on the part of the child and the parent. Both should form a very close partnership with the treating doctor so that all are working cooperatively toward achieving good control of the illness. Sports participation should only be undertaken with the approval of your child's physician.

Some people with asthma seem to show no patterns to their symptoms. Others appear to manifest asthmatic symptoms only under certain conditions. For example, some people develop symptoms only when they are engaged in strenuous activity. This is called exercise-induced asthma. Others seem only to show symptoms when they are out in extremely cold weather. Some experience respiratory distress such as wheezing and shortness of breath when exposed to a specific histamine they are allergic to. For instance, some people develop asthma symptoms only after continued exposure to cat dander for several hours. For others, it may be only when they are outdoors, when the pollen count is high, or when they are exposed to some specific plant or weed they are allergic to.

If your child has asthma, it is important to know what kind of environments trigger asthmatic symptoms or attacks. This knowledge may be critical as you consider a sport for the child. For example, swimming is generally considered a good sport for asthmatics to take up because it helps them learn to control their breathing and the humid pool air helps them breathe better. Playing outdoor winter sports or sports played in the cold tends to be discouraged since asthmatics seem to have more trouble breathing in the cold. So skiing, figure skating, speed skating, and ice hockey are examples of sports that might be problematic for children with asthma.

With the permission of your child's doctor, consider her sport interests and proceed to explore those sports, providing they are not played in settings that are potentially dangerous for her. She also should be responsible about taking her medications. Almost all asthmatics use a minimum of two medications: one is a long-acting medication taken daily that controls the bronchial inflammation that is often the root cause of asthma; the other is fast-acting inhaled medication that relieves acute asthma symptoms. Your child should be able to identify the first symptoms indicating that she might be experiencing respiratory distress so that she quickly takes the correct medication. Make sure she is not reluctant or embarrassed to use her medications in front of teammates or coaches.

Her coaches or instructors should be informed that she has asthma so that they can take action if they notice symptoms of distress before she does. Tell other parents that your child has asthma so that if you are not present at a practice or game, they can keep an eye on her.

Children with exercise-induced asthma should obtain special instructions from their doctors with respect to playing sports and dealing with their asthma. While instructions may vary somewhat across people, generally athletes with exercise-induced asthma will use their fast-acting inhaler about fifteen minutes prior to exercise. They should warm up for six to ten minutes before beginning a full exercise or sport program and drink plenty of fluids. If symptoms arise, they should stop exercising. Cooling down at the end of their exercise is important, and actually, all athletes should do this.

Sports with intermittent periods of activity are considered best for children with exercise-induced asthma. These types of sports are less likely to cause symptoms, and they allow them to regain control of their breathing. Some of these sports include swimming, bowling, baseball, and golf.

As with other serious medical conditions, many famous athletes have asthma. They practically have a medical degree when it comes to their understanding of asthma. They are knowledgeable about the various medications in their arsenal. In short, they know how to manage their illness yet compete at very high performance levels. Bill Koch was an Olympic skier with asthma. Olympic gold medalist runner Jackie Joyner Kersee had asthma. Not only did he have diabetes, but famous baseball pitcher Catfish Hunter also coped with asthma!

*Amy Van Dyken won gold medals at the
2000 Olympics despite being able to take in
only 35 percent as much oxygen as persons
without asthma. In addition, because steroids
are banned in swimming competitions, she
could only take asthma medication that did
not work as well as steroids.*[30]

Children with Other Chronic Illnesses or Conditions

A number of children with chronic illnesses or conditions wish to participate in sports. Some of these conditions include spina bifida, cerebral palsy, and muscular dystrophy. Whether they can play regular mainstream sports depends on the sport they would like to play, and the nature, severity, and limitations of their conditions. Children with mild forms of these illnesses and/or few limitations of movement may be able to find a team or individual sport that they can enjoy and do well in. Keep in mind, with some conditions, a contact sport may be contraindicated and you may have to consider noncontact sports like swimming, bowling, and golf.

Some children with these chronic conditions may find more success in Special Olympics or Paralympic organizations and sports, or other, condition-specific organizations or associations. Again, a lot will depend on the specific condition, severity, and limitations as well as the resources in your community. Check also with local organizations such as cerebral palsy and muscular dystrophy associations.

Ideally, we want all children who want to play a sport, no matter what their physical condition, illness, or limitation, to find the right sport for them, to find the right venue or level (mainstream youth sports, Special Olympics, Paralympics), and to find enjoyment and success.

Special Situations

I WANT TO TOUCH on some special situations that may arise after your child has picked a sport, found a team or instructor, and has begun learning or playing the sport. Some of these situations are more likely to appear when playing team sports, but many of them are possible no matter what type of sport—individual or team—your child is playing. There will be situations that, without intervention, may jeopardize your child's choice of sport and team; he may want to quit the sport or team, or he may be asked to leave the team or sport.

Bullying

While the incidence of bullying probably varies somewhat from locale to locale, let's look at some recent statistics for the state of Colorado. A 2002 study by the Colorado Trust showed that "46 percent of kids were hit, shoved, kicked or tripped in a three-month period; and 18 percent had it happen five times or more in a month."[31]

We know that some athletes are bullies. Some of them bully their peers who do not play sports, a behavior that is part of what is called "jock culture." Others may bully their teammates or other kids at the gym. Whether to call certain behavior true bullying is, at times, contextual—you may have to witness the behavior and the context yourself to render an opinion. I have occasionally seen an older child say "boo" to a younger child when lining up during tae kwon do practice. Later the younger child is in line with the same older child and they are talking and laughing. The younger child is clearly neither afraid of nor intimidated by the older child. I think we have to be careful about labeling every questionable behavior as bullying.

You should assess three pieces of information to make a decision as to whether your child was bullied: the behavior toward him, his reaction at the time, and his relationship with the "bully" during practices and games over a period of time. Most bullying behavior is verbal rather than physical. Bullying is usually for the purpose, when there is a purpose, of annoying, intimidating, having control over, or making the victim feel afraid. If none of these seem to be taking place and your child is clearly comfortable with his teammate, then the behavior may be immature, it may be inappropriate, but it may not be bullying.

There will be times when the action is clearly bullying behavior: your child seems afraid around the teammate, goes out of his way to avoid him, and he begins to talk about quitting the lessons or the team. The psychological effects of bullying can vary with the nature of the bullying and the emotional makeup of the child. The effects can cause minor distress but at their worst, can lead to post-traumatic stress disorder or, in a few cases, suicide.

Sometimes just ignoring the bully is enough. Some bullies are fed by the reaction of their victims. By eliminating this reinforcement pattern, the bully no longer gets what he wants and reduces his bullying behavior. Sometimes it helps when other children or teammates stand together against the bully. There is strength in numbers, and this can often deter the bully from further unwanted behavior. To the extent that he can, your child should try to avoid the bully and never be caught alone with him.

When none of these efforts stops the bully, you should talk to the coach about what is happening. Some coaches have their antennae out for bullying behavior, others seem clueless, and yet others seem to turn a blind eye. The clueless types will need to be informed. In most instances, coaches will put a stop to bullying. Few coaches will tolerate a kid disrupting practice or the game by bullying other players. They also don't want any confusion as to who's in charge.

Admittedly, in some instances a coach may look the other way if the star athlete on the team is the bully. We may see this more in certain parts of the country than others. If this is the case and the coach continues to resist intervention, you have some options. One is to investigate the legal ramifications when a coach has been told of bullying behavior, yet does nothing. Look up the state criminal code as well as county and local ordinances. Document all bullying incidents: dates and locations, detailed description of what happened, and names of witnesses. Take photos if there has been any physical injury. If the bullying took place in a school program, see if your school district has an antibullying policy. If so, make sure it is enforced. Another option is for your child to look for another team or instructor. This will be unfortunate if you and your child have put in many hours researching sports and locating a team or instructor. But, playing sports must be fun and safe—safe physically *and* emotionally.

Teammates Who Are a Bad Influence

You may find that there are children in your child's gymnastics class or kids on his baseball team who are a bad influence on him and perhaps the other kids in the class or on the team. You may disapprove of some of their behavior. They may curse; they may be too aggressive. You may have heard that they do drugs or alcohol. Maybe they're terrible students who always boast about doing poorly or cutting class, even suggesting that your child play hooky with them.

It's important to know your child before you consider what to do about this situation. Some children are quite resilient and impervious to being dragged into bad behavior. They have a strong sense of self and a strong sense of values. Kids like this are seldom swayed into delinquent behavior. To the contrary, sometimes these kids are able to set a good example, and soon the "bad" kids are straightening up.

But, even if your child has his feet on the ground, be sure to monitor how the other kids' questionable behavior is affecting him. Does he speak about their behavior to you? Does he disapprove of their behavior? Keep your lines of communication open so that you know how he is reacting to his trouble-seeking teammates.

What if your child doesn't seem sure of himself and in the past you have worried that he may be more of a follower than a leader? Maybe you've seen him pick up bad habits from other kids. You're worried that one or two teammates may lead him astray.

A starting place is to have a conversation with your child. Tell him what you've been observing on the field, at a game, or at practice. Invite him to tell you his thoughts and feelings about this behavior. He may already have some very negative reactions toward these kids and their behavior. It's OK to tell him that you don't want him to pick up their bad habits. You may have to help him develop some assertiveness so he can rebuff the attempts of these kids who try to get him to join them in their shenanigans. You can find books that lay out, in simple ways, how children can become more assertive and how to stand up to peer pressure.

Point out some of the cool players and leaders on the team. They are probably doing better because they are paying more attention, working harder, and playing in a more cooperative manner. Encourage your child to emulate them. Remind him that he loves the sport. Praise his hard work to date. Tell him that if he wants to continue to progress in the sport and to become a better player, it makes sense not to be distracted by the behavior of a few kids and certainly not to allow himself to be influenced by them.

Look for the coach to intervene with some of these kids. Good coaches are good leaders. They set up a team or learning environment that is positive and healthy. If coaches see a few kids challenging this learning atmosphere, they will make it clear that the kids have to live up to certain expectations if they wish to remain on the team or continue with lessons. Many school teams as well as nonschool leagues do have some sanctions when a player's grades slip or when his behavior is unacceptable. As a parent, make sure such expectations or sports eligibility requirements are enforced.

If your child has already begun to display some of the unacceptable behaviors you are concerned about, *he* may be asked to leave the team or be placed on probation. If not, you can require him to leave the sport until you're assured that he will not revert to old ways. If he really enjoys playing, this action on your part may seem harsh, but it may be the only thing that motivates him to take responsibility for his behavior and not let a few kids influence him and jeopardize his playing. Playing sports is not a right. It's not mandatory. As the parent you want to make sure that playing sports is a positive experience. Stand your ground if you feel that your child is not reaping positive benefits from participation in a particular sport.

Your Child's Team Loses Consistently

Sometimes your child's team loses all its games. Your child seems to be losing interest also.

There are several scenarios for this situation. First, if it is the beginning of the season and the team has lost eight straight games, wait. I've seen many teams lose most or all of their initial games. Then, as the players begin to get better and gel as a team, they begin winning some games. Try to have some patience and see how the season progresses.

Sometimes teams that lose a lot are perhaps playing at the wrong level or in the wrong division. Ask around. Other leagues or divisions may be available for the team to join where it can be more competitive.

Occasionally, the addition of one or two new players can advance the team's chances. The coach may know of other kids who are good athletes who may be interested in joining the team. As a last resort, it is possible that your child is good enough to join a better team. You can explore this, but don't do it automatically before you gauge the impact on him. It's not good for a child to learn to bail out just because he's playing on a losing team.

There will be times that a team is just not good enough to win. In my experience, most kids on such teams struggle a little with their enthusiasm for the sport, but if they are having fun playing, they seem to take losing in stride. One kid told me that it wasn't fun losing but that he really liked his teammates, he was getting better, and he was having fun. He also said that he thought they'd win some games next year. Talk about the power of positive thinking!

So, if your child becomes discouraged when playing on a losing team, try to point out some of the positives. Praise him for how he is improving. Tell him what a good teammate he has become and how he's not hogging the ball like he used to. Remind him that losing is a part of life, and we can't win all of life's events.

Your Athletically Talented Child Plays with Minimally Talented Teammates

This is a common situation for the athletically gifted child. Early on, many teams take all comers and with the minimum play rule, all children, no matter their athletic talent, play the same amount of time. Some leagues rate each player as excellent, average, or below average. When putting together each team in the league, an equal number of players in each category are assigned to a team. The goal is to have evenly matched teams and thus more fairness in competition.

Of course, many leagues don't deliberately structure their teams to have players of varying abilities, yet that is often the outcome.

When this happens, it is understandable that children who are outstanding athletes may find playing with less talented teammates frustrating. (I have had this experience when playing volleyball recreationally and finding myself to be the best player on my team.) This can be frustrating for a variety of reasons. For one, the child's team may be less likely to win. For another, playing may become less enjoyable because one of the thrills of being a good player is having teammates who also are playing at a high level. This brings out the best in all players. Also, there are certain situations in which playing with weaker teammates may force the child to play down, below his usual level of play. For example, if a pitcher has a blazing fastball but his catcher can't catch it, he may have to ease up on his pitching. In soccer, a midfielder might not kick the ball as far forward if he feels his teammate is not fast enough to catch up with it before it goes out of bounds. If children become too frustrated or lose interest in playing, their parents may begin to hear them express the desire to quit the team.

In truth, this situation mirrors most adult life and work situations. Schools have master teachers and so-so teachers. In business, there are great managers and weak managers. Research labs have scientists who have the talent to win Nobel Prizes some day and scientists whose work is important but who will never make the scientific breakthroughs all researchers strive for. Even professional sports teams have the stars, above average players, and average players.

That said, how does the parent deal with the athletically talented child whose teammates are not on his level? Try to point out that as he progresses it is likely that he will be on teams in the future where the range between the better players and the weaker players is much narrower. It is also possible that by being one of the better players on the team, he is more likely to be chosen as the captain. He can hone his leadership skills. His coach may ask him to help teach some of the weaker players. This way, he can develop his leadership *and* teaching skills.

You might look into his playing in another league or on a different team, maybe in addition to the current team. If his playing level seems to plateau because he's not being challenged enough, besides seeking out another team, look into high-level clinics or camps for his sport—ones that only take the better players. Another possibility is to consider changing to or adding another sport.

Not every situation in life will be to our liking. But even less than desirable situations are tests of how we handle them, providing lessons we can learn from them. Can we make lemonade out of lemons? So empathize with your child, but help him figure out some solutions that make sense to him and encourage him to continue playing.

Your Child Loses Consistently

What if your child participates in an individual sport and loses consistently? You will need to figure out the reasons for this and also evaluate the impact losing is having on her. Let's begin with some of the more common reasons for losing:

1. Your child is at the bottom of her age bracket. Often competitions are by age. For example, swimming events are organized by age: six and under, seven and eight, nine and ten, and so on. It's not uncommon for swimmers at the bottom of their age bracket to do less well. When they're at the top of their age bracket, they do better.

2. Your child is competing against children who are clearly much better than she is. It may be that the level or division she is competing in is not appropriate for her. She may need to find a level where she can be competitive—meaning that she can

place occasionally. If this is the case, see if you can find a more appropriate competitive level for her.

3. There may be personal factors. She may have missed a lot of practices, or she may be recovering from an illness or injury. Once she attends more practices and/or is no longer suffering from the effects of an illness or injury, she may find that she is more competitive.

4. You may feel that her competitors seem to show better form. It may be that your child would benefit from more practice or a new coach.

5. If she seems to lose by close margins, it may be that she falters at the end. Talk to her and her coach about this. It's possible that she's caving in psychologically, or choking, and she may need some help to figure out why she is doing this and to help her break out of this pattern.

6. She may have too much on her plate and doesn't have enough time to put in the required efforts to get better. She may want to explore how important the sport is for her and whether she would like to give up a couple of other activities and direct more of her energies to the sport.

7. She may not have that competitive drive or motivation. (See chapter 7, "Competitiveness.")

8. Consider the possibility that she is competing in the wrong event or the wrong sport for her abilities. A sprinter who loses her swimming events may do better in long-distance events. A gymnast who struggles on the balance beam may find more success focusing on the vault. Perhaps she can look into a different individual sport or a team sport.

Those are the more common reasons why a child might be losing consistently. If the reasons are such that the problem can be corrected, fine. If, however, you can't figure out the reasons and/or after taking steps to correct the situation she is still losing, then you should see how losing is affecting her.

As mentioned, for some kids, just playing is the payoff. Winning or placing is not important to them. Clearly some children are really OK with this. They seem to enjoy playing the sport, they're having fun, and they're enjoying the interaction with other competitors or teammates. They feel like they're doing their best, and this gives them some satisfaction. They don't appear to be down or losing self-confidence. If this is the case, it may be fine for them to remain where they are. If, on the other hand, they are becoming discouraged, frustrated, angry, or disappointed, some change may be in order, especially if the hurt of always losing is stronger than the benefits of the sport. They can think about playing another sport—one they may be better at—or finding another league, team, or level at which they can be more competitive.

If you do find out that your child is quite upset over always losing, ask her what she wants to do. She may have some ideas in mind. If she can't come up with some ideas, you should come up with some options for her, laying them out in a neutral manner. Some of these options may include quitting sports completely, taking a break, changing coaches or leagues, changing her schedule so she has more time to practice, or taking up another sport. You may be quite surprised by how maturely she responds. She may even come up with some ideas you hadn't thought of. If they are reasonable ideas, try to support them.

Even if she chooses to quit sports entirely, this may have been a positive learning experience for her. It's OK for kids to learn that they may be good in some things and not as good in other things. Many children are not particularly athletic but play sports. They may not have experienced winning, but they have had some fun. They may have made some new friends, they've learned that some sports are harder than they look, and they may have reached a level of basic competence in a sport—they can swim, they can play tennis, or they can bowl. They may not be competitive in the sport, but they can pursue it recreationally, solely for pleasure. Depending on the sport, they may participate in it the rest of their lives. Maybe they'll be fans of the sport as adults. This can bring them considerable pleasure in the years ahead.

Your Child Is the Star of the Team or Wins All the Time in His Individual Sport

For the most part, this should be a cause for joy and not a problem. However, in some instances changes may need to be considered or discussed.

If your child is far and away the star of his team, it may be best for him and his development in the sport to consider joining a team that is a notch up and where the players are performing nearer to his level of play. When an athlete plays with teammates who are at his level or better, it usually brings out his best. He works harder and pushes himself more. He is unlikely to improve if his level of play is such that he can play at 75 percent and still be the star. Of course, there may not be a team or league appropriate to his level of play.

When a child is in an individual sport and he always wins and no competitor even comes close, the same concerns about his personal development in the sport arise. It may be that he is not playing in a league or division that most closely matches his performance level. Many individual sports have different divisions based on the prior times or records of the competitors. Be sure your child is enrolled at a level that provides appropriate competition so that he has an incentive to work hard and strive to achieve his personal best.

There's another reason why you might want to try to bump your child up to another team or a higher level of an individual sport. Sometimes resentment builds when teammates can never come close to playing as well as another player. Competition is always better and fairer when competitors are, within a range, comparable in ability.

Of course, your child may be participating at the highest levels of the sport possible and he wins all the time. If this is the case, smile and support his achievements. He may be good enough to play in college and even to win a college athletic scholarship. Colleges look for students with promise in individual sports, and more individual sports than ever are commanding scholarship monies.

Your Child Is Always Second String

Some children attend practices faithfully, work hard, and are motivated and enthusiastic. They have improved significantly since they first began playing. They have to play just as hard at practices as the starters since they have to be prepared and ready to go into the game. Also, they contribute to the team by pushing the first team in practice scrimmages. Most coaches do recognize their role and encourage them to help make the whole team better. But they are still second stringers.

Time and again, second stringers sit on the bench during games, and if they play at all, it is only for a few minutes. Most cheer their teammates on though they may feel a bit overlooked and unappreciated. They may have to struggle with feelings of disappointment and anger. Their parents may experience frustration, and at times behave inappropriately. A newspaper reported that a high school principal allegedly assaulted the volleyball coach because the principal thought his daughter spent too much time on the bench.

This situation happens mostly with competitive teams, including many high school teams. These teams do not follow the minimum play rule. The teams often play in leagues or divisions that participate in playoffs and state championships. The coaches, schools, players, and parents want to field the best players in order to increase the chances of winning.

If it becomes apparent to you that being second string is bothering your child, you and he should look at this situation to see if any options are available that might not only help him feel better but also improve his chances for more playing time.

A child may be consigned to the bench and see little playing time for several common reasons. One is that the child just is not good enough at his position to warrant much time on the field or court. A second occurs when the coach is not satisfied with your child's attitude or work ethic. Last, favoritism on the part of the coach can translate into less playing time.

The first reason may be clear to the coach and other players but perhaps difficult to see or admit to if you are the benched child or his parent. Both of you need to look at his performance and abilities objectively and compare them with his teammates. Perhaps he just needs to practice more. Or it may be that he has some weakness that a little extra work or practice can result in catching the coach's attention. A discussion with the coach can be helpful—he can identify where the weaknesses are and propose a way to get in some extra coaching or practice time. If your child is interested, think about sending him to a summer sports camp. He may improve enough to be a starter next season. It may be that just a little needed improvement prevents him from being a starter.

Another approach is to consider whether your child is playing in the right position. A child who is a forward in basketball may be better suited to be a guard. A child who plays offense may be a natural on defense. I have seen significant improvements in performance after a child has shifted positions.

After all the ways to improve his performance have been identified and implemented, it may be that he still is not good enough to play more. At this point you might want to consider another team or another sport that is more suited to his athletic skills. Research your choices. There may be a league or division in which the performance level of the players is closer to that of your child's, or there may be a team that plays by the minimum play rule.

If after your evaluation you still feel your child is as good as some of his teammates who are playing, you or your child should ask the coach about this. You may find out that he has not been happy with your child's attitude. Perhaps he doesn't play cooperatively. Maybe the coach feels that he doesn't try hard enough. Your child may be a goof-off during practices. If any of these are the case, ask the coach to speak with your child, to let him know of his specific concerns. Your child will need to weigh his desire to play against his poor attitude. It comes down to showing the coach that he really does want to play by making the necessary changes in his attitude.

Sadly, there are instances of coach favoritism. While infrequent, it is a tough situation to change. Even when the favoritism is obvious, it's a rare coach who will admit to it. If the favoritism seems obvious to all, it may help if you speak with the coach or league officials or the principal if it is a school team. Check with your child first. She may not want you to take any action. Your need to obtain justice for her is understandable, but other dynamics may be in play that may make doing nothing the wiser course. If this is the case, she may want to stick it out. She may be

disappointed at not playing more, but she may be reaping other benefits—being with her friends, enjoying the practices, and getting exercise
and becoming fit. And, if she is on a school team, she'll probably get her
letter at the end of the year whether she's second string or the star of the
team. Many college admissions deans like to see an applicant who has
played a sport for several years and lettered in it. Besides her decent
grades, they see that she has been able to manage her time well and that
she is not just a bookworm. And they don't have to know that she was
second string—unless she makes that the topic of her admissions essay!

Then again, she may be interested in finding a team whose coach
doesn't play favorites and she has the opportunity of more playing
time. If you find another team that is right for her, ask the parents
about coach favoritism before you sign her up. No need to go through
this situation twice!

Conflict with the Coach

This is one of the hardest situations to deal with. Not only must you
and your child view this situation honestly so that you understand
some of what is going on, but both of you will have to decide what
steps to take. Should either of you speak with the coach? Which one?
Perhaps doing nothing is best.

A high school basketball point guard spoke with me about his
coach. He talked about incidents when the coach would bench him
immediately after he missed a shot. This isn't too unusual by itself;
many coaches employ this technique when a player is not performing
well. However, he said that when teammates missed their shots, the
coach rarely benched them. The coach would also tell him to shoot
whenever he was open. At other times he would remind him that the
point guard's task is to direct the play by setting his teammates up for
shots and passing to them when they are open. (The point guard is
sometimes called the on-court coach.) I asked if these directions confused him, and he said yes. He no longer knew if he should shoot or
if he should set up the play by passing the ball to his teammates—his
confidence in himself was shaken. Further discussion revealed that over
time he had become anxious and his field goal percentage was down.

To him, the coach was sending mixed messages. He wanted to please the coach, but he didn't know what to do. It seemed that he couldn't do anything right even though he had been one of the better players on the team. He began to develop stomach pains that had been checked out medically. This is when he first came to see me.

Many different scenarios point to conflict with the coach. Talk with your child about how he sees the conflict. Try to see what role, if any, he has played in the conflict and what role the coach played. If you can help him disentangle the threads of the conflict, a solution may become evident.

Underlying some of these conflicts is the strong desire of the coach to win. In any game there are 101 decisions to make, both tactical and strategic. Under pressure, the coach may not always be able to make the best decisions. Coaches are human, and while we hope that they treat all the players equally, some may find certain players easier to coach than others. A coach may be unsure of how to deal with a child who generally plays well but who does not do well in clutch situations. An athlete's playing style might remind the coach of own style from his own playing days, and the coach might end up—consciously or unconsciously—favoring this player or giving him more attention. The stars of the team may be allowed more freedom to make decisions; the other players may find their moves second-guessed.

Some conflicts are outgrowths of what people prosaically call personality conflicts. A hardheaded coach may buck horns with a strong-willed player. A coach may feel that one of his players is a bit of a wimp and lashes out at him, perhaps thinking he can toughen him up.

As you can see, these conflicts can be extremely complicated. Figuring them out and finding solutions is difficult. Sometimes a coach should be challenged and called on his behavior. Often it is best that the child do this, especially if he is in high school. He has to learn to stand on his own two feet. He may find doing this scary and intimidating, but you can role-play with him before he meets with the coach. Help him come across constructively, pointing out the conflict but with little blaming (even though there may be good reasons to blame the coach). The gist of your child's message should be, "You want me to do well. I want to do well. How can we work together to bring this about?" If you have reason to believe that your child has done something in the past to help set up this conflict, help him overcome his pride so that he can admit his role in it. That can go a long way toward setting up the right context and tone when speaking with the coach.

After evaluating the conflict, you may come to feel that there is no easy solution to it. If you feel that to continue with this coach is really harmful to your child either psychologically and/or in his development as a player, then he may need to consider finding a new coach. This decision should not be made quickly.

I would suggest that you speak with the coach about the conflict if your child is in grade school or middle school. Again, I recommend presenting your observations in a calm, non-accusatory manner. When coaches are attacked, they can become defensive. Try to sound like you're problem solving and that you want to be helpful but you'd like his help also. Remind him that what you both want is a good team, and a team where all the players can do their best.

Conflicts with coaches of individual sports can be more difficult to resolve. The relationship between coach and athlete is often close. Sometimes a child has worked with the coach for years, and a bond may exist in spite of the conflict. The coach may be known for his expertise and for his record in producing top athletes in the field. Leaving this coach may leave you with few other coaches to choose from.

John achieved his black belt a few months short of his ninth birthday. His first and only tae kwon do instructor was a famous master who was a ninth-degree black belt. John respected him, and a bond had been built up over six years. It seemed that the master, because he was fond of John, held higher expectations of him than he did of his other students. However, the teacher was overly strict and rigid, and as John grew older, he felt stifled. He wanted to ask his master some questions but was too intimidated. He found that he could never relax during practices. John and his parents were in a quandary. John felt loyal to his master—a part of him wanted to leave and a part of him wanted to stay. By now John had his second-degree black belt.

This dilemma was finally solved when the master moved his tae kwon do studio to another city. If John had been entirely comfortable with the master, his parents would have found a way to drive the extra distance. Because of the conflict, they saw this as an opportunity to find another instructor. After some research, they located a well-regarded instructor, and John started with him. It has been two years since John made this move, and he has blossomed and has been much happier, though there is still some sadness, and maybe some guilt, at leaving his master.

This was a personality conflict that probably was not resolvable. John's master was elderly, his English was barely understandable, and he was authoritarian. Neither John nor his parents could picture having a conversation with him about this. Ultimately John came to feel that his master was the right instructor for him for those first six years. Later, John's needs were different and his master was no longer the right person for him.

Not all coach-player conflicts can be resolved. Do your best to analyze the conflict with your child; consider the impact it is having on him. Speak with the coach if it seems like the right thing to do. If the conflict can be resolved or at best ameliorated, fine. Sometimes adjustments on both sides can go a long way toward reducing the conflict.

If it can't be reduced and you feel the conflict is harmful to your child, finding another coach may be in your child's best interest.

Cutthroat Soccer (or Basketball or Hockey)

Certain sports, both team and individual, have teams or clubs that are considered elite. These teams select only the most advanced players. More children are rejected than are accepted. Both players and their parents often see these elite teams or travel clubs as the best path to success in the sport and a way to increase the chances for college athletic scholarships. Certain clubs and coaches are known for producing stars. College coaches and athletic directors troll these clubs, on the lookout for next season's standouts.

There are two problems with these teams. One is that some begin recruiting third graders. Some parents wonder how healthy it is when their eight-year-old child is subjected to a cutthroat tryout and selection process. A second concern is the intensity of the competition and the demands such teams place on its players. Practices are often five to sixdays a week, many of these teams travel extensively for games, and a whole family's life can revolve around the child's team or club. Other children in the family may come to feel that their needs are being neglected.

To be sure, many children are selected for these teams or clubs at an early age and play on them through high school. They excel early on and thrive on the competition and the high performance level demanded. Some are good enough to be offered college athletic scholarships.

However, parents and their kids need to consider some of the possible downsides to participation at this level.

For starters, many youth experts such as pediatricians and sports psychologists feel that this level of competition is not appropriate for children under ten. Some would say twelve is the earliest age a child should play at this level. They question whether very young children can emotionally handle the pressure of heavy competition when winning is the only goal. The physical demands of such teams can be daunting. These teams force a young athlete to specialize too soon; many experts point out that it's best for young athletes to play several sports at a time and then only specialize in one sport when they are older, perhaps when they reach late middle school or high school. One of the advantages of doing this is the likelihood of finding the right sport. After playing several sports for a few years, the child can make a better decision about which sport is his best sport. Then he can direct his efforts toward that sport.

Another downside is that in spite of considerable talent and hard work, your child may not be accepted on the team. This type of losing may be worse than if his team loses, because it is personal. He may feel devastated or angry. Parents have to deal with their disconsolate child. Picking up the pieces and trying to figure out the next step may be a challenge. Speak with your child about his various options. One may be to think about trying out again. Many athletes recall that they had to try out for a team repeatedly before being accepted. If your child really isn't good enough for the team, look for another league or team just below the level of the one he was rejected by. Once he's playing again he will feel better. If he is playing only this one sport, it may be a good time to encourage him to go out for another sport, either in addition to the current sport or instead of it.

Reassure him that you love him no matter what, and praise him for his hard work and for his dreams. Point out that not all dreams come true but that having dreams and working hard to realize them is a good life experience, and sports reflect life.

Parents should look at their own motives before encouraging their children to try out for one of these clubs. Sometimes parents become intoxicated with the glory of their child's play on the field. There can be some vicarious pleasure and excitement when their children are stars. Ironically, some of the same parents who at one point had reservations about elite teams are the very parents who push their children onto such teams.

Competition between kids turns into competition between parents and towns. Bob Bigelow, a former NBA player, has spoken out against this: "It's purely about adult ego—we have to keep up with the other towns. Soon we'll have prenatal soccer in this country." [32]

Before encouraging a child to try out for one of these teams, make sure that her abilities seem to match the level of play of the elite teams, especially the level of the team she is trying out for. Does she appear to thrive on pushing herself to get better and better? Does she love to practice; does she like to put in extra time practicing, even beyond what is required?

*Wynton Marsalis, the famous trumpeter,
said, "If you want to be different, you got to
do something different. If you practice an
hour a day, you'll be like everybody who practices an hour a day. If you want to be great,
you be the one doing five hours a day."* [33]

How does she handle losing? Does she have that competitive drive? Does she want to notch up and try out for one of these teams? Is she aware that she may be rejected? Does she have the right perspective if she is not chosen?

There are risks when very young children play on elite teams. Parents should consider them before moving ahead. Even though your child may look ready, he may not be. Of course, it may not be possible to anticipate this beforehand. If he is all enthusiasm but there are little clues that he is not ready, do not ignore these signs. Are his expectations realistic? He may be good enough for an elite team, but he may never be good enough to play in college or compete on the professional level. After playing on a demanding team or participating in a highly competitive individual sport for four or five years, he may become burned out and reject the sport entirely. After playing since they were four or five, many thirteen-year-olds have had enough and leave organized youth sports. A number of children quit because of the pressure to win. It just isn't fun anymore. Quitting at this age is sad for a number of reasons but especially because they lose out on the high school sports experience— generally a positive experience for many athletes.

Perhaps the biggest risk is the possibility that your stated values— learn a sport, enjoy, have fun—may go by the wayside. Your child and you may succumb to the "winning is all" motto and all the pressures associated with that. He may rehash a loss for days on end or continually blame himself for an error on the field or for a fall on the ice. He may be tense and stressed most of the time, but especially before competition. Life becomes like a pressure cooker. All of this happens so gradually that you can barely remember the simple pleasures you and your child experienced when he first took lessons or played on his first team. You may wake up one morning and realize that this doesn't feel very healthy or balanced. So watch to see if your values have become but a dim memory. If so, you can help your child change course and look for a different level of competition.

Once you've taken into account the risks and you've assured yourself that your child is physically and emotionally ready to upgrade to an elite team, some practical considerations are in order. Can you afford the costs involved? They can be substantial—one travel soccer club in the New York suburbs costs $1,600 a year and there are many additional expenses on top of that. Some parents pay out thousands of dollars a year to send their children to elite sports camps or to attend sport schools year-round. What about the time requirements? These teams are time burners and can consume hours of your time—transporting your child to and from practices, and traveling to and attending games or meets. Family vacations may become a thing of the past. Many of these teams play year-round and penalize players who go off on family vacations. Can your child balance the pressures of playing for one of these teams and keep his grades up at the same time? If the other children in the family are not into sports but are involved with other extra-curricular activities, is there enough time left over for you to be involved in their activities? Will you be able to attend their school plays, musicals, dance recitals, or concerts? Parental attention and involvement is often in short supply, especially with single parents or families whose parents both work. Some families can handle having many balls in the air without any dropping to the floor. Other families don't do as well, and some kids can get lost in the shuffle. Make sure that there is enough of you to go around.

I Just Want to Play Baseball (or Soccer or Basketball)

Some athletic children resist any attempt on your part for them to play more than one sport. They don't seem interested in other sports, and they may give various reasons for this. They may be very good at the one sport and are quite content to stay with it. Most of their friends play on the team or club. Some kids have a bias against certain sports. While a second sport really fits your child's athletic abilities and talents, he may feel that it's not cool. Whatever the rationales given, if the child is under twelve, tell him about the benefits of playing a second or third sport. What are these benefits?

- Certain sports are not played year-round; some are played only one season a year. Taking up another sport helps keep him fit year-round.

- Other sports help build up other abilities—abilities that might help play the primary sport at a higher level. This is a cross-training benefit.

- When the child is ready to specialize in a sport, he will make a better decision on which one he likes the best or which is his best sport.

- Sometimes a child will suffer an injury that can end his playing days in one sport, yet the injury does not prevent him from playing another. A hand injury might be devastating for a child who is a pitcher, but he can still play soccer.

- Burnout is less likely if a child plays more than one sport, then concentrates on one or two of them when he is older.

- A child's interests may change over time, and he may become less interested in his chosen sport. Now that he's ready to play another sport, it may be too late. Some sports cannot be taken up in eighth or ninth grade. The learning curve and experience necessary to compete in the sport at this level is just too great.

Youth sports experts and psychologists all agree that young athletes should not specialize in one sport. They differ somewhat on the age that specialization is appropriate, but many feel it should not begin before high school. Even so, a number of these experts prefer for children to play more than one sport through high school.

There are other reasons a child should not play only one sport. Doctors are seeing a dramatic increase in overuse injuries in young athletes. When more than two dozen sports medicine doctors were interviewed, they cited one factor as the prime cause for the surge in overuse injuries in children: "specialization in one sport at an early age and the year-round, almost manic, training for it that often follows."[34] Children are candidates for overuse injuries when they play one sport, practice several hours every day, play year-round, and play this sport on a school team, two travel teams, and attend several camps for their sport if and when the season is over.

Also, I've had a number of adults tell me that they wished they had played more than one sport when they were kids. On looking back they have come to realize there were other sports they might have been better at if only they had branched out and tried them when they were younger. There's no way of finding this out if a child plays only one sport.

A number of Olympic and professional athletes played multiple sports when young but eventually focused on one sport. Some postponed making this difficult decision until professional recruiters from two different sports approached them. John Elway played baseball and football in college. Professional teams of both sports drafted him. Fortunately for the Denver Broncos, he chose to specialize in football and led the team to two consecutive Super Bowl wins.

If you are able to convince your child to take up other sports, how does he go about figuring out which one or ones to add to his repertoire?

His sports interests as well as specific athletic skills will often determine which additional sport(s) he will choose. He may only play one additional sport because of time constraints. In general, if only two sports are going to be played, I like kids to have the experience of playing an individual and a team sport because some of the psychological and personality benefits differ. If he plays three or more sports, often only one individual sport is in the mix, with the rest being team sports that he plays in different seasons. However, some young athletes are able to play more than one individual sport. A soccer player may also play golf and tennis—each played at different times of the year.

If your child is somewhat neutral about which sport to add, both of you can research those sports that may best give him a leg up in his primary sport, or that give him some variety, or that force him to develop very different skills. Maybe his primary sport is not particularly strenuous. Perhaps a second sport should be one that really gives his cardiovascular system a workout and increases stamina. If his first sport is running, perhaps the second sport can involve his upper body more. One sport may require a short burst of energy with little or no thinking required. Maybe the second sport can be one that requires some analytical skills and strategizing. One sport may be a strenuous contact sport like lacrosse, the other a moderately strenuous, noncontact sport like golf. If he is playing a gross-motor sport like basketball, the second sport can be a fine-motor sport such as archery. Realistically, an athlete will probably play certain sports only in his younger years. Football and field hockey are examples. Because of this, it's wise to choose a second sport that can be a lifelong sport. Golf and swimming can be pursued well into a person's eighties or longer.

If your child is going to play two sports, there is value in choosing ones somewhat opposite in nature, such as some of the above examples. By playing two very different sports, your child is less likely to burn out in either one. In sports, variety can be the spice of life.

As you can see, lots of different combinations of sports can be considered. Over a period of five or six years, children with above average athletic skills may have tried a number of different sports. By doing this, they have probably learned which sports are the right ones for them. They can engage in multiple sports until the time comes when they want to specialize in only one. Or, there may come a time when other, nonathletic interests appear and they want to reduce their sports involvement. They may choose to focus on only one of their sports.

Are there instances when it is OK for the young child to zero in on only one sport? There are several. Your child may be minimally athletic. In this case, he may not be capable of learning more than one sport at a time. If he's found a sport he's interested in and he can play adequately, then it may not make sense for him to learn other sports. Ironically, the less seriously the child pursues athletics, the more it makes sense to pursue fewer sports. He's just playing mainly for fun and he's not interested in making elite teams or advancing to higher competition levels. Another child may have other interests that are more important to him than sports, but maybe he wants to play for fun and social reasons, for example, his friends play.

Many decisions must be made along the way, and a wise and sports-knowledgeable parent can help guide his child during these years. Since so much of a child's life is wrapped up in sports, parents should be involved with these decisions, whether directly or indirectly. Some children need some direct, hands-on guidance. Other children are capable of making good decisions mostly on their own, but they may want their parents to be hovering around, sort of like genies, invisible, but there if needed.

Playing sports can build character, increase personal responsibility, and promote emotional growth. With all the hours a child (and you) invests in sports, be sure that the decisions are healthy ones.

Raising a Champion

Perhaps few other topics in youth sports can stir up as much controversy as the efforts on the part of some parents to groom their athletic two-year-olds to be elite athletes and champions. One parent suggested that if it's OK to push your child to be a doctor, why is it so wrong to push another child to be a professional quarterback?[35] Let's look at two scenarios.

The Academic Track

Jim's parents are both professionals; one is a physician, the other is a professor of economics at an Ivy League school. They believe Jim is very bright, and they wanted the best academic opportunities for him. They enrolled him in a well-regarded preschool, known for its strong emphasis on academics, especially for its motto, "Kids read by four." Graduates of this preschool are more likely to be admitted to the Great Books grade school. Ninety percent of its graduates are accepted at the Premier Studies high school. Eighty percent of its graduates make it into an Ivy League college. Jim's school years are all mapped out by the time he is two.

As it happens, Jim *is* quite bright, and he sails through these various private schools. In high school he was a whiz kid in science, and because his school was known for its excellent science program, a number of professors from Harvard often attended the school's science fair. A Harvard professor came, saw Jim's work, and immediately told the admissions dean at Harvard to try to woo Jim to go to the university with a complete tuition and room-and-board scholarship. Jim was accepted by several Ivy League schools, and eventually he did choose Harvard. Jim now has a PhD in physics and is thought to be on track to win a Nobel Prize for his research.

The Athletic Track

Mark's parents were both star athletes in college, and his mother went on to play on the U.S. Olympic basketball team. His father was a national champion gymnast before he suffered a career-ending injury. They saw that, at age two, Mark seemed to be well coordinated. He ran fast, he could throw and catch a ball, and ride his bike. They bought a children's basketball set, with the basket about five feet off the ground. One day they noticed that Mark was making all his shots. When he turned three, they decided to start him in a Basketball for Tots program taught by a retired college coach. Graduates of this program played on a club team coached by a former NCAA player. Scouts from the various high school basketball powerhouses in the area often attended the games played by this team. They knew the players were talented and well coached. In turn, some of the Division I colleges scouted several of the high schools in the area. They knew that many of the players came up through this elite system, and they wanted to make sure they didn't miss any future stars. Of course, some of these colleges were known to produce NBA-worthy players. Mark did begin playing basketball with Basketball for Tots, and he eventually was good enough to be drafted by one of the NBA teams. He played for several years before he retired.

In both tracks, the parents believed that their child was or could be exceptional in an area, and they laid out plans to give the child the most opportunities to advance in that area. Jim's parents saw to it that Jim had the finest educational opportunities. Mark's parents saw to it that Mark had the finest athletic opportunities. Both children benefited from these opportunities and were able to expand their talents. Both are happy adults and very grateful for their parents' efforts and sacrifices.

Is there anything wrong with these scenarios? On the face of it, no. There doesn't seem to be anything wrong with a parent who sees that his child has some special talent or ability and for him to help the child develop that ability. Both boys were obviously exceptional from a young age. Their parents saw their talent and pursued ways to encourage their natural abilities and to maximize their chances to stand out. If either child wasn't interested, wasn't talented, or wasn't motivated to excel, he wouldn't have accomplished what he did. Might either one have achieved what he did if he wasn't exposed to all those opportunities? We will never know for sure, but it is likely that some children like Jim and Mark would have achieved greatness without all the additional, special opportunities and some would not have.

Having said this, there are a lot of scenarios to consider—any one of which can abruptly derail the path to athletic greatness.

1. A two-year-old athletic prodigy may not look so exceptional when she is eight. The motor skills of her peers have developed and caught up with hers. She is still a natural athlete, but her exceptional abilities when she was two are no longer as exceptional.

2. A child's figure skating abilities are such that from age four until age twelve, he wins most of his contests. At twelve, he begins to lose more often because now he is expected to do certain jumps and axels. In spite of considerable effort and practice, it seems that he just is not able to do the jumps required for competition. His parents consult with a sports physiologist, and after taking some leg measurements and putting him through other tests, he concludes that the child probably will not be able to perform the needed jumps because of some physical limitations due to the length of certain leg muscles and tendons and poor jump height because of his lack of power. Another child has excelled in basketball until he was fifteen. His peers shoot up in height but he doesn't. He is now one of the shortest players, and defenders who are six feet tall easily block his shots. In spite of having been a star player up

to this point, he realizes that he is not good enough to continue playing basketball at his height and skill level and that he will have to switch to a sport where height is not a factor. (A short basketball player can make it to the professional level, but he has to be a truly outstanding player. The Denver Nuggets have a player who is five feet five.)

3. It takes much more than sheer athletic ability to become a champion. A champion will need to sustain his motivation and interest in the sport over many years. He will have to make countless sacrifices over the years. Long hours of practice are ahead of him—working out when other kids seem to be off doing fun things. He has to have mental toughness. He will have to overcome plateau periods—times when he is not improving. There will be injuries and surgeries with weeks of physical therapy and recovery, and times when he loses even though he is clearly one of the best. Only a fraction of those children who start out looking like they will make it to the top are able to stay the course.

Many child athletic stars have quit in their teens. Some have burned out, others have maxed out—they are no longer improving, or they have grown too big or too tall, or haven't grown big enough or tall enough for their sport. Others lost interest in the sport. Whatever the reason, their rising star has fallen. Some quit the sport completely; others go on to enjoy the sport on purely a recreational basis.

Mindful of all of these potential pitfalls—many of which are not in your control—how should parents proceed when they think they have the next Michael Jordan or Maria Sharapova on their hands?

• Keep your grip on reality. The odds are very slim that a child of two will ever reach the professional ranks or make it to the Olympics. For example, of the thirty NBA teams, each team can have a maximum of 15 players on its active roster, so the total number of men who play professional basketball in this country at any one time is 450. The NBA is global, and it recruits players from all over the world, not just the United States. Similar odds pertain to almost all sports, including individual sports.

- Be aware that it's easy for your child to look wonderful in the early years of competition. As the level of play or performance becomes greater or more difficult, what was a snap at five may not be a snap at ten.

- The kids who were playing with him in the early years may have just been enjoying a taste of the sport. They were not necessarily serious players. Now they have dropped out, and the remaining players are better.

- Make sure your child loves the sport and enjoys competing. It's important that he is motivated and that you don't have to push or cajole him to practice.

- Look for signs that your child may not be enjoying it as much. If you see such signs, talk to him about this. He may want to quit. Tell him that this is OK. He may need to hear this from you. It may be that he has continued playing because of you—he thought you'd be disappointed or angry with him if he quit. He may have been sticking with the sport because he saw that it was a big part of your life.

- If you think your child's interest in the sport is waning, present several options. Taking a break, adding another sport, changing coaches or teams, reducing the level of competition—these and other options more specific to your situation should be explored. Listen to what your child is saying. Don't attack his reasoning. He may not be able to express his feelings or thoughts in the most logical or understandable manner. He may quit the sport for good. Or he may quit and then later realize that he really misses it and wants to go back. Interestingly, girls drop out of competitive sports at a rate that is six times higher than that of boys.

- As children reach their teen years, they may begin to rebel. If you have pushed your child year after year to stay with a sport he has come to dislike, he will probably rebel against playing the sport. He can do this in many ways other than quitting. Deliberately losing or not doing his best are great ways to thwart his parent's wishes.

- Remember that your child's development and interests are not static. As she grows older, she may want to pursue other interests, some of which may not include sports. She may decide that her interest in theater is stronger than her interest in volleyball. Continuing in volleyball, even though she is very good, would not allow her time to attend rehearsals and perform in the school plays. You may see years of hard work go down the drain. She's ready to move on, and who knows? Her acting talents may be considerable. Wherever acting takes her, she knows firsthand the importance of practice and dedication. She may go on and play volleyball recreationally. Or she may become a volleyball coach—if she's not performing on Broadway.

- Even though you feel your child has the potential to be a champion, you may see indications that suggest to you that expectations should be lowered. He may show signs that the level of performance or competition required is having an impact on other areas of his life in negative ways. He seems unhappy, he's hanging out with the wrong kids, his grades are slipping, he's moody and acting depressed, or he's unduly stressed a week before competition. These may be signs that he's not emotionally able to handle the high performance demands of his sport. Maybe the pressure of trying to be a star is too much for him. It may be that he would be happier notching downward and playing the sport at a lower level of competition. It's important to talk with your child about this situation. Letting him drop out of the path to being a champion may the best move. Sometimes a sports psychologist can help with this situation and help clarify what the child really wants to do.

The well-known sports psychologist Harvey Dorfman[36] suggests the following paradigm for success in life and sports:

Dorfman notes that desire alone is not enough to succeed in sports; the athlete must be willing to "translate desire into action." He needs to set down the goals required to bring about success, then dedicate himself mentally and physically to the actions that will enable him to meet his goals.

The goals cannot be too vague or general, for example, "I want to swim faster." (All competitive swimmers want to swim faster.) Rather, the goals should be more specific and a behavioral action should be set forth to meet the goal—"I want to cut two seconds off my time in the hundred meters. My turns are the weakest part of my race. I plan to practice my turns for thirty minutes after every practice." The first statement is the goal, the second identifies the weak link or problem, and the third specifies a behavior or action the athlete is going to take to bring about the goal.

Simply put, does your child have the desire and the right goals and shows the necessary determination to be a champion? A child who says he wants to win yet goofs off during practice or displays other self-defeating behaviors is not translating desire into action. Athletes need to learn to make realistic goals, but aiming a little higher than what they feel they are actually capable of doesn't hurt.

"Success is aiming for the stars, because if you fall short, you're going to land on the moon, and there are not too many people on the moon now, are there?"

—Olympic gold medal swimmer Amy Van Dyken

Both the parents and the child must be in agreement on the goals and the steps that are necessary to reach those goals. Parents must be vigilant—see to it that their child is handling the pressures that increase incrementally as he advances to yet higher levels of performance.

The history of sports is replete with many instances of tragedies that come from the inordinate pressures of high-level training and performance. Top athletes have been known to suffer from serious depression and even become suicidal after failing to win the desired medal or failing to qualify for the Olympics.

Al Heppner's race was the 50-kilometer walk, and he wanted to compete in the 2004 Athens Olympics. However, six months before the Olympics, he came in fifth in the qualifying event. A few days later, he killed himself by jumping off a bridge.

Canadian backstroker Elaine Tanner seemed a sure bet to win the gold in the 100-meter backstroke event in the 1968 Olympic Games in Mexico City. She set the Olympic record in both qualifying races before the final. Right before the final race, her inexperienced coach gave her advice that her competitor overheard. That competitor won the gold. Though Tanner did win two silvers and a bronze, she could not cope with missing the gold. For the next twenty years she suffered severe depression, anorexia, two failed marriages, dead-end jobs, and losing contact with her children.[37] Gymnasts who have shown great promise have either died or ruined their health and left the sport because of extreme dieting or starvation in their effort to keep their weight down.

The training that these athletes go through and the pressures and stresses of trying to win can be too much for some, especially for those whose whole life is dedicated to winning the gold. If these older and more experienced athletes cannot handle the pressures of high-stakes competitions, make sure your child can, or help him find ways to reduce the pressure.

Athletes at this level must be driven. But if their happiness and sense of worth depend solely upon winning, then they obviously have lost a healthy perspective on themselves and on life. Make sure that as your child proceeds along the path to broken records and gold medals that he never loses the sense that at the end, his sport is a game. Moreover, athletic careers for most Olympians or professional players are over by age thirty-five, for many, sooner. The child has a whole lifetime ahead of him, and his career or main efforts are not going to be athletic performances. Make sure that he's having fun and enjoying himself and that winning doesn't become a do-or-die endeavor. Tennis superstar Martina Navratilova cautions the athlete who only lives to win, "The moment of victory is much too short to live for that and nothing else."

> *Norwegian speed skater Aadne Sondral
> referred to advice he was once given. "If
> I am not man enough without the medal,
> I will never be man enough with it."
> Sondral went on to say after winning the
> gold in the 1998 Olympic Games, "I'm
> the same guy I was an hour ago. The only
> difference is that I skated some fast laps."* [38]

Make sure your child knows about athletes who have developed a healthy perspective toward their sports and toward winning and losing. Their stories are often inspiring, and your child can learn important lessons from them.

In summary, if you placed your child on the "champion track" when she was quite young, you should acknowledge that this was your agenda and goal, even if it was well meaning. There are many reasons why she may go off track. Be sure to allow her many escape hatches to leave her sport and to pursue other interests. Make sure that you don't pressure her to stay on track. At thirteen, or twenty, she is not the same person who showed great promise when she was two.

Obviously, not every child is able to make it to the top or achieve his dreams. What happens when the child tops out short of the goals he has been working toward for years? Grooming a potential champion is often a whole family enterprise. For years, family life, time, and finances have been taken up by this child's goal. If he quits the sport or stays with the sport but at a lower, less pressured and competitive level, there may be relief but there may also be a letdown. Family members may even find themselves grieving at the loss of a dream. Take this opportunity to reassure your child that it is really OK. Keep a close eye on him to make sure that his disappointment does not turn into despair or depression. Don't let him take on some demanding new goal too soon. This may be a good time for everyone in the family to relax for a while. Eventually, it's good to review all the interests of family members, how much time has been freed up, and how to redirect the family's energies.

How Do I Know If My Child Is Doing Too Much?

Parents of natural athletes want their child to do well in sports. But most parents also want their kids to do well in school and to have other interests besides sports. In short, they want their child to be well rounded and balanced. Let's take a look at a well-rounded athlete.

Max is a sophomore and an athlete at Cherry Creek High School, where he carries a 4.0 grade-point average. He started competitive athletics when he began running middle distances of 5,000 and 10,000 meters at age five. At ages eight and nine, Max set two records for 5,000 meters in the eleven and under division in two Arizona races: the Race for the Cure and the Fiesta Bowl Distance Classic. His Race for the Cure record still stands.

Max trains year-round for baseball, and this past spring and summer he was a catcher on his high school baseball team. He holds a black belt in tae kwon do, and he has competed more than 150 times, winning two gold medals, a silver, and a bronze in four United States Taekwondo Junior Olympics. He also won a gold medal at the U.S. Open. He holds seven state championships from Colorado, Arizona, Nevada, and Hawaii.

This year Max is taking three honors courses and an advanced placement course in economics. When he was a freshman, he was a straight-A student and took three honors courses. He also received an award of distinction in honors language arts and served as a member of his school's Gifted and Talented Advisory Committee.

He mentored an autistic boy. For two years, Max sorted food for the homeless at a food ministries organization and did cleanup work at a nearby state park. Max's hobbies are astronomy and fly-fishing, and he is a member of an astronomy club at school.39

Whew! Didn't you get tired just reading about Max? Since he has the same twenty-four-hour day the rest of us have, how can he do it and still be emotionally balanced?

Kids like Max are obviously special. They seem to thrive on doing a lot of things and excel in many of their sports and extracurricular activities while keeping their grades up. They appear to have lots of friends and relate well to both peers and adults. From all outward appearances, they look physically and emotionally healthy. The problem is that while many of the kids *are* healthy and emotionally sound, some may not be.

If you have a child like Max, what should you look for to make sure he is healthy and balanced? A starting place is to determine if he is facing unhealthy pressure to accomplish or overachieve. If you decide that there is pressure, see if you can figure out whether it's coming from you or him. If it's coming from you, you'll want to look at all the verbal and nonverbal messages you've sent him over the years and may still be sending. If he's internalized these messages and he is driven to achieve because of them, there is a risk that he may one day realize this. At that time, he may decide that he's been achieving for you, not for him. He may become resentful or unhappy.

If the pressure is coming from him, take a look at how he handles defeat or disappointment. If he handles them in healthy ways and can regroup and move on, this is good. On the other hand, if he becomes depressed, angry, or withdrawn, he may need help learning how to cope better or to reduce his expectations.

Next, look for the signs of healthy, balanced athletes. They are happy, they laugh, they don't always take themselves too seriously, they get up when the alarm goes off, they get to school and practices on time. Their personalities are stable; they tend not to be moody. They seem to genuinely enjoy all that they do—they never speak of their efforts as chores. They take defeats or disappointments in stride, reacting as though they are just part of life. They have great friends, and they are good friends to others. Their health is good; they do not get sick often, and they seldom complain of somatic symptoms other than when they are injured. They are rarely depressed or anxious or overly stressed. They are able to keep their grades up.

As long as your achieving child seems to show most of these qualities, you can be fairly confident that he's not juggling too many activities. (Realistically, as your child gets older, his studies and sports at the next level become more demanding. He will probably need to reduce the number of activities he pursues.) But if negative behaviors or emotions or personality traits begin to emerge, it's imperative that he slow down and perhaps be evaluated. If the price of success is too high, it's time to consider whether he is doing too much. The worst-case scenario, no intervention, might lead to suicide. At best, he may only need to modify his schedule—drop some sports or activities—to feel better.

The problem of doing too much is more common with teenagers than children. Teenagers think they're invincible. Many take on too much and are often slow to realize that they can't handle it all. They want to taste a little bit of everything that interests them. A wise parent allows his child to pursue sports and activities in which he has interest and talent. But the same wise parent must sometimes step in and point out to his child that he may be overdoing it. Be prepared to tell him the signs you have observed that suggest to you that he is pushing too hard. Ideally, the child will pull back himself; if not, you may have to set some limits. Be prepared to discuss your expectations. Emphasize your wish that he be happy and emotionally healthy. After he cuts back, point out how he seems less stressed and happier.

If other psychological problems have developed, make sure to have a counselor or psychologist evaluate him. Sometimes emotional problems that seem to be caused by a too demanding schedule may, in fact, be because of deeper, underlying problems that have been present for a long time but are only noticed now.

It may be that your child is like Max. You've inventoried the sources of any pressure, and you've looked carefully to see if he's shown any signs that he is not coping well. He looks happy and balanced. If so, take pleasure in having such a special kid! His ability to do all that he does will serve him well in adulthood. He is probably a pro in time management, he can deal with successes and failures, and he knows that hard work pays off. He will have learned most of life's lessons by the time he graduates from high school. Post-high school he will face new challenges, but he should be able to deal with them because of his accomplishments in school, sports, and other activities.

My Kid's Not Aggressive Enough

Parents sometimes notice that their child does not seem aggressive enough when playing a team or individual sport. This lack of aggressiveness is more common in contact team sports, though it can also occur in noncontact individual sports. With some children, the reason for this situation is obvious. With others, the reason is not quite as apparent.

Some kids are afraid of getting hurt. If they are playing a contact sport with the possibility of injury, then this fear has some basis in reality. Even so, most children know the potential for injury but play full throttle nevertheless. What's the difference between these two types of kids?

If a child has been overprotected and sheltered from experiences that could result in injury, he may have learned to hold back and be overly cautious. I've seen parents who don't allow their child to climb trees, prevent him from engaging in activities because he may get dirty (playing in sandboxes with water is out), and make a big fuss every time he scrapes his knees. Little wonder that this same child will not break past a row of defenders on the basketball court or will not run through home plate if the catcher is waiting to tag him. In tennis, he will rarely pursue a ball if he has to run very fast to get to it. If questioned, he will admit that he was afraid he'd trip, fall, and hurt himself while going after the ball.

Working with overprotected and coddled kids can be frustrating. Coaches wonder if they will ever show even a smidgen of the aggressiveness required in the sport. Teammates learn not to count on them. Worse, they may be ridiculed and called names.

There are several tacks to take with this child. First, make sure he is not playing a high-contact sport with high rates of injuries—football, basketball, or lacrosse. (Keep in mind that while football has the highest rate of injury, a child is less likely to be injured playing it at eight than at fifteen. The size and speed differentials between players at fifteen are more likely to result in injuries than at eight.) Next, consider a different sport—one where physical contact or the chances of injury are minimal. Golf, archery, and some of the martial arts come to mind. Or think about a sport where aggressiveness, while called for occasionally, is not a requisite for lower levels of performance or competition. Swimming, running, bowling, and rowing are other noncontact sports where aggressiveness is not absolutely required in order to participate.

Another possibility is to consult with a sports psychologist. The psychologist may be able to help the child who is fearful of getting hurt.

A number of therapeutic techniques can reduce the child's fears. These include visualization, relaxation, role-playing, and positive self-talk.

After talking with your child, you might find out that it's not so much that he's afraid of getting hurt, but he's afraid of hurting other players. This causes him to pull back and play cautiously. Usually you can reassure him that any injury he causes will probably be minor, like sprained ankles or cuts and abrasions, or at worst a broken finger or arm. You can also point out that small injuries are a part of the game but that good training, coaching, and equipment can keep these injuries to a minimum. If these points don't seem to make a difference, he can consider playing other low-contact, low-injury sports.

If none of these reasons appears to explain why your child is not aggressive enough and he is not willing to change sports, perhaps a sports psychologist can help him identify other explanations for his reluctance to play more aggressively. Some of these explanations may be quite easy to address, others may not be.

The Foul-Tempered Athlete

We have all witnessed star athletes becoming upset or hot-tempered, especially over calls they think were incorrect. We especially empathize with them when countless replays show that the referee or umpire clearly made the wrong call against the athlete. At the 2004 French Open quarterfinals, Serena Williams contested a couple of shots that were ruled against her. Seeing the replays, viewers could only marvel at her relative restraint given the egregious miscalls. One of those miscalls was over a crucial point that may have cost her the game and, ultimately, the match. Tennis star John McEnroe often reacted with belligerence and name-calling when umpires ruled against him. In high-stakes games or matches, recovering and regrouping after wrong calls or perceived wrong calls can be difficult.

Anger can be used as a motivational tool. When I was in my doctoral program, I met another student who was told in high school that he wasn't college material. He did a slow burn ever since, vowing that after he received his college diploma he would go back to his high school and shove his diploma into his teacher's face. When he did receive his sheepskin, he decided that he would wait until he received his

PhD, and then shove it into the teacher's face. After he received his doctorate, he no longer had the need to hunt down his teacher. But this anger fantasy propelled him on for many years of study. So, it's best if children can learn to deal with their anger in a manner that does not cause self-defeating behavior and can help them bring out their best. This kind of anger is sometimes called controlled or constructive anger.

Youth athletes can show intemperate behavior on the field. They may throw their bats in such a way that they endanger teammates, they may stomp off the court, or they may toss their golf clubs into the air and possibly hurt a fan or themselves. Sometimes their anger causes them to be too distracted and too emotional. As a result, they play poorly for the rest of the game or match. In other instances, they may take their frustrations and anger out on officials, coaches, or fans, often by yelling, cussing, arguing, pushing, or punching. Teams often pay a penalty for the player's behavior. A team may have to forfeit a point or game. Officials may eject a star player and the team loses one of its better scorers. Sometimes a player is suspended for a number of games. Sometimes an angry athlete injures himself and cannot play. His team may lose important games because of this. The player doesn't win any points from his coach or his teammates for losing control.

If your child shows the beginning signs of not handling his frustration or emotions appropriately, it's important to step in early and to try to stop this behavior before it becomes a habit and before he hurts himself or others. The aim is not to eliminate anger, or other heightened emotions, but to help the child learn to moderate his anger to lower levels and to redirect or channel his emotional energy in acceptable ways.

Many different situations might bring on out-of-control anger or temper tantrums:

- In an individual sport, the child loses by a hairbreadth. She is frustrated and angry with herself. She stomps off and throws things around.

- The umpire calls the base stealer out at second base. It's a close call, and the player is angry with the umpire, yells at him, and calls him a dimwit. The umpire ejects him.

- The pitcher becomes angry at the shortstop for making an error that results in a run for the other team. He yells at the shortstop. The shortstop stops speaking to the pitcher. Teamwork suffers.

- The coach tells the child that he's not working hard enough during practice and that he's not going to be a starter in the soccer game on Saturday. The player begins to cuss at the coach.

Sometimes a child's emotional maturity does not match his physical and athletic abilities. This can happen if he advances quite rapidly in his sport but is not emotionally ready to handle the pressure of the game at the level it is being played. He may be an excellent athlete, but he may not be able to modulate his emotions adequately. We encourage him to play with passion, yet we also say, "Control your emotions." This can be confusing to a young athlete. In some cases it helps to reduce the level of the game, to join another team or league until his emotional maturity improves.

Some children routinely become angry whenever they are frustrated. They haven't learned how to react or cope when things become difficult or don't go their way. Often this behavior is seen in other areas of the child's life, not just when playing sports. Sometimes it is a learned behavior. (When the child has seen a parent respond to frustration with anger or violence, it should not be too surprising when the child begins to show the same behavior.) Consultation with a psychologist may be necessary.

Some kids' temper tantrums are for show or intimidation. There is an audience effect, and sometimes teammates think such kids are cool. Coaches should put a stop to these types of tantrums, using different interventions including benching—not to punish, but to give the child a chance to cool off, think about his behavior, and regain control.

Tension or inability to relax can lead to the build-up of frustration and anger. This type of problem calls for relaxation training and other strategies for reducing tension. Relaxation tapes, visualization techniques, and music may help. If none of this helps, a sports psychologist may be able to determine the best ways to help the child.

Irritability and anger can be signs of depression. Children and adolescents don't always show the more typical signs of depression the way adults do. Boredom and acting out behaviors can signal possible depression. If you suspect your child is depressed, have him screened and evaluated by a mental health professional.

Unfortunately, some adolescents begin to experiment with drugs and/or alcohol, which sometimes accounts for belligerent and unacceptable aggressive behavior. Many teams bench such players or suspend them indefinitely. If the child appears to be addicted, prompt professional help is imperative.

Whatever the underlying reason for a child's temper outbursts, try to help him see that his temper is self-defeating, especially if he is playing an individual sport. If he is playing a team sport, help him realize that he's not helping himself or his team. Both you and his coach or instructor should make it clear that his behavior is unacceptable and that if he wants to continue playing, he will have to show a significant improvement in his ability to control himself. He may need the help of a psychologist or a sports psychologist. A number of treatment approaches can help the athlete learn to manage his temper or anger more effectively. It would be a shame if an otherwise excellent athlete had to leave the sport because of his temper.

When Do You Consult With a Sports Psychologist?

Professional sports teams, Olympic teams, and college teams all have sports psychologists working with their athletes. The psychologist often works with the athletes on an ongoing basis, especially in the case of Olympic athletes in individual sports when winning is measured in hundredths of a second or in millimeters. Many performance situations require the skills of a sports psychologist. At this level, many of these psychologists have doctorates in sports psychology. Often they also have advanced training in kinesiology, sports medicine, and/or fitness training. Some are former competitive athletes.

For children, the sports psychologist may be a psychologist, but some are not—they may have advanced training in some clinical area such as social work or nursing. Some have degrees in exercise physiology and training. They may be former coaches who now specialize in working with athletes. Depending upon their training, some sports psychologists focus on the motivational aspects of athletic performance. Others are very familiar with the research findings on athletic skills, exercise physiology, biomechanics, and performance enhancement techniques. For example, one sports psychologist pointed out to a golfer that he was gripping his club too hard. Doing so restricted blood flow to the capillaries of the hands and fingers, and this resulted in his problem with distance accuracy.[40] Of course, some sports psychologists are competent in both areas and combine the two when they work with athletes.

What situations call for the skills of a sports psychologist or therapist? Sports psychologists deal with many of the special situations discussed in this section. One of the common areas is performance enhancement. The psychologist has a number of techniques in her arsenal to use with an athlete to help maximize his performance. Some of these include relaxation training, visualization, various cognitive techniques, and special breathing exercises. Sometimes just speaking with a child may be enough. The child may say some things to the sports psychologist that he might not be willing to say to a coach or a parent. In some instances, the coach or the parent is too close to see some things that may be obvious to the psychologist.

Champion golfer Annika Sorenstam utilizes visualization techniques to help her with her game.

"I close my eyes and see the shot. I look at the ball and see the type of shot I have in my mind. I see it fly and I see it land. It's a way of seeing the result before you do it. I visualize the end result."

What if your child experiences extreme anxiety before meets or games? A sports psychologist will work with him to help identify why he is becoming so anxious and help him learn how to turn his anxiety into useful stress. Overanxiousness may be expressed in emotional ways, or some somatic or bodily signs may appear, like vomiting, skin rashes, welts, headaches, and stomachaches.

Some children begin to lose interest. They begin missing practices, don't go to sleep early enough the night before races, or begin to eat improperly. A parent or coach may be able to help identify the problem. If not, sometimes a sports psychologist can help figure out what's wrong and map out appropriate steps to take to help a child recover his motivation.

A number of athletes struggle with inner conflicts such as fear of failing, fear of being too aggressive, or fear of being hurt. Wrestling with these worries can have a dramatic impact upon their performance. A sports psychologist can often help with these concerns.

Some athletes are the most talented players on their team, yet they play inconsistently time and again. When they win, they're the star of the team or they break records. But they do poorly as many times as they do well. Sports psychologists can help these athletes identify the reasons for their yo-yo performances.

Some athletes seem to do well all during a race or game but appear to choke at the end or the finish line, or when they are executing a particularly difficult dive or triple axel, or when they are the last chance for their team to win. Sports psychologists can often look like miracle workers when they work with such children.

Another common situation is that of burnout (sometimes referred to as overtraining syndrome). A child who was very enthusiastic now seems less motivated or disinterested. His performance has dropped off noticeably. Or a child may be tired all the time yet a night or two of good sleep doesn't seem to help. He no longer seems to be having any fun. These are just some of the possible signs of burnout. Most good coaches try to make sure that this doesn't happen; they know how much training is appropriate, and they design training or practices that reflect this. However, what are good training methods for most children may not be appropriate for some children. Also, some children sneak in extra training that the coach doesn't know about and in so doing, overdo it. Children may conclude that if one hundred laps during practice is good, then another hundred laps after practice is twice as good. If doing ten reps helps build muscles, then doing twenty reps should build muscles twice as fast. This is rarely the case. There may be other, more psychological reasons for burnout, and a sports psychologist can often get to the bottom of them.

A sports psychologist can be helpful after an athlete suffers a serious injury. There may be a long road to recovery. Sometimes the recovery process is very demanding—physical therapy three or four times a week, and the child is tired after each session. The child may become discouraged, wondering if he will ever be able to return to the game. Other injured children may seem less motivated to return to the game—they may be fearful of being injured again. The injured player has different needs and emotions. The sports psychologist can help him deal with his recovery in a healthy way.

Usually it's best to consult with a sports psychologist after you and the coach have tried to deal with the problem or situation. Sometimes just taking a break will solve some of these situations. Exhaust the simple approaches first. If there is still a problem and if your child is interested in getting some help, then find out the name of a sports psychologist who works with children. Coaches may be able to provide you with names. Your state psychological association can give you the names of sports psychologists in your community.

Many other special situations can arise when your child is active in sports, especially organized sports. I've covered some of the more common ones. Generally, try to be objective: step back, gather information, and use some common sense. If you do these things, you should be able to handle many of these situations with your child.

A Final Word

WHETHER IT'S FOR A FEW MONTHS or for many years, all children who are interested should have the opportunity to learn and play one or more sports. Whether your child is an athletic prodigy or quite awkward physically, or is physically, emotionally, or developmentally disabled, there are many benefits of youth sports. Many successful people credit their early participation in sports for teaching them the values of hard work, perseverance, dedication, setting goals, doing their best, and never giving up—values that helped them succeed in their adult lives. Some were natural athletes and played varsity in high school and for their colleges; others felt that they had little athletic ability though they enjoyed some modest success as an athlete. Most speak proudly and fondly of their playing days and how they took the lessons they learned from sports and carried them into their everyday lives.

Director and screenwriter Ron Shelton played baseball and basketball when younger. He summarized what sports did for him: "Almost everything I know that's worthwhile I learned from playing sports. All the critical lessons, from the time I was a boy through college and my years in the pros, came from athletics . . . Sports teach you so much: how to lose—not be happy with it, mind you—but how to deal with it. For instance, in marriage you have ups and downs, and in your work life you have ups and downs, and sports teaches you how to deal with those ups and downs without lessening your commitment."[41]

Others believe that their playing days helped them get through emotionally and physically harrowing life situations—situations that were not part of everyday life. U.S. Senator John McCain wrestled and boxed in high school and boxed at the U.S. Naval Academy. He believes that his boxing experiences helped him survive five and a half years of torture when he was a prisoner of the North Vietnamese. When in prison "the first time I got knocked around by the Vietnamese, it did not come as a total shock . . . I got beat up a lot. It wasn't easy, but I'm sure glad I had the experience of contact sports because I learned perseverance and how to recover."[42]

For many children, playing sports will consume almost as much time, and for some, more hours than they spend in school. Because of the lessons kids can learn and because of the time sports take up in children's lives, parents surely want their sports involvement to be a positive experience. I hope parents and children have found this book helpful in their quest to find the right sport, team, and coach. May your children experience achievement, great satisfaction, enjoyment, and fun!

In 1988, U.S. Senator Joseph Biden was facing surgery for double cranial aneurysms. Speaking with his sons shortly before surgery he told them, "If I die, I don't want any of this senator stuff and chairman stuff on my tombstone. I just want four things on the tombstone: husband, father, son, athlete." [43]

Notes

Chapter 1

1. Michael D. Lemonick, "How We Grew So Big," *Time*, June 7, 2004.

2. "Panel Tackles Obesity Problem Among Students," *Denver Post*, September 29, 2004.

3. Rick Reilly, "The Fat of the Land," *Sports Illustrated*, September 22, 2003, p. 84.

4. Barbara Yost, "Kids' Obesity a Call to Arms," *Arizona Republic*, October 15, 2003, p. A16.

Chapter 2

5. Suzanne Sievert, "It's Not Just How We Play That Matters," *Newsweek*, March 19, 2001, p. 12.

6. Nancy Gibbs, "Parents Behaving Badly," *Time*, February 21, 2005, pgs. 40–49.

7. Alexander Wolff, "The American Athlete Age 10," *Sports Illustrated*, October 6, 2003, pgs. 59–75.

8. Kieran Nicholson, "Pulling No Punches," *Denver Post*, October 5, 2003, p. 27A, 34A.

Chapter 4

9. Theresa Smith, "Child's Play," *Denver Post*, July 16, 2002, p. 10D.

Chapter 5

10. Michael Specter, "The Long Ride," *New Yorker*, July 15, 2002, pgs. 48–58.

11. Tara Parker-Pope, "Why Gym Class Matters: Kids' Attitudes Toward Sports Affect Their Adult Health," *Wall Street Journal*, September 2, 2003.

12. Alexander Wolff, "The American Athlete Age 10," *Sports Illustrated*, pgs. 59–75.

13. "We Can't All Win the World Cup, *New York Times*, July 18, 1999.

Chapter 6
14. John Wukovits, *The Encyclopedia of the Winter Olympics*, 2001.

Chapter 10
15. Phil Jackson and Hugh Delehanty, *Sacred Hoops: Spiritual Lessons of a Hardwood Warrior* (New York: Hyperion, 1995).

16. Bill Briggs, "Kid Athletes Stressed Out," *Denver Post*, July 2, 2001, p. 1F.

17. Alexander Wolff, "The American Athlete Age 10," *Sports Illustrated*, pgs. 59–75.

18. Dan Benardot, *Nutrition for Serious Athletes* (Champaign, IL: Human Kinetics, 2000).

19. Alexander Wolff, "The American Athlete Age 10," *Sports Illustrated*, pgs. 59–75.

Chapter 13
20. Gary Mack, *Mind Gym*, 2001.

21. National Alliance Web Survey, www.nays.org/IntMain.cfm. Accessed March 8, 2005, and March 16, 2005.

22. Bruce Weber, "Ice Time: For Players, Fast Pulses; For Parents, Raw Nerves," *New York Times*, January 22, 2005.

23. Cal Ripken, Jr., "The Dedication of a Sportsman," *Sports Illustrated*, October 20, 2003.

24. Adam Schefter, "Know Her From Adam Julie Foudy," *Denver Post*, September 12, 2003.

Part 2: Guide to Sports
25. Eric Small, MD. *Kids & Sports: Everything You and Your Child Need to Know About Sports, Physical Activity, Nutrition, and Good Health—A Doctor's Guide for Parents and Coaches.*

Part 3: Special Issues and Situations
26. Gary Mack, *Mind Gym*, 2001.

27. Centers for Disease Control, Youth Risk Behavior Survey, 2003.

28. National Institute on Drug Abuse, "Anabolic Steroids Use in Teens," www.drugabuse.gov/NIDA. Accessed April 7, 2005.

29. Tom Foreman, *Q&A: Blind Mountain Climber on Summiting Everest*, http://news.nationalgeographic.com/news/2003/07/0730_030730 _everest.html. Interview took place on July 30, 2003.

30. Michael A. Paré, *Sports Stars Series 3* (Detroit: UXL, 1997).

31. Elizabeth Aguilera, "Middle-School Taunts Take Frightening Turn," *Denver Post*, January 13, 2005, p. 15A.

32. Peter Applebome, "What's to Come, Soccer Tryouts in the Cradle?," *New York Times*, October 17, 2004, p. 28.

33. "The Music Man," *New York Times Magazine*, October 3, 2004.

34. Bill Pennington, "Doctors See a Big Rise in Injuries for Young Athletes," *New York Times*, February 22, 2005.

35. Gordon Marino, "In [Self-] Defense of the Fanatical Sports Parent," *New York Times Magazine*, January 26, 2003, p. 38, 40–41.

36. Dorfman and Kuehl, *The Mental Game of Baseball*.

37. Clay Latimer, "When Failure Isn't an Option," *Rocky Mountain News*, August 27, 2004, pgs. 6S–7S.

38. Wukovits, *The Encyclopedia of the Winter Olympics*, 2001.

39. "Top Kid," *Denver Post*, October 18, 2004, p. 2B.

40. Chris Lewis, "This Head Coach Is Hot," *Sports Illustrated*, January 31, 2005.

A Final Word

41. Brian Kilmeade, *The Games Do Count: America's Best and Brightest on the Power of Sports*, 2004.

42. Ibid.

43. Ibid.

Further Reading

Bigelow, Bob, Tom Moroney, and Linda Hall. *Just Let the Kids Play: How to Stop Other Adults from Ruining Your Child's Fun and Success in Youth Sports*. Dearfield Beach, FL: Health Communications, 2001.

An important book that emphasizes the parents' role in youth sports.

Brown, Fern G. *Special Olympics*. New York: Franklin Watts, 1992.

A good overview of the Special Olympics program.

Brown, Jim. *Sports Talent: How To Identify and Develop Outstanding Athletes*. Champaign, IL: Human Kinetics, 2001.

Brown's book will help parents evaluate their child's natural abilities and how these abilities translate to various sports.

Chastain, Brandi. *It's Not about the Bra: Play Hard, Play Fair, and Put the Fun Back into Competition*. New York: HarperCollins, 2004.

Chastain is the soccer player famous for her game-winning kick in the 1999 World Cup finals against China. She writes about how important it is to remove some of the pressures of organized youth sports. She stresses the importance of children having fun when playing sports.

Clifford, Craig, and Randolph Feezell. *Coaching for Character: Reclaiming the Principles of Sportsmanship*. Champaign, IL: Human Kinetics, 1997.

The authors show how and why sportsmanship is an intrinsic part of sports. They provide many examples of how sportsmanship can be taught.

Doren, Kim, and Charlie Jones. *If Winning Were Easy, Everyone Would Do It: Motivational Quotes for Athletes*. Kansas City, MO: Andrews McMeel Publishing, 2002.

Filled with motivational quotes by famous athletes, coaches, and sport psychologists. Many of the boxed quotations in this book came from it.

Doren, Kim, and Charlie Jones. *You Go Girl! The Winning Way*. Santa Anna, CA: Seven Locks Press, 2003.

Female athletes are enthusiastically encouraged to do their best and find their "winning way." Several of the boxed quotes in this book come from their book.

Dorfman, H. A. *Coaching the Mental Game: Leadership Philosophies and Strategies for Peak Performance in Sports—and Everyday Life*. Lanham, MD: Taylor Trade Publishing, 2003.

Dorfman emphasizes the importance of the mental part of sports. While written for the full-time coach, volunteer parent coaches will find Dorfman's advice to coaches quite helpful.

Dorfman, H. A., and Karl Kuehl. *The Mental Game of Baseball: A Guide to Peak Performance*. Lanham, MD: Diamond Communications, 2002.

Though the authors focus on the mental game of baseball, much of the advice applies to the mental game of many sports.

Engh, Fred. *Why Johnny Hates Sports: Why Organized Youth Sports Are Failing Our Children and What We Can Do About It*. Garden City Park, NJ: Avery Publishing Group, 1999.

An excellent book about the proper role of parents and coaches in youth sports. Engh is the president of the National Alliance for Youth Sports.

Fortin, François. *Sports: The Complete Visual Reference*. Willowdale, Ontario: Firefly Books, 2000.

This is a useful and comprehensive visual guide to sports. While this book does not present the rules, regulations, and events of various sports at the beginner level, a child and parent can obtain a good idea of what a sport is like by reading it. Some of the historical facts in this book about each sport came from this.

Jackson, Colin. *The Young Track and Field Athlete*. New York: DK Publishing, 1996.

An excellent book that provides a good introduction to track and field events for the young child or teen.

Karlin, Len. *The Guide to Careers in Sports*. 2nd ed. New York: E. M. Guild, 1997.

This book has a complete compilation of careers in the sports industry.

Kennedy, Mike. *Special Olympics*. New York: Children's Press, 2002.

This book, written for children, is a good introduction to the Special Olympics program.

Kilmeade, Brian. *The Games Do Count: America's Best and Brightest on the Power of Sports*. New York: Regan Books, 2004.

Kilmeade asked many achievers in various areas of work to write about their youth experiences in sports. They all wax nostalgic about their athletic years and how playing sports when they were young had an impact on their adult lives today.

Mack, Gary, with David Casstevens. *Mind Gym: An Athlete's Guide to Inner Excellence*. New York: Contemporary Books, 2001.

A good book that covers the mental and emotional part of playing sports.

National Alliance for Youth Sports. *Your First Coaching Book: A Practical Guide for Volunteer Coaches*. Garden City Park, NY: Square One Publishers, 2002.

A great book for parents who would be volunteer coaches.

Norton, Jerry. *Mom, Can I Play Football?: An Introspective View of the Game for Parents and Coaches*. Ponte Vedra Beach, FL: Sideline Press, 1999.

The wisdom of this book goes beyond the sport of football. It presents much useful, common sense advice about how to be a supportive parent of a child playing any sport.

Phillips, Laurel, and Barbara Stahl. *Parenting, SportsMom Style: Real-Life Solutions for Surviving the Youth Sports Scene*. Maumee, OH: 307 Books, 2000.

A witty book for moms who have children in youth sports. Between them, the authors have had five children in various sports.

Sanders, Summer. *Champions Are Raised, Not Born: How My Parents Made Me a Success*. New York: Delacorte Press, 1999.

The title can mislead the reader. Summer Sanders does not approve of the overinvolved parent. Rather, she feels that a parent needs to support his child in appropriate ways. She has a great deal to say about how the inappropriate behaviors and pressure of many parents can drive their children away from sports.

Sheehy, Harry. *Raising A Team Player*. North Adams, MA: Storey Books, 2002.

Sheehy's book provides some good ideas and advice about how to raise a team player. He believes that the behaviors good team players learn in childhood are essential in adulthood.

Small, Eric, MD. *Kids & Sports: Everything You and Your Child Need to Know About Sports, Physical Activity, Nutrition, and Good Health—A Doctor's Guide for Parents and Coaches*. New York: Newmarket Press, 2002.

A sports medicine pediatrician, Small focuses on developmental and health issues for kids of all abilities participating in sports. He emphasizes the importance of physical activity starting in infancy.

Storm, Hannah. *Go Girl! Raising Confident and Successful Girls through Sports*. Naperville, IL: Sourcebooks, 2002.

Storm suggests that girls can develop confidence through sports. She also has a section in the book describing many sports that girls play.

Sundberg, Jim, and Janet Sundberg. *How to Win at Sports Parenting*. Colorado Springs, CO: Waterbrook Press, 2000.

The authors stress the role of parents of children in sports.

Wolff, Rick. *Good Sports: The Concerned Parent's Guide to Competitive Youth Sports*. Champaign, IL: Coaches Choice, 1997.

An excellent introduction to organized youth sports leagues by a well-known and knowledgeable youth sports psychologist.

Wukovits, John. *The Encyclopedia of the Winter Olympics*. New York: Franklin Watts, 2001.

Gives the history and basic information about twelve Olympic winter sports. The book also has interesting and sometimes moving stories of twenty-seven gold medalists.

Zimmerman, Jean, and Gil Reakjvill. *Raising Our Athletic Daughters*. New York: Doubleday, 1998.

Since society tends not to support girl athletes in the same way it supports boys, these authors describe ways parents can encourage their daughters' participation in sports.

Other Resources

www.positivecoach.org
Positive Coaching Alliance
Department of Athletics
Stanford University
Palo Alto, CA 94305

www.fogdog.com
FogDog
Guide for selecting proper equipment for your sport.

www.nays.org
1-800-729-2057
The National Alliance for Youth Sports
2050 Vista Parkway
West Palm Beach, FL 33411
Provides educational programs for parents.

www.nays.org (click on Start Smart icon)
Start Smart Sports Development Program
Starter classes for young children, three to five and five to seven. If there are
no Start Smart programs in your community, the Web site gives you instructions on how to develop Start Smart classes where you live.

www.SportsID.com
View hundreds of coaching videos on more than ninety sports.

www.sportsparents.com
A site for parents that covers sportsmanship and sports psychology.

www.bam.gov
This Web site encourages children to be more physically active; it also includes
a personality quiz to help them choose a sport.

http://ed-web3.educ.msu.edu/ysi/
The Institute for the Study of Youth Sports is based at Michigan State University. Check the Web site for good articles on youth sports for parents and coaches. Its six-page newsletter is free to Michigan residents and only $5 a year to nonresidents.

www.nyscagoldcoach.nays.org
National Youth Sports Coaches Association Parent members can take a course online to learn how to be volunteer coaches. Topics include philosophy and ethics, sports safety and injury prevention, physical preparation and conditioning, growth and development, teaching and communication, organization and administration, skills and tactics, and evaluation. A certificate of completion is issued after completing the course. The cost of the course is $60.

www.sportsmom.com
Useful information on various youth sports topics such as health, nutrition, handling difficult situations, and other issues.

Index

About the Author

Nicole Sperekas, PhD, is a child psychologist and was the Director of Child Mental Health Services for Denver Health Medical Center. Now in private practice, she works with children and adolescents and their parents. Dr. Sperekas is a former competitive swimmer and swim team coach. She still swims, plays tennis, climbs the Rocky Mountains, and is an enthusiastic fan of many sports.